T0301857

PROBLEM SOLVING IN ECONOMICS

A Quantitative Approach

PROBLEM SOLVING IN ECONOMICS

A Quantitative Approach

Monojit Chatterji

University of Cambridge, UK

NEW JERSEY • LONDON • SINGAPORE • BEIJING • SHANGHAI • HONG KONG • TAIPEI • CHENNAI • TOKYO

Published by

World Scientific Publishing Co. Pte. Ltd.
5 Toh Tuck Link, Singapore 596224
USA office: 27 Warren Street, Suite 401-402, Hackensack, NJ 07601
UK office: 57 Shelton Street, Covent Garden, London WC2H 9HE

Library of Congress Cataloging-in-Publication Data
Names: Chatterji, Monojit, author.
Title: Problem solving in economics : a quantitative approach /
Monojit Chatterji, University of Cambridge, UK.
Description: New Jersey : World Scientific, [2024] | Includes index.
Identifiers: LCCN 2023009945 | ISBN 9789811273353 (hardcover) |
ISBN 9789811273360 (ebook) | ISBN 9789811273377 (ebook other)
Subjects: LCSH: Econometrics. | Economics--Decision making. |
Economics--Mathematical models.
Classification: LCC HB139 .C44 2024 | DDC 330.01/5195--dc23/eng/20230302
LC record available at https://lccn.loc.gov/2023009945

British Library Cataloguing-in-Publication Data
A catalogue record for this book is available from the British Library.

For any available supplementary material, please visit
https://www.worldscientific.com/worldscibooks/10.1142/13334#t=suppl

Desk Editors: Logeshwaran Arumugam/Geysilla Jean/Claire Lum

Typeset by Stallion Press
Email: enquiries@stallionpress.com

Printed in Singapore

This book is dedicated to the memory of my parents who were my first teachers of English and Mathematics and many other things.

Preface

This book has grown out of conversations with my students — past and present — at the University of Cambridge. In many years of supervising very able students who all knew basic calculus, I discovered that mathematical knowledge and fluency did not always translate smoothly into problem-solving ability. In fact, the students themselves frequently said to me that they were not as confident with applying their mathematical knowledge to solving economic problems. The same was true for some of the more gifted students I taught at the New College of the Humanities in London (now renamed as North Eastern University, London).

Though aimed at undergraduates in the early stages of studying economics, this book would be of use to converting graduate students too. In the UK, there are several good advanced diploma programmes which are designed as conversion courses for students who already have a first degree in another subject. This book could usefully be used by them too.

The mathematical techniques used are fairly rudimentary — optimisation methods and equation solving are the primary tools used. A brief explanation of constrained optimisation using Lagrange multipliers is provided. Important concepts are highlighted in bold when they are first introduced. Important results are also highlighted.

This book is not a book about economic theory but rather reinforces understanding by showing how basic mathematics is used to construct models of the economy. Students will get the most out of this book if they first attempt the problems without looking at the solution. The many problems with detailed solutions will encourage active reading and independent thought. Both microeconomics and macroeconomics are covered. This book is ideally suited for self-study.

In matter and form, this book owes most to my students. I am very grateful to my colleagues at Cambridge notably Charles Brendon, Chryssi Giannitsorou, Robert Evans, Pontus Rendahl, Aytek Erdil and Mikhail Safranov for their generosity in allowing me to adapt some of their supervision problems for the purpose of this book. I am also grateful to my former NCH student Aleksander Mielnikow for help with constructing the diagrams. My greatest debt is to Jonathan James of Swansea University who gave me extremely helpful detailed feedback on early drafts. Responsibility for errors and ambiguities remains with me. Finally, I am grateful to my wife Anjum and my children Kaya, Mohinoor and Priyanaz who encouraged me to stay with the writing of this book and then to write others.

About the Author

Monojit Chatterji teaches Economics at the University of Cambridge. He has supervised Cambridge undergraduates in both Microeconomics and Macroeconomics for the past twelve years and gives lectures on Macroeconomics to graduate students. Until recently, he was also giving lectures on introductory Microeconomics and Macroeconomics at the New College of the Humanities in London. He is also honorary professor at Heriot-Watt University in Edinburgh. His teaching experience over 50 years has encompassed leading universities in the UK, Australia, USA, India and Mexico.

Contents

Chapter 1

Fundamental Concepts of Consumer Theory

The conventional economic model of the consumer postulates a self-seeking individual who does the best she can, subject to affordability. When faced with a choice of how much of each good to buy, the consumer chooses the "best" bundle of goods that is affordable. We start by focusing on a precise meaning of affordability leaving a description of what is meant by the "best" till later.

1.1 Budget Sets

We denote by x and y the quantities of two goods X and Y that are consumed. Alternatively, we write the consumption bundle as (x, y). If the unit prices of the two goods are fixed at £p and £q per unit of X and Y respectively, then the consumer's expenditure is £$(px + qy)$. If consumer money income is £m, then the set of affordable bundles, called the budget set, is given by

$$px + qy \leq m. \tag{1.1}$$

Example 1.1: Joe has an income of £100. Burgers cost £5 each and pizzas cost £4 each. Call burgers good X and pizza good Y. Describe his budget set and illustrate diagrammatically.

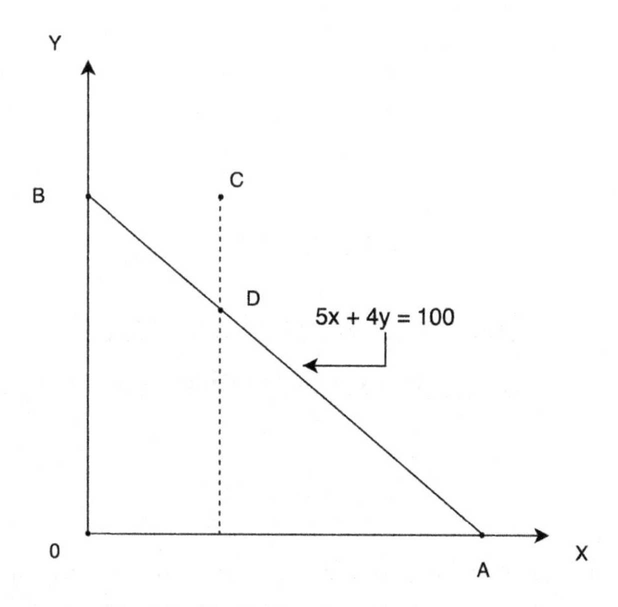

Fig. 1.1 The Budget Set with Fixed Prices

From Eq. (1.1), the budget set is

$$5x + 4y \leq 100. \tag{1.2}$$

Figure 1.1 illustrates the budget set with fixed prices.

In Figure 1.1, the X axis measures burgers and the Y axis measures pizzas. The budget set is the triangle 0AB. All points within the triangle including those on the line segments 0A, AB and 0B are affordable whereas a point like C to the northeast of AB is not affordable. The equation of the straight line AB is

$$5x + 4y = 100, \tag{1.3}$$

and represents all points at which the budget of £100 is fully exhausted. AB is the boundary of the budget set and is called the budget line or budget constraint. Its downward slope shows that there is a trade-off between X and Y. More of one implies less of the other. The slope of AB is −5/4 obtained by rewriting Eq. (1.3) as

$$y = 25 - (5/4)x. \tag{1.4}$$

The absolute value of the slope (ignoring the sign) measures the **relative price** of good X compared to good Y. As the budget line is downward sloping, its slope is always negative. However, as our interest focuses on the numerical value of the slope only, we sometimes use the word "slope" somewhat loosely to mean the absolute value of the slope. It measures how many extra units of Y can be obtained by giving up one unit of X. If Joe spent all his income on Y, he would have 25 pizzas which is the intercept on the Y axis represented by point B in Figure 1.1. This number is real income measured in pizzas. It measures the value of income not in money but in terms of a real commodity — in this case, pizzas.

How does one know that C is not in the budget set? Consider C and D. Both have the same x value, i.e., both involve the same number of burgers. But C involves more pizza than D. Hence, for any set of prices, expenditure at C is greater than expenditure at D. But expenditure at D is exactly £100 since D is on AB. Hence, expenditure at C exceeds £100 and is therefore unaffordable.

Finally, note that just as B measures real income in terms of pizzas, so A measures real income in terms of burgers. It's the maximum number of burgers that can be bought given money income and price of burgers. Thus, A is 20 burgers. The real income of the consumer can be expressed as either 20 burgers or 25 pizzas.

Example 1.2: Redo Example 1.1 but with prices £p and £q (instead of £5 and £4) and income of £m (instead of £100). What happens as prices and income change?

Figure 1.1 is unchanged except the equation of AB is now

$$px + qy = m, \tag{1.5}$$

or

$$y = (m/q) - (p/q)x. \tag{1.6}$$

The slope is now (p/q). A is (m/p) and B is (m/q). If p rises, the slope increases shifting A inwards towards 0 but B is unchanged.

The maximum amount of burgers that can be bought has shrunk. AB is steeper. If q rises, A does not change but B shifts downwards towards 0; the slope decreases and AB is flatter. If only m increases, AB shifts parallel to itself, and there is no change in the slope. What if all three — p, q and m — change simultaneously? One special case of interest is when both prices and money income change by the same proportional amount, for example, all three double. From Eq. (1.6), it is clear that if p, q and m all increase by a factor t, then there is no change at all to the budget line as the t factor cancels out from both the slope and the intercept term! This is an important result.

The above examples have used a simple model with only two goods. In reality of course, there are many goods. If we interpret good X as burgers and good Y as "Everything Else", then the model extends to many goods. This "Everything Else" is referred to as a **composite good**. Its price is conveniently set to 1. In Eqs. (1.5) and (1.6), we simply set $q = £1$ and everything about the budget set continues to hold. The slope is now just p since the absolute and relative price of good X is the same since the price of good Y has been set to £1. Good Y is known as the "**numeraire**" — it is the yardstick for relative price measurement. Good Y is strictly measured in "numeraire units" but for convenience, we simply measure the numeraire good in its money equivalent since its price is always £1 per unit.

In the analysis of budget sets so far, we have assumed constant prices. But in many situations, the pricing structure is more complicated. For example, offers involving bulk buying like "Buy 2 units, get further units at half price" are not uncommon. Similarly, situations where one has to pay a joining fee to access a good or service, e.g., a gym or a borrowing library or a wine club. See Examples 1.3 and 1.4.

Example 1.3: Shampoo bottles in a store cost £4 each for the first two bottles but £2 per bottle thereafter. Joe has an income of £100. Describe the budget set facing the consumer.

Measure shampoo bottles on the X axis and the composite good (the numeraire) on the Y axis. The budget set is shown in Figure 1.2.

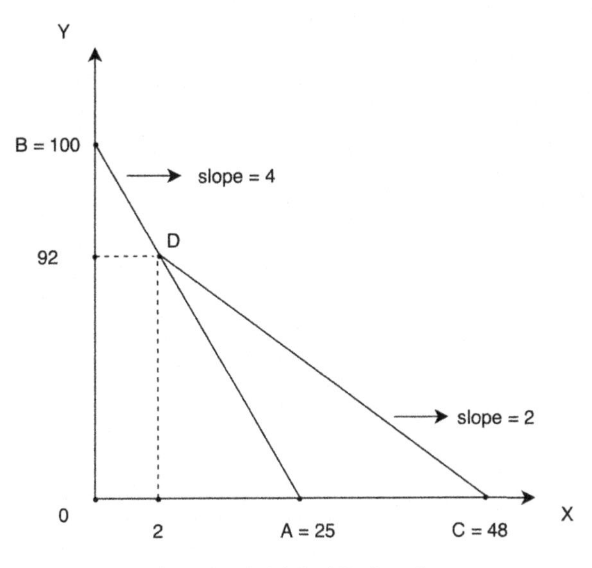

Fig. 1.2 A Kinked Budget Set

If Joe spends all his income on the other (composite) good *Y*, he will have £100 worth of the composite good and no shampoo. This is point B in Figure 1.2. If the price of shampoo was constant at £4 per bottle, and Joe spent all his income on shampoo, he would have 100/4 = 25 bottles of shampoo and none of the composite good. This is point A. The conventional constant price budget set is 0AB. However, the price of shampoo falls after 2 bottles have been consumed. This costs £8, so Joe still has an income of £(100 – 8) = £92 left. And at £2 per bottle, he can buy a further 92/2 = 46 bottles. Hence, the maximum amount of shampoo he can consume is 2 (at £4 per bottle) and a further 46 (at £2 per bottle) making 48 in total. This is point C. Consider point D which is (2, 92). The slope along BD is 4. But along DC, it is only 2 reflecting the lower price. The budget line BDC is continuous BUT there is a kink at D where the slope changes.

Example 1.4: A wine club charges £4 a bottle to members who must pay a fee of £40 to join the club. Non-members pay £10 per bottle. Ann has an income of £120. Will Ann join the club?

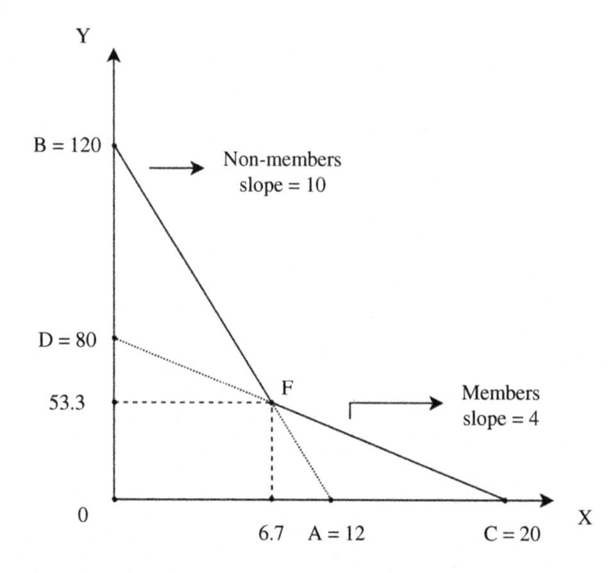

Fig. 1.3 Budget Set with Membership Fee

Figure 1.3 illustrates budget set with membership fee.

Wine is measured on the X axis and the composite good alternative on the Y axis. The non-member budget set is the standard constant price budget set with budget line AB where A is 12 (bottles of wine) and the maximum amount of the composite good available is £120. The equation of AB is

$$10x + y = 120. \tag{1.7}$$

For members, the maximum amount of the composite good available is only £80 because of the membership charge of £40. But at £4 a bottle, the maximum amount of wine she can buy is (80/4) = 20 bottles of wine. Hence, the budget line is DC where D is £80 and C is 20 bottles of wine. The equation of DC is

$$4x + y = 80. \tag{1.8}$$

Consider the intersection of the two different budget lines at F. From the equation of each budget line (Eqs. (1.7) and (1.8)), F is the point

(6.7, 53.3) obtained by solving (1.7) and (1.8) as a pair of linear simultaneous equations. F is the break-even point between the two regimes of member and non-member. The overall budget line is BFC — continuous but with a kink.

If Ann plans to consume 6 bottles of wine or less, she should not join the club. By not joining, she has a greater amount of the composite good for the same wine — the segment BF lies above DF. The converse is true if she plans to buy 7 or more bottles of wine — the line segment FC is above FA. If wine bottles are infinitely divisible, then her break-even point is 6.7 bottles of wine. Thus, Ann's choice depends on her planned consumption — which will depend on her preferences ("love of wine") which we now must analyse. In effect, the consumer will choose which part of the budget set to use.

1.2 Consumer Preferences

In the previous section, we had a thorough description of affordability which depended on measurable concepts like prices and consumer income. However, as we saw, the budget sets contain an infinite number of points. How does the consumer choose among these infinitely many affordable bundles? For this, we need to construct a theory of consumer preferences. For convenience, we refer to bundles of two goods as A, B, C,..., where A is the bundle (x_a, y_a), B is the bundle (x_b, y_b), etc. We say that A is strictly preferred to B if given a free choice between A and B, he will definitely pick A. If the consumer is indifferent between A and B, it means that he gets equal satisfaction from both bundles. Given a free choice between A and B, he might as well toss a coin to decide. Finally, if a consumer either strictly prefers A to B or is indifferent between A and B, then he is said to weakly prefer A to B.

The conventional theory of consumer behaviour assumes that preferences are of the following nature:

I. For every pair of bundles A and B, the consumer will always be able to say whether A is weakly preferred to B or vice versa or both — in which case, A is indifferent to B. The technical name for this assumption is completeness.

II. For any three bundles A, B and C, then if A is weakly preferred to B and B is weakly preferred to C, then A must be weakly preferred to C. The technical name for this assumption is transitivity.

III. Every bundle A is weakly preferred to itself.

IV. More is preferred to less so that if A has the same x amount as B (i.e., $x_a = x_b$) and if A has more Y than B (i.e., $y_a > y_b$), then A is strictly preferred to B. Other more technical assumptions are made and used but these are the basics.

A convenient graphical representation of preferences is through a device called an **indifference curve**. This is a curve in (X, Y) space which connects all bundles that give the consumer equal satisfaction; he is indifferent between all bundles that lie on the same indifference curve. By the "more is preferred to less" assumption, an indifference curve must be downward sloping. If A and B are on the same indifference curve and $x_a > x_b$, then it follows that $y_a < y_b$ which implies a downward-sloping curve.

Example 1.5: Which of the following functions can be a representation of an indifference curve when both x and y are non-negative?

(a) $y = 1/x$; (b) $y = a - bx$ (with $b > 0$); (c) $x^2 + y^2 = 9$; (d) $y = \ln x + 1$.

All four of the functions are familiar shapes. Thus, (a) is a downward-sloping rectangular hyperbola (slope is $dy/dx = -1/x^2$); (b) is a downward-sloping straight line (slope $= -b$); (c) is the arc of a circle from (3, 0) to (0, 3) (slope $= -x/y$); (d) is an upward sloping curve (slope $= +1/x$). Therefore, (d) CANNOT represent an indifference curve while the other three can. Figure 1.4 illustrates the three potential indifference curve types.

In Figure 1.4, the three potential indifference curves are labelled (A), (B) and (C). Although they are all downward sloping, they have very

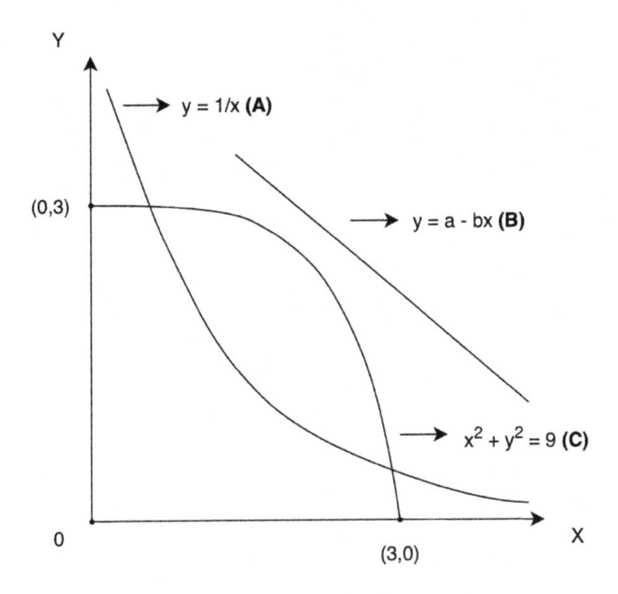

Fig. 1.4 Three Possible Indifference Curves

different **curvatures**. (A) is said to be convex (bowed in towards the origin) while (C) is said to be concave (bowed outwards from the origin) while (B) is the intermediate case between (A) and (C). These distinctions of curvature will be very important as we shall see later.

Each indifference curve represents a single distinct level of satisfaction. And no two indifference curves representing different levels of satisfaction can cross. Figure 1.5 shows why indifference curves cannot cross.

In Figure 1.5, the two indifference curves intersect at A. Because they are on the same indifference curve, A is indifferent to B. Similarly, A is also indifferent to C. By transitivity, B is indifferent to C. But this is impossible since C has the same amount of X but more Y and hence is preferred to B. This contradiction implies that the starting assumption must be wrong. Hence, indifference curves cannot cross.

How do points not on an indifference curve compare with those which are? Once again, "more is better" and "transitivity" will resolve this issue. Figure 1.6 illustrates indifference curves and "more is better".

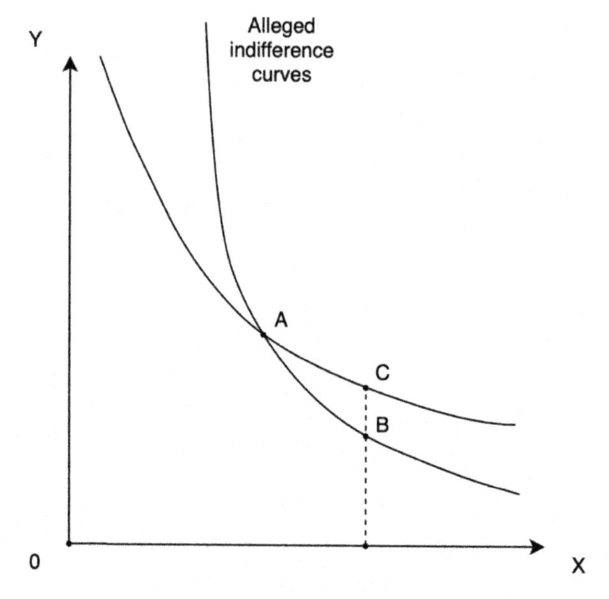

Fig. 1.5 Indifference Curves Cannot Cross

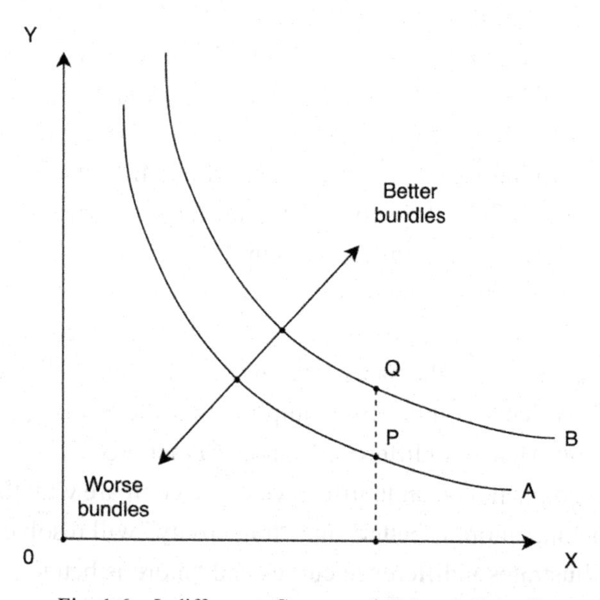

Fig. 1.6 Indifference Curves and "More is Better"

In Figure 1.6, all points on indifference curve A are as equally valued as P. Consider the points P and Q. Since Q is vertically above P, it is preferred to P as it has more Y but same X as P. Every point on B which is a higher indifference curve than A is valued the same as Q. Thus, every point on B is preferred to every point on A. The arrows indicate bundles that are worse and better than those on A. Moving northeast produces better bundles.

Example 1.6: Compare the two indifference curves (A) $y = 1/x$ and (B) $y = 2/x$.

For any value of x, (B) yields exactly twice as much Y as (A). Hence, B is a higher indifference curve as shown in Figure 1.6.

Example 1.7: Joe and Ann are both indifferent between bundles A and B. A is (6, 2) and B is (2, 6). However, Joe prefers C (4, 4) to both A and B, while Ann prefers A and B to C. What can be deduced about their indifference curves?

The first point to note is that C lies exactly halfway between A and B. It is the midpoint of the straight-line joining A and B. For Joe, C lies on a higher IC than the one joining AB. Conversely for Ann, as shown in Figure 1.7.

In Figure 1.7, Joe is indifferent between A and B but (strictly) prefers C to both. Consider P, the point on Joe's indifference curve AB when $x = 4$. It must be lower than C since C is (strictly) preferred to both A and B. Thus, Joe's indifference curve is APB — which is (strictly) **convex**. By similar argument, the point Q on Ann's indifference curve AB when $x = 4$ must be higher than C as C is worse than A and B. Hence, Ann's indifference curve is AQB — which is (strictly) **concave**. This helps clarify what convex and concave ICs are about. Convex ICs imply that averages are preferred to extremes (like Joe). Concave ICs imply the opposite — extremes are preferred to averages (like Ann). When the preference for averages over extremes is strict rather than weak, we use the phrase "strictly convex" (as opposed to just "convex"). Similarly, for concave preferences.

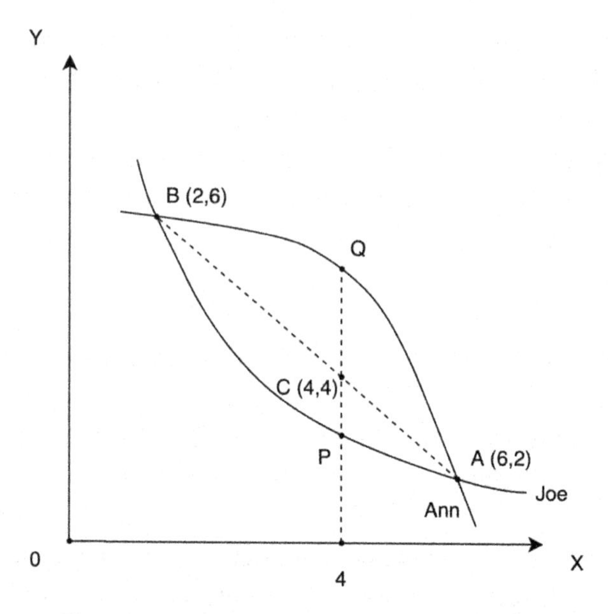

Fig. 1.7 Convex and Concave Indifference Curves

Whether indifference curves are convex or concave has deep implications for consumer choice and consumer demand. We discuss this in detail later. Economists often refer to preferences embodied in convex indifference curves as "well behaved" for reasons that will become clear.

1.3 Utility and Preferences

A convenient way to describe preferences is through a utility function which assigns a number to every possible bundle of goods such that more preferred bundles get assigned a higher number. The utility function is peculiar to each consumer. For example, suppose Ann's utility function is given by $U = xy$ where x is burgers, y is pizzas and U is utility measured in a subjective unit which we will call utils. Then, consider bundles A (2, 4) and B (4, 3). Which is preferred by Ann? Clearly, A gives Ann 8 utils but B gives Ann 12 utils, so she prefers B to A as 12 is bigger than 8. Note, however, that all this function does is rank bundles unambiguously. There is no meaning to the statement bundle B is worth 4 utils more than bundle A. In technical language, we call the utility measure ordinal because it assigns an order to bundles. Since we are only interested in ranking bundles, any monotonic transformation of a given utility function will represent exactly the same preferences.

There is considerable information contained in the slope of an IC. To fully appreciate the significance of the slope of an indifference curve, we need to exploit the concept of utility and changes in utility. To examine this further, let $U = F(x, y)$ be a utility function. Examples could be $U = xy$ or $U = x + \ln Y$ or $U = x^2 + y^2$. In each case, the function assigns a unique utility number measured in utils to every (x, y) combination which represents a bundle of goods. A natural question to ask is how much does U rise if starting from (x, y), there is a small increase in x but y is held constant. This quantity is called the marginal utility of X. If y is unchanged and x increases by a small amount Δx and consequently U increases by ΔU, then the marginal utility of x is calculated as $(\Delta U/\Delta x)$, an expression which is interpreted as "the rate of change of U per unit change in x, holding y constant". If Δx is small, then $(\Delta U/\Delta x)$ becomes what is known as the **partial derivative** of U with respect to x and is written as $(\partial U/\partial x)$. Exactly similar considerations apply when y changes but x is constant. Thus, we may write as definitions that

Marginal utility of $X = (\partial U/\partial x)$ and marginal utility of $Y = (\partial U/\partial y)$

Example 1.8: For each of the utility functions (a), (b) and (c), calculate Marginal Utility of X (MU_X) and Marginal Utility of Y (MU_Y):

(a) $U = xy$; (b) $U = x + \ln y$; (c) $U = x^2 + y^2$.
(b) For $U = xy$, $\text{MU}_X = (\partial U/\partial x) = y$ and $\text{MU}_Y = (\partial U/\partial y) = x$.
(c) For $U = x + \ln y$, $\text{MU}_X = (\partial U/\partial x) = 1$ and $\text{MU}_Y = (\partial U/\partial y) = (1/y)$.
(d) For $U = x^2 + y^2$, $\text{MU}_X = (\partial U/\partial x) = 2x$ and $\text{MU}_Y = (\partial U/\partial y) = 2y$.

In calculating partial derivatives with respect to say x, all we do is differentiate with respect to x as normal and treat y as a constant. Conversely when we partially differentiate with respect to y. Note that marginal utilities are not fixed numbers, rather they are themselves functions of x and y which will take on particular numerical values only if we assign numerical values to x and y.

Example 1.9: For each of the utility functions in Example 1.8, find MU_X and MU_Y when $x = 2$ and $y = 1$.

Substituting $x = 2$ and $y = 1$ into the answers for MU_X and MU_Y in (1.7), we get

(a) $MU_X = 1$, $MU_Y = 2$; (b) $MU_X = 1$, $MU_Y = 1$; (c) $MU_X = 4$, $MU_Y = 2$.

Along any IC, the utility value of every (x, y) bundle must be the same. Hence, to draw an IC, we simply set the utility level. Hence, in general, we write the equation of an indifference curve as $F(x, y) = k$, where k is the utility level. For example, if we set $k = 1$, then the IC corresponding to this for (a), (b) and (c) is given by (a) $xy = 1$ or $y = 1/x$; (b) $x + \ln y = 1$ or $\ln y = 1 - x$ or $y = \exp(1 - x)$; (c) $x^2 + y^2 = 1$ or $y = \sqrt{(1 - x^2)}$. In all three of these cases, we are able to write the IC explicitly as $y = \varphi(x, k)$. But it is not always possible to write the equation of an IC explicitly in this form. Hence, our focus lies on the slope of an IC which can generally be calculated as the following example illustrates.

Example 1.10: For the utility function $U = F(x, y)$, find the slope of any IC.

Consider the IC $F(x, y) = 1$. In Figure 1.8, two points on the IC are A (x_A, y_A) and $B(x_B, y_B)$.

Consider a movement from A to B. The consumption of x increases by $\Delta x = (x_B - x_A)$. The consumption of Y changes by $\Delta y = (y_A - y_B)$ which is a negative number. Hence, the slope of the chord AB is $(\Delta y/\Delta x)$ which is negative. And if we shrink the chord AB by moving B closer and closer to A, we get the slope of the IC at A to be the limit of $(\Delta y/\Delta x)$ which is of course just the **derivative** (dy/dx). This calculation of the slope is intimately related to the marginal utilities as we will see. Imagine the movement from A to B occurring in two steps: first from A to D and then from

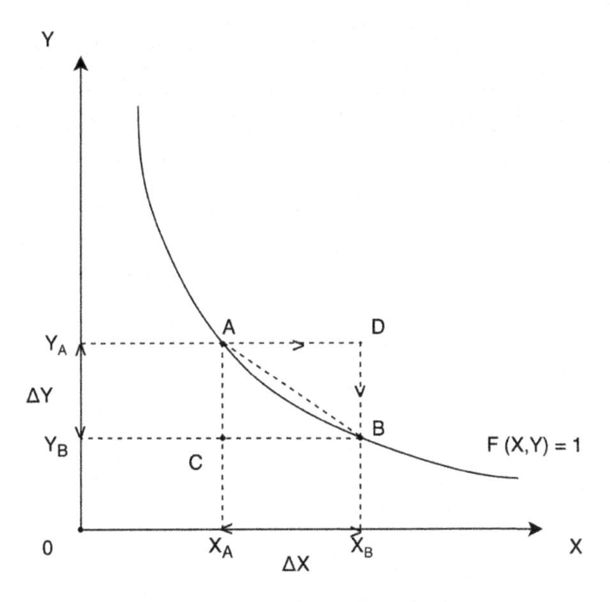

Fig. 1.8 Slope of an IC

D to B. Holding y constant at y_A, let x increase from x_A to x_B. This movement from A to D involves holding y constant at y_A but increasing x from x_A to x_B. At D, utility is higher by $[(\Delta U/\Delta x) \times (\Delta x)]$ or by $[(\text{MU}_X) \times (\Delta x)]$. The second movement from D to B involves holding x constant at x_B but decreasing y from y_A to y_B. This movement involves a fall in utility compared to D. This fall is measured as $[(\Delta U/\Delta y) \times (\Delta y)]$ or $[\text{MU}_Y \times (\Delta y)]$ which is of course negative since Δy is negative. The total change in utility from these two steps starting at A and ending at B is the sum of these two utility changes and is thus given by

$$\Delta U = [(\text{MU}_X) \times (\Delta x)] + [\text{MU}_Y \times (\Delta y)]. \tag{1.9}$$

But as A and B lie on the same IC, the change in utility must be zero. Hence, setting the right-hand side (RHS) of Eq. (1.9) equal to zero, we get the fundamental result that $[(\Delta y)/(\Delta x)] = -[(\text{MU}_X)/(\text{MU}_Y)]$. And if we suppose that the movement from A to B is "small", then we can replace $[(\Delta y)/(\Delta x)]$ with the derivative dy/dx to obtain the important result that *the* ***slope of an indifference*** **curve, *dy/dx*, is measured as $-[(\mathrm{MU}_X)/(\mathrm{MU}_Y)]$**. It is interpreted as the amount of Y one is prepared to give up in order to acquire an extra unit of X and still remain on the same indifference curve. It is the consumer's subjective rate of exchange. The slope of an IC is called the **Marginal Rate of Substitution (MRS)**. Strictly speaking, it is of course a negative number but we will frequently be interested in the absolute value only. Note that calculation of MRS does not require one to first find the explicit equation for an IC in the form $y = \phi(x)$.

Example 1.11: For each of the utility functions (a) $U = xy$; (b) $U = x + \ln y$; (c) $U = x^2 + y^2$, find the MRS using the formula **MRS= $-[(\mathrm{MU}_X)/(\mathrm{MU}_Y)]$** and verify by direct differentiation of the equation of the IC, $y = \phi(x)$.

From Example 1.8, we already have the marginal utilities, so let us use those calculations to obtain MRS in each case. Thus,

$$\text{(a) MRS} = -(y/x); \quad \text{(b) MRS} = -y; \quad \text{and} \quad \text{(c) MRS} = -x/y.$$

For direct differentiation, we first need the explicit IC equation, $y = \phi(x, k)$ in each case. These are as follows:

(a) $y = k/x$; (b) $\ln y = k - x$; (c) $y = \sqrt{(k - x^2)}$. Note that for (c), we must have $x < \sqrt{k}$ so that both x and y are positive. By direct differentiation (using function of a function rule for (b) and (c)) and some manipulation, we get back exactly the same results as by using **MRS = $-[(\mathrm{MU}_X)/(\mathrm{MU}_Y)]$**.

Example 1.12: Evaluate the behaviour of the MRS of ICs for the utility functions (a) $U = xy$ and (b) $U = x^2 + y^2$.

Let the arbitrary level of utility be fixed at k so that we are examining the ICs $xy = k$ and $x^2 + y^2 = k$ and the MRS calculations are as before, i.e.,

$$\text{MRS}_a = -(y/x) \quad \text{and} \quad \text{MRS}_b = -(x/y).$$

If we ignore the signs, we see that MRS_a is decreasing as x increases but MRS_b does exactly the opposite. Figure 1.9 illustrates changing MRS.

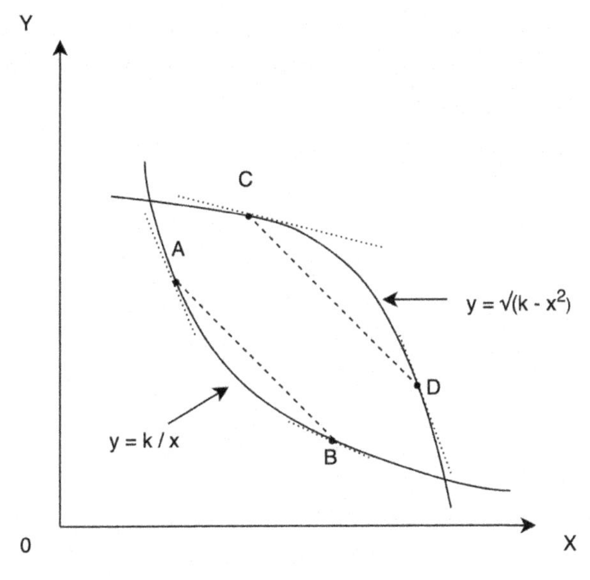

Fig. 1.9 Changing MRS

For IC given by $y = k/x$, note how the tangent to IC gets flatter as we move from A to B. This means absolute value of slope is getting smaller, i.e., MRS falls as x increases. Note how for the IC given by $y = \sqrt{(k - x^2)}$, the absolute value of the slope is getting bigger as we go from C to D by increasing x. By comparison with Example 1.7 and Figure 1.7, we note that when MRS is decreasing in absolute value, we have convex indifference curves and conversely when MRS is increasing in absolute value, we have concave indifference curves. The straight line AB (excluding the end points A and B) which represents all weighted averages of A and B lies on a higher IC than A or B. The converse is true for the dotted line joining CD. Thus, $y = k/x$ represents convex IC but $y = \sqrt{(k - x^2)}$ represents a concave IC.

1.4 Summary

- Budget sets of consumers are straight lines when prices are fixed but can take on different shapes if prices are variable.

- Consumer preferences can be represented by an ordinal utility function $U = F(x, y)$. A bundle with higher utility value is preferred to one with a lower utility value.
- An indifference curve (IC) connects all points with the same utility value.
- More is better implies ICs must be downward sloping. It also implies that any monotonic transformation of a utility function will produce the same ranking as the original (untransformed) utility function.
- The slope of an IC at any point measures the MRS between two goods at that point. It can be calculated by using the formula

$$\mathbf{MRS = -[(MU_X)/(MU_Y)]}.$$

- ICs which show a consumer preferring averages to extremes are convex. They have diminishing MRS (absolute value of slope falls as x increases).
- ICs which show a consumer preferring extremes to averages are concave. They have increasing MRS (absolute value of slope rises as x increases).

In the following chapter, we put together the properties of budget sets and consumer preferences to arrive at a theory of choice.

Chapter 2

Consumer Optimum and Demand

In this chapter, we use the concepts developed in Chapter 1 to analyse the consumer's **optimum choice bundle**. Specifically, we will address the question of how the consumer's optimum bundle is characterised and whether the characterisation depends on the nature of preferences (utility function). We illustrate different possibilities in the examples. We also create examples to illustrate how the optimum changes as prices or money income change.

2.1 Consumer Optimum

The following examples illustrate the method for finding the solutions under varying assumptions about preferences and budget sets. Some important special cases are examined.

Example 2.1: Joe desires burgers (X) and pizzas (Y). He has utility function given by $U = xy$. His income is £100. The price of burgers is £4 each and pizzas is £2 each. Find Joe's optimum consumption bundle of burgers and pizzas.

From Example 1.12, the properties of this utility function are known. All indifference curves are rectangular hyperbolae of the form $y = (k/x)$ and the MRS (in absolute value) is y/x which decreases as x increases.

Higher values of k represent higher levels of utility. The budget constraint is analogous to Eq. (1.5) and is given by

$$4x + 2y = 100. \tag{2.1}$$

The relative price ratio is thus $(4/2) = 2$. The consumer's problem now reduces to finding the highest indifference curve he can get to without violating his budget constraint. Figure 2.1 illustrates the tangency optimum.

It is clear from Figure 2.1 that a point like C in the **interior** of the budget set cannot be an optimum for Joe as he can have more of at least one commodity without losing any of the others by simply moving horizontally or vertically from C — as shown by the broken arrows. Hence, his optimum MUST lie on AB. Now, consider points like F and G. Clearly, Joe is indifferent between F and G as they both effect and lie on the convex indifference curve IC_1. Neither F nor G can be an optimum since by the convexity of the IC, every point on the chord FG must be preferred (averages are better than extremes) and all such points are **feasible**

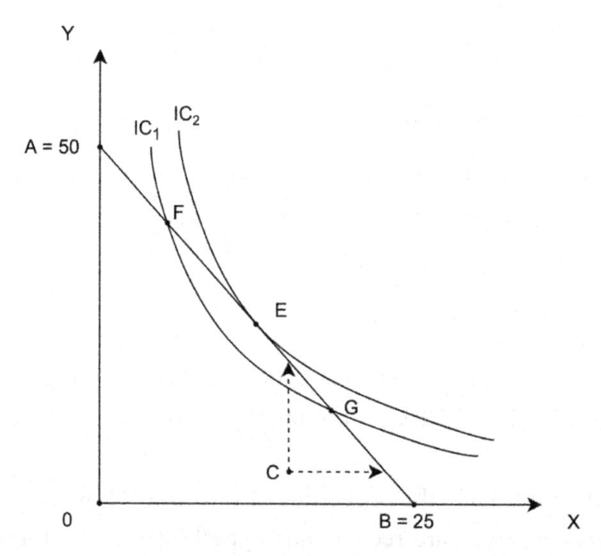

Fig. 2.1 The Tangency Optimum

(affordable). By exactly the same argument, the optimum can never lie on any indifference curve which cuts the budget line AB at two distinct points. Therefore, the optimum must be at a tangency, i.e., at E on IC_2, where the slopes of the indifference curve and the budget line are equal. Hence, the optimum is characterised by **MRS = relative price ratio**. This equality is sometimes referred to as the **tangency condition or the first-order condition**.

Using the tangency condition, the optimum is where $(y/x) = 2$ or $y = 2x$. But all (x, y) combinations must also satisfy the budget constraint (2.1). Hence, substituting $y = 2x$ into (2.1) gives the optimum values of x and y as $x^* = 12.5$ and $y^* = 25$ which are the coordinates of E.

Example 2.2: Repeat Example 2.1 but with prices p and q and money income m and a general utility function $U(x, y)$ which has convex indifference curves.

The same diagram (Figure 2.1) applies and the logic is exactly the same so that the optimum is characterised by a tangency. Hence, the solutions for optimal x and y must simultaneously satisfy
and

$$MU_x/MU_y = p/q. \tag{2.2a}$$

$$px + qy = m. \tag{2.2b}$$

Equation (2.2b) is linear but (2.2a) is not typically linear, even though in Example 2.1 it is linear. Hence these equations are not always easy to solve.

Example 2.3: Joe desires burgers (X) and pizzas (Y). He has utility function given by $U = x^2y^2$. His income is £100. The price of burgers is £4 each and pizzas is £2 each. Find Joe's optimum consumption bundle of burgers and pizzas.

First, note that the IC given $x^2y^2 = k$ can be written as $y = (\sqrt{k})/x$ and is thus convex and very similar to $y = k/x$ in Example 2.1. Hence, the tangency solution will hold. To find the MRS, we first find the marginal utilities MU_x and MU_y which by partial differentiation of U are $2xy^2$ and $2x^2y$ respectively and hence MRS = y/x as in Example 2.1 and hence the solutions are the same.

An alternative route would be to take a monotonic transformation of U by taking square root, i.e., let $V = \sqrt{U}$ and then we just work with $V = xy$ which is of course the same as in Example 2.1 and yields identical answers.

Example 2.4: Joe desires burgers (X) and pizzas (Y). He has utility function given by $U = x^a y^b$. His income is £m. The price of burgers is £p each and pizzas is £q each. Find Joe's optimum consumption bundle of burgers and pizzas.

Start by taking a monotonic transformation of U. Let $V = \ln U = a \ln x + b \ln y$ where ln stands for natural logarithms. Then, MRS = (V_x/V_y) where the notation V_z means the "partial derivative of the function V with respect to the variable z". Hence, MRS= $[(a/b)\ (y/x)]$ which behaves like (y/x) and hence justifies the search for a tangency solution. Thus, we must simultaneously solve

$$(a/b)(y/x) = p/q,$$

and

$$px + qy = m.$$

The solutions are $\boldsymbol{x^* = [a/(a + b)]\ [m/p]}$ **and** $\boldsymbol{y^* = [b/(a + b)]\ [m/q]}$.

Note that Examples 2.1 and 2.3 are special cases of Example 2.4. By putting in the numerical values for a, b, p, q and m into the answers for Example 2.4, we get the numerical answers for Examples 2.1 and 2.3. Note however that the solution to Example 2.4 has the odd feature that the consumption of X in no way depends on the price of Y and vice versa. This is a property of the particular utility function we chose. It is by no means a general result as the following example illustrates.

Example 2.5: Joe desires burgers (X) and pizzas (Y). He has utility function given by $U = \sqrt{x} + a\sqrt{y}$. His income is £m. The price of burgers is £p each and pizzas is £q each. Find Joe's optimum consumption bundle of burgers and pizzas.

As before, we start by examining MRS. By partial differentiation of U with respect to x and y, we obtain

$\mathrm{MU}_x = \frac{1}{2\sqrt{x}}$ and $\mathrm{MU}_y = \frac{a}{2\sqrt{y}}$ and hence MRS (absolute value) $= \frac{\sqrt{y}}{a\sqrt{x}}$. Since as x increases and y decreases, $\sqrt{y}$ falls and $\sqrt{x}$ increases, then MRS (absolute value) falls. This declining MRS (absolute value) implies convex indifference curve and justifies a search for a tangency solution. The full solution as earlier is given by

$$\mathrm{MU}_x/\mathrm{MU}_y = p/q. \tag{2.2a}$$

and

$$px + qy = m. \tag{2.2b}$$

By substituting the value of MRS (absolute value) into (2.2a), we get the solutions as

$$x^* = [m]/[p + a^2p^2/q] \text{ and } y^* = (ma^2p^2/q^2)/[p + a^2p^2/q].$$

Clearly, both x^* and y^* depend on both prices p and q as well as m — which is the general result.

Example 2.6: Ann desires burgers (X) and pizzas (Y). She has utility function given by $U = v(x) + y$ where $v(x)$ is an increasing function of x. Her income is £m. The price of burgers is £p each and pizzas is £q each. Find Ann's optimum consumption bundle of burgers and pizzas.

Again, we start by calculating MRS. By partial differentiation of U with respect to x and y, we obtain

$\mathrm{MU}_x = \frac{dv}{dx}$ which, in notation, we write as $v'(x)$; and obviously, $\mathrm{MU}_y = 1$. Hence, MRS (absolute value) $= v'(x)$. For MRS to be decreasing, we require $v'(x)$ to be decreasing or equivalently the second derivative of $v(x)$ written as $v''(x)$ must be negative. Examples include $v(x) = \ln x$ or $v(x) = \sqrt{x}$. If $v''(x) < 0$, MRS (absolute value) is decreasing and we can write the usual tangency solution as

$$v'(x) = (p/q),$$

which solves immediately for x^* *without reference to the budget constraint.* For instance, if $v(x) = \ln x$, then $v'(x) = 1/x$ and hence $x^* = q/p$. Once x^* is known, y^* is obtained from the budget constraint. Thus, if $v(x) = \ln x$ so that $x^* = q/p$, then from the budget constraint, $p\,(q/p) + qy^* = m$ so that $y^* = [(m - q)/q]$. Note that for this class of utility functions — which are called **quasi-linear** as they are linear in y but not in x — the optimum choice of x depends only on relative price while all remaining income after x^* is bought is spent on Y. The solution is of course only valid if px^* is less than m.

In all of the examples above, the solution has been characterised by a tangency between the budget line and an indifference curve. This solution has worked because of the strict convexity of the indifference curve which guaranteed a declining absolute value of MRS as we moved down the indifference curve consuming more x but less y. In the following few examples, we analyse what happens to consumer choice when this condition of continuously declining absolute value of MRS is not satisfied.

Example 2.7: Ann desires burgers (X) and coffee (Y). She has utility function given by $U = \min\,[ax, y]$. Her income is £m. The price of burgers is £p each and coffee is £q each cup. Find Ann's optimum consumption bundle of burgers and coffee.

This utility function describes goods that are perfect complements. To see that this works, suppose $a = 1$ and consider three bundles $A \equiv (10, 10)$, $B \equiv (10, 11)$ and $C \equiv (11, 10)$. Given the utility function, all three give the same utility which is 10. The "extra" amounts of X and Y in B and C are redundant. Since the consumer would never pay for redundant objects, the optimum must be characterised by $y = ax$. Substituting in the budget constraint, we can obtain x^* and y^* as $x^* = m/[p + qa]$ and $y^* = am/[p + qa]$. Figure 2.2 illustrates optimum with perfect complements.

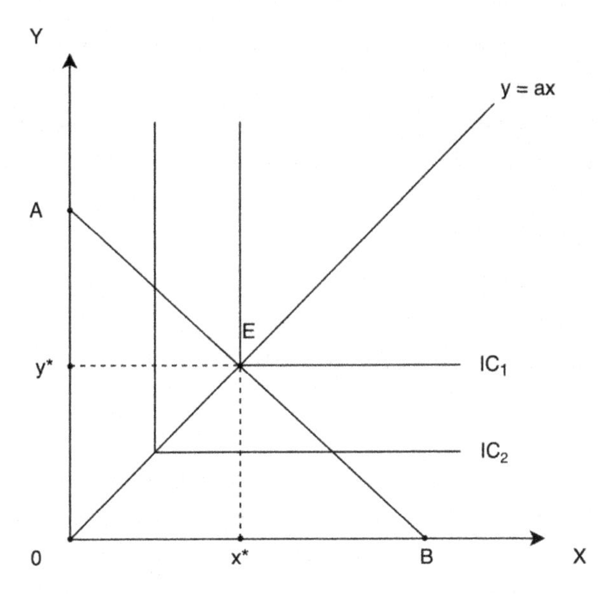

Fig. 2.2 Optimum with Perfect Complements

The indifference curve through any point will be L-shaped like IC_1 and IC_2 reflecting the assumption that "extra" of any one good is of no help. The optimum is clearly at E on the line $y = ax$. This is the highest IC she can reach while not breaking the budget. Note that although there is no unique tangent to IC_1 at E, it is still true that IC_1 is the only IC which does not cut the budget line twice — we can think of the budget line as a quasi-tangent! Note that there are infinitely many budget lines which can act as a quasi-tangent at E. Any straight line with negative slope passing through E will do the job! While there is no tangency condition, note that it is still the case that at the optimum, the IC does not pass through the budget line.

Example 2.8: Ann desires burgers (X) and pizzas (Y). She has utility function given by $U = [ax + y]$. Her income is £m. The price of burgers is £p each and pizzas is £q each. Find Ann's optimum consumption bundle of burgers and pizzas.

This utility function characterises perfect substitutes. Ann is willing to substitute one for the other at a constant rate. In the special case, when

$a = 1$, then all that matters to Ann is the total $(x + y)$, however the total is made up.

In this case, since $MU_x = a$ and $MU_y = 1$, (absolute value) MRS $= a$ and is constant. It is not decreasing! The indifference curves are straight lines of the form $y = k - ax$. They are not strictly convex. Figure 2.3 illustrates optimum with perfect substitutes.

AB is the budget line. The absolute value of the slope is (p/q). IC_1, IC_2 and IC_3 are indifference curves all with absolute value of slope being a. As drawn, a is less than (p/q). AB is steeper than IC_1, IC_2 and IC_3. Clearly, the highest indifference curve that can be achieved is IC_3 and the equilibrium is at B. Ann consumes only pizzas and no burgers. If on the other hand, Joe has similar preferences but a high value of a so that his ICs are the parallel dashed lines, then Joe would consume only burgers. The general point is complete specialisation will occur. No one will consume both burgers and pizzas! This is an immediate consequence of abandoning the strict convexity assumption. Once again at the optimum, the IC will not cross the budget line.

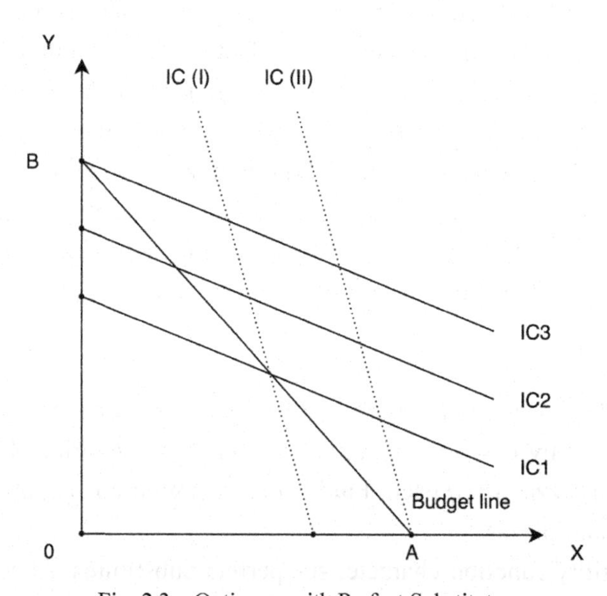

Fig. 2.3 Optimum with Perfect Substitutes

Example 2.9: Ann desires gin (X) and whiskey (Y). She has utility function given by $U = x^2 + y^2$. Her income is £m. The price of gin is £p each and whisky is £q each. Find Ann's optimum consumption bundle of burgers and pizzas.

$MU_x = 2x$ and $MU_y = 2y$ so that (absolute value) MRS = (x/y) which is *increasing* as we move down an IC by increasing x and lowering y. Thus, the ICs are not convex but concave. Tangency is not a solution. In fact, each IC is a quarter circle. Figure 2.4 illustrates optimum with concave indifference curves.

The tangency at E is the worst point on AB. Any movement away from E (towards A or B) puts Ann on a higher IC. Since averaging makes Ann worse off, her optimum will be at a corner. Which one, A or B? As drawn, it is B (all whiskey, no gin) as that puts her on a higher IC. If on the other hand prices were such that the budget line was BD, the optimum would be in the other corner at D (all gin, no whiskey). Either way, we get complete specialisation. Note that it is still true that at the optimal point at the corner, the IC will not cross the budget line!

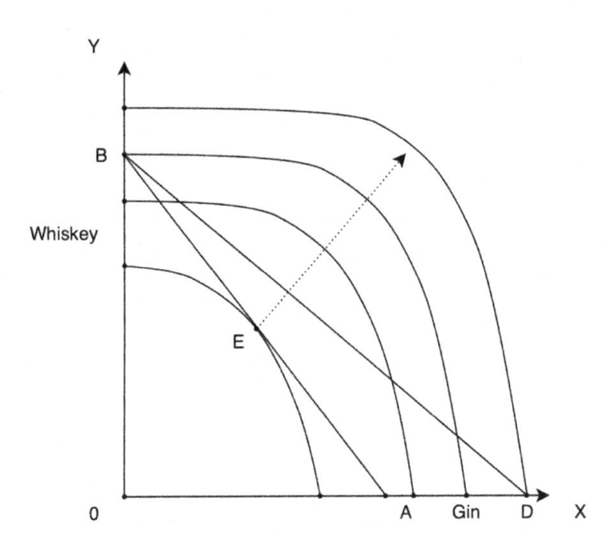

Fig. 2.4 Optimum with Concave Indifference Curves

Example 2.10: Joe desires wine (X) and a composite good called "other" whose price is £1 per unit. Initially, he buys wine from the supermarket at £10 per bottle and he buys 20 bottles per month. His monthly income is £1,500 and his indifference curves are known to be "smooth". A wine club opens charging a monthly membership of £100 but sells wine at £5 per bottle. Will Joe join the club?

Joe has a choice of two regimes: buy at supermarket or join the wine club. The monthly cost of 20 bottles from supermarket is £200. The monthly cost of 20 bottles from wine club is £100 (membership) plus £100 (20 bottles at £5 each) which is also £200. Superficially, it appears neutral. But why should Joe continue to consume 20 bottles at the wine club?

Joe's MRS must equal $10/1 = 10$ when buying from supermarket. Therefore, Joe's MRS at wine = 20 bottles must be 10. But at the wine club, his MRS will equal 5 at the optimum. But this must mean more wine consumption to lower the MRS. Figure 2.5 illustrates choice in different regimes.

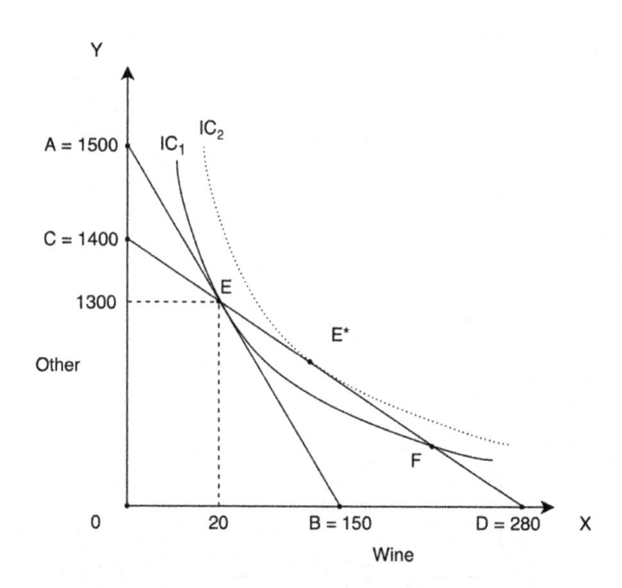

Fig. 2.5 Choice in Different Regimes

In Figure 2.5, wine is measured on the *X* axis and "other" on the *Y* axis. AB is the budget line if buying from supermarket. Initial equilibrium is at E with 20 bottles of wine consumed (and 1,300 units of "other"). The IC at E is convex because E is an interior point on budget line. The wine club budget line is CD. Note that it starts at 1,400 on the *Y* axis because of the membership fee of £100. E is also a point on the wine club budget line. The slope of CD is 5 compared to AB which is 10.

Under the supermarket deal, E is preferred to every other point on AE because all those were available when Joe chose E. And every point on AE is preferred to every point on CE (except at E). Therefore, Joe has in effect rejected the rest of CE if E is available — which it is under the wine club deal. Therefore, Joe will stay at E or move rightwards along ED. Since the IC through E has a slope of 10, it must cut the line CED which has a slope of 5. Hence, E cannot be an optimum under the wine club deal. The optimum must be on ED — every point of which is preferred to EB (excepting E). Thus, he is better off by joining the wine club!

Since Joe's ICs are convex, the IC which is tangent at E cuts CD twice: once at E and once at F as shown. By convexity arguments, every point on the wine club budget line between E and F is preferred to E or F. Hence, on CD, the optimum must occur at a point like E* which is on a higher IC than E. The slope of the indifference through E* is 5. Ergo, Joe joins the club and buys more wine than 20 bottles and less "other" than 1,300. It is the possibility of substitution on more favourable terms which makes Joe better off by joining the club. Note that what has been compared is Joe's best position under each regime. On that basis, the wine club regime is preferred.

2.2 Demand Analysis

In Section 2.1, we solved the problem of the consumer's optimal choice in a variety of settings. What we analyse in this section is how the optimal choice changes as parts of the setting change. This is known as demand analysis. In Example 2.5, we showed that the optimal choices were given by

$$x^* = [m]/[p + a^2p^2/q] \text{ and } y^* = (ma^2p^2/q^2)/[p + a^2p^2/q]. \qquad (2.2c)$$

Note that both optimal choices depend on p, q and m. Equation (2.2c) describes what are called **demand functions for X and Y**. It shows how x^* and y^* vary as prices or incomes vary either separately or together. If in (2.2c) we multiply p, q and m by the same factor k, neither x^* nor y^* will change. The factor k simply cancels out. This is a general property of all demand functions and it follows directly from the fact that an equi-proportional change in p, q and m leaves the budget set unaltered, and hence the optimal choice unaltered. This property is formally referred to as "homogeneity of degree zero". It can easily be checked that in Examples 2.1–2.9, the demand function has this property. We are often particularly interested in the impact of a change in the price of a good on its optimal consumption holding other things constant. This is what is called the **demand curve** (as opposed to the demand function defined earlier). The following diagrammatic examples illustrate the various possibilities as prices and/or income changes.

Example 2.11: Ann desires burgers (X) and pizzas (Y). Her preferences are strictly convex. The price of burgers falls. Illustrate how Ann's demand for burgers and pizzas changes. Is she better off?

Figure 2.6 illustrates demand after price change.

The initial budget line is AB. A fall in the price of X (burgers) means the budget line expands to CB. Clearly, CB encompasses more options than AB; Ann is better off. In effect, Ann is now richer in real terms. With the new price, she might move to a point like F and consume more of both or to G where she consumes more burgers but less pizzas, or even to a point like H where she consumes fewer burgers and more pizzas! The only possibility which can be ruled out is consuming less of both! Decomposing the price change into constituent parts will help understand the possibilities.

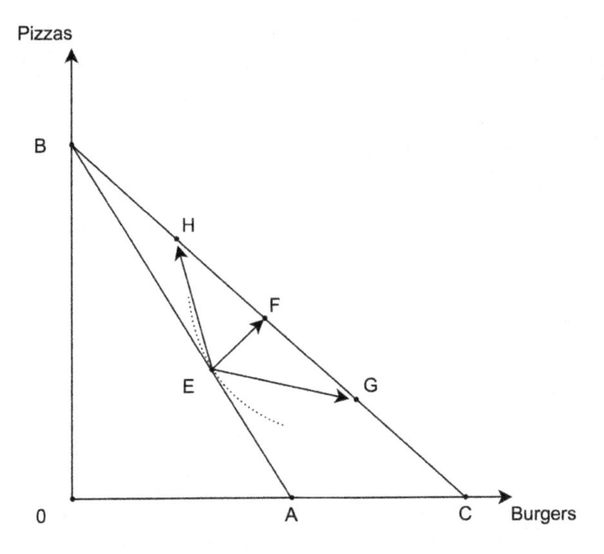

Fig. 2.6 Demand After Price Change

Example 2.12: Ann desires burgers (X) and pizzas (Y). Her preferences are given by $U = \sqrt{x} + \sqrt{y}$. The prices of burgers and of pizzas are p and q, respectively. Her income is m. Find the demand functions. Also, find the demand curve when $q = 4$ and $m = 160$. Illustrate how Ann's demand curve for burgers shifts if m rises to 320.

From Example 2.5 and setting $a = 1$, we get the demand functions as

$$x^* = [m]/[p + p^2/q] \text{ and } y^* = [mp^2/q^2]/[p + p^2/q],$$

When $q = 4$ and $m = 160$, the demand curve is given by $x^* = [640/(4p + p^2)]$.

When $q = 4$ and $m = 320$, the demand curve is given by $x^* = [1{,}280/(4p + p^2)]$.

The impact of higher income is to shift the demand curve upwards and rightwards as illustrated in Figure 2.7.

In Figure 2.7, demand x is measured on the vertical axis and price p on the horizontal. Since p drives x, this would be the normal mathematical way of drawing the demand curve. However, for various historical reasons, economists typically draw the **inverse demand curve**, $p = f(x)$ with

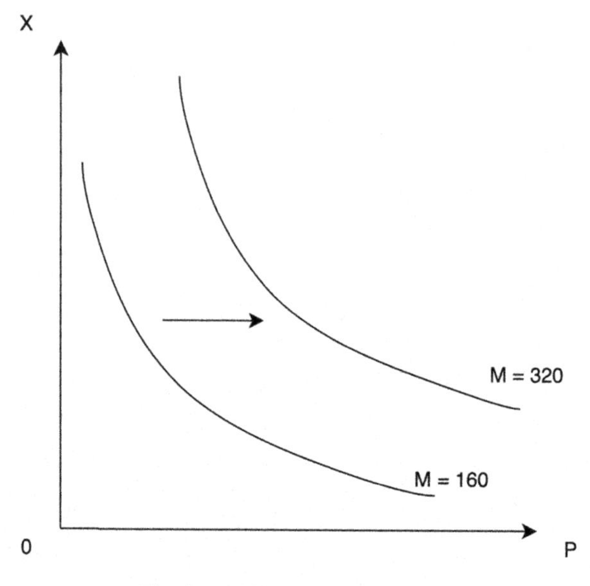

Fig. 2.7 Shift in Demand Curve

price (p) on the vertical axis, and the quantity demanded (x) on the horizontal axis. Both versions contain the same information.

2.3 Demand and Decomposition

In this section, we analyse the different elements which drive the impact of price changes. A price change alters relative prices (the slope of the budget line changes) but also real income (the size of the budget set changes). Both these influence the change in demand as the following example illustrates.

Example 2.13: Ann desires burgers (X) and pizzas (Y). Her preferences are given by $U = xy$. The prices of burgers and of pizzas are p and q, respectively. And her income is m.

(a) If m is 160, $p = 2$ and $q = 4$, find her optimal consumption of x, y and her consequent maximum utility. Illustrate on a diagram as point E. Call the optimum x as x^*.

(b) Repeat if p now rises to 4, all else constant. Illustrate on a diagram as point F. By how much does x^* fall? Compare to (a). Call this new optimum x as x^{**}.
(c) By how much will x^* fall, if after the price change, Ann is compensated by an increase in income which leaves her utility level the same as in (a)? Illustrate on a diagram as point D. Call this x^*_s.
(d) What increase in income, all else constant, will propel Ann from point F to point D?
(e) Will $x^* > x^*_s > x^{**}$, for all consumers whenever price of x rises?

This is a complex but highly instructive example. Since MRS = y/x, the solution in general is $(y/x = p/q)$ and $px + qy = m$ which solves for $x = (m/2p)$ and $y = (m/2q)$.

For (a), we substitute $p = 2$, $q = 4$ and $m = 160$ to get

$$x^* = 40, y^* = 20 \text{ and maximum utility } U^* = 800.$$

For (b), by substitution, we get $x^{**} = 20$, $y^{**} = 20$ and $U^{**} = 400$. Ann is worse off.

For (c), note that $y/x = 1$ or $y = x$ and $U = 800$ as in (a). Substitute $y = x$ into U to get $x^2 = 800$ so that $x^*_s = 20\sqrt{2} = 28$ (approx.), $y^*_s = 28$ (approx.) and $U = 800$.

For (d), we must find the value of m which given $p = q = 4$ will generate x^*_s as an optimum. That is to say, it's that m which solves $x = y$ and $4x + 4y = m$, where $x = 28$. This gives $m = 8\,[20\sqrt{2}] = 226$ (approximately). So, if prices were $p = q = 4$, an income of 226 would induce Ann to consume at $x = y = 28$ and be just as well off with $U = 800$ as she was in (a).

Figure 2.8 illustrates the **decomposition** of the price effect on x consumption.

AB is the initial budget line with relative price = 1/2 and initial optimum is at E on IC_1 with $x^* = 40$ and $y^* = 20$. After the price rise of X from 2 to 4, the new budget line is CB reflecting relative price of 1 and new optimum is at F on IC_2 with $x^{**} = 20$ and $y^{**} = 20$. The movement from E to F can be decomposed into two movements. First, a movement from E to D and then another from D to F. The movement from E to D is what

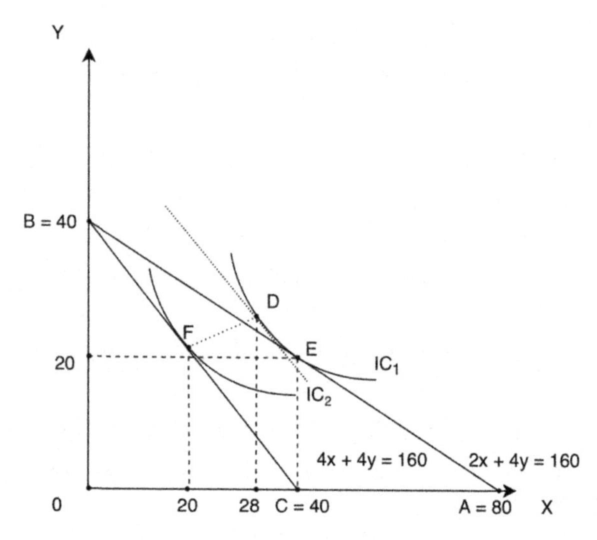

Fig. 2.8 Decomposing the Price Effect

is called **the substitution effect** of a price change. It calculates the change in x due purely to change in relative prices holding utility constant. This is the amount (40 – 28) = 12. The second movement from D to F is called the **income effect**. It is the change in x due to an implicit change in income or purchasing power holding prices constant. Thus, the pseudo budget line through D is parallel to the one through F, reflecting constant relative price of 1. In this example, $x^* = 40$, $x^*_s = 28$ and $x^{**} = 20$. The substitution effect is negative going in opposite direction to the price change; it lowers x by 12 following the price rise. The income effect in this example is positive — it changes x in the same direction as the implicit income change; it lowers x by a further 8 as the price rise reduces real income. The two effects reinforce each other. Both lower x. The sum of the two effects makes up the total effect of a price change.

For (e), we note that in this example, $x^* = 40 > x^*_s = 28 > x^{**} = 20$. But this ordering does not uniformly hold. The income effect is not always positive. Goods in which the income effect is positive are called **normal goods** while those in which income effect is negative are called **inferior goods**. For such inferior goods, a rise in income, all else constant, will lead to a fall in demand for that good. Examples might be bread, potatoes or other basic goods. And what is inferior for one individual might not be inferior for another individual.

Example 2.14: Rani consumes rice (X) and a "composite good" (Y) whose price is unity. Rice is an inferior good. The price of rice rises. Will Rani consume more or less rice?

The price rise raises the relative price of rice and reduces the budget set — implicitly income falls. The rise in relative price of rice will lead to a substitution effect due to which Rani consumes less rice. But the fall in income leads to a rise in rice consumption since rice is an inferior good for Rani. The overall effect is the sum of these two separate effects. If the income effect is stronger than the substitution effect, then rice consumption rises despite the price rise. In this case, rice is not only an inferior good but sufficiently strongly inferior to be a **Giffen** good. These goods are a subset of inferior goods with such strong income effects that they outweigh the substitution effect. Giffen goods have upward-sloping demand curves — price rises lead to consumption rises. Giffen goods are rare in practice in rich countries.

2.4 Some Special Cases

In the decomposition analysed in Section 2.3, we showed the role played by income and substitution effects in what may be deemed to be a standard case. In this section, we look at two special cases which are of importance. In the first special case, income effects will always be zero so that only the substitution effect matters in determining the changes in demand. In the second special case, the rise in price will expand rather than shrink the budget set. See the following examples.

Example 2.15: Ari has utility function $U = \ln x + y$ where "ln" stands for natural logarithms. The price of X is £p per unit, and the price of Y is £q per unit. His income is £m. Find his demand functions for X and Y and discuss how demand changes as income changes.

The equation of an IC will be $y = k - \ln x$ and hence MRS = absolute value of $dy/dx = (1/x)$ which decreases as x gets bigger. Hence, strict convexity of IC is assured and we can search for the tangency solution. This is given by $(1/x) = (p/q)$ so that $x^* = (q/p)$ which is the demand function for X. Note that m does not figure in the demand function which means that the income effect is zero! Substituting $x^* = (q/p)$ into the budget constraint, we solve for y^* as $y^* = (m - q)/q$. Any increase in m is fully reflected in increased Y consumption while x^* remains constant! As the income effect on X consumption is zero, we know that the demand curve for X will always slope downwards due to the substitution effect. Example 2.16 generalises this case.

Example 2.16: Rani has utility function $U = V(x) + y$. The price of X is £p per unit, and the price of Y is £q per unit. Her income is £m. Find her demand functions for X and Y and discuss how demand changes as income changes.

The IC can be written as $y = k - V(x)$ so that MRS = absolute value of slope of IC = $V'(x)$ which must be positive. For strict convexity, we require MRS to be decreasing and so we must have $V''(x) < 0$. Given these conditions, the tangency solution requires $V'(x) = (p/q)$ which solves for x^* independently of the value of m. The income effect is zero. As Rani gets richer, all extra income is spent on Y while X consumption remains constant.

Example 2.15 is a special case of Example 2.16 with $V(x) = \ln x$. Both examples are characterised by utility functions that are called quasi-linear utility functions because the term in y is linear but not the term in x. The indifference curves corresponding to such functions are simply parallel vertically shifted versions of each other. Quasi-linear utility functions are not particularly realistic but are very convenient to work with because we can forget about the complications caused by non-zero income effects.

We end this section by examining a practical policy problem, the solution to which requires an understanding of income and substitution effects.

Example 2.17: Rani is a senior citizen whose pension income is £1,200. She consumes only electricity (X) and a composite good (Y) whose price is £1 per unit. The price of electricity is £0.50 per unit and she spends £400 on electricity.

(a) If her utility function is known to be $U = xy^{\alpha}$, find the value of α.
(b) The electricity company raises the price of electricity to £0.6 per unit. The government is concerned to maintain Rani's well-being. One government adviser, Mr A, says that her pension income should be raised by £80. How does he arrive at this figure? Another adviser, Ms B, says it should be raised by less than £80. Who is right?
(c) Ms B further says that she can find the exact amount of increased pension required. Explain B's thinking using a diagram and find her exact answer.

(a) Since Rani consumes at an interior point on her budget line, with electricity = 400/0.5 = 800 units, her preferences are convex. Hence, we focus on tangency solutions. Consumption of Y is (1200 – 400)/1 = 800 units.

   $\text{MRS} = \text{MU}_X/\text{MU}_Y = (y/\alpha x) = 0.5/1 = (1/2)$. But we know $x^* = 800$ and $y^* = 800$. Substituting these values into the MRS = relative price condition, $(y/\alpha x) = (1/2)$, yields $\alpha = 2$. Thus, Rani's utility function is $U = xy^2$.

(b) For Rani to purchase the original bundle of (800, 800) would now cost £0.1 more per unit of X (since price of y is constant), i.e., £(800×0.1) = £80. This is the basis of A's calculation. It assumes that the way to maintain Rani's well-being is to **compensate** her with enough income to purchase the original bundle she was buying before the price rise. It ignores Rani's ability to substitute the composite good for electricity. On the other hand, B explicitly recognises that Rani can and will substitute some composite good for electricity. Hence, B argues for a **subsidy** of less than £80 as Rani will not consume 800 units of electricity at the new prices.

(c) To calculate the exact subsidy, B uses the substitution/income effect decomposition. At the original optimum, Rani had utility = $xy^2 = 800 \times 800^2 = 800^3$. At the new prices, tangency solution requires $(y/2x) = 0.6$ or $y = 1.2x$ which then gives utility $= x(1.2x)^2 = 1.44x^3$. If Rani's well-being is to be maintained, then this new utility of $1.44x^3$ must equal the old utility of 800^3. Setting these equal to reach other, i.e., $1.44x^3 = 800^3$ or $x = [800/(1.44^{0.333})] = 708$. From $y = 1.2x$, we get $y = 850$ when $x = 708$. Thus, the bundle (708, 850) gives the same utility as (800, 800). This new bundle costs £[(708 × 0.6) + (850 × 1)] = £1,275. In other words, if Rani had an income of £1,275 and faced prices (0.6, 1), she would optimally choose the bundle (708, 850) and get the same utility as before. Hence, the required subsidy is only £75 NOT £80. Figure 2.9 illustrates compensation policy.

In Figure 2.9, electricity is measured on the *X* axis and the composite good on the *Y* axis. Since the composite good has a price of unity, the *Y* axis also measures total expenditure. CD is the original budget line reflecting an electricity price of £0.5 per unit. Rani's consumption is at E where she buys 800 units of electricity and 800 units of the composite

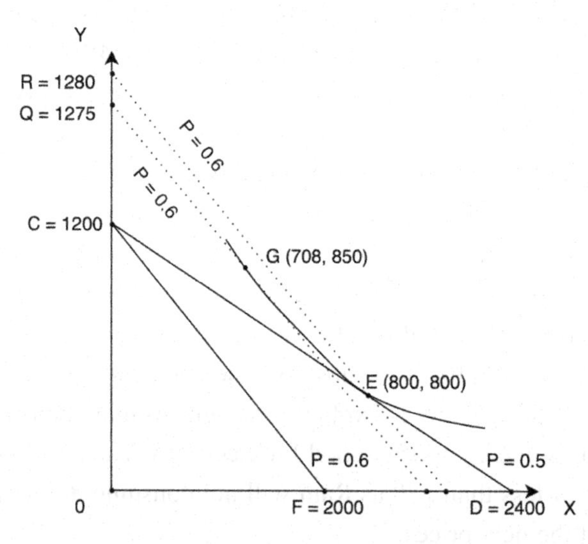

Fig. 2.9 Compensation Policy

good. CF is the new budget line reflecting an electricity price of 0.6. A's solution requires Rani to be able to afford E at the new prices — the budget line RE achieves this. Note that R on the Y axis is £1,280 which is the amount of income required to consume E when the price of electricity is £0.6 per unit. However, B takes advantage of the substitution effect which shows that consumption at G on QG (which also embodies an electricity price of 0.6) yields the same utility as at E. Thus, G maintains Rani's well-being. But from the intercept Q on the Y axis, we see that expenditure at G is less than expenditure at R. Hence, B's solution involves a lower income subsidy and still enables Rani to maintain her well-being.

2.5 Responsiveness of Demand

We have seen how the quantity demanded of a commodity depends on the price of the commodity, the price of the substitute good and income. Let the demand function be $x = F(p, q, m)$ where p, q and m stand respectively for price of X, price of substitute Y and money income. Examples of the above abound in previous sections. A natural question to ask is as follows: "How much does demand respond when one of its determinants changes?" One way of capturing this idea of "the degree of responsiveness" is by looking at the slope of the demand curves. Greater responsiveness of quantity to a price change is reflected in a flatter (inverse) demand. Higher quantity responsiveness is associated with lower (absolute value) of slopes of the (inverse) curves. So, we could use absolute slope to measure responsiveness. But the problem with that is that the slope depends on the units of measurement — which is not an attractive property.

So, we modify slightly and use the concept economists call "**elasticity**". This concept measures the proportionate increase in quantity demanded due to a 1% change in its price, holding all else constant. Formally, holding q and m constant, if price p changes by Δp and the consequent change in quantity demanded x is given by Δx, we define the **price elasticity** of demand as being given by

$$\xi_{x,\,p} = (\Delta x/x)/(\Delta p/p).$$

In the definition above, the elasticity measure $\xi_{x,p}$ is read as "the elasticity of demand x with respect to price p" or, in short, as price elasticity of demand. The numerator is the percentage increase in demand while the denominator is the percentage change in price. We can rewrite $\xi_{x,p}$ as

$$\xi_{x,p} = (\Delta x/\Delta p)\ (p/x).$$

And if the change in p (and in x) is small, the ratio of small changes approximates to a derivative so that

$$\xi_{x,p} = (dx/dp)\ (p/x).$$

Example 2.18: Find the price elasticity of demand for each of the following demand curves: (a) $x = Ap^{\alpha}$ and (b) $x = \beta - \alpha p$ for $p < \beta/\alpha$

In (a), $(dx/dp) = -\alpha Ap^{\alpha-1}$ and hence $\xi_{x,p} = (dx/dp)\ (p/x)$
$= -[\alpha Ap^{\alpha-1}]\ [p/Ap^{\alpha}] = -\alpha,$

In (b) $\xi_{x,p} = -\alpha p/[\beta - \alpha p]$.

The comparison between (a) and (b) is instructive. In both cases, elasticity is negative. However, in (a), the demand curve is negative exponential and the price elasticity is a constant. In (b), however, the demand curve is linear and elasticity varies with price p. As p gets bigger, the value of elasticity in absolute terms rises.

Since we expect demand curves to be downward sloping, we expect price elasticities to be negative as in Example 2.18. However, for the most part, we use the elasticity concept in absolute value format ignoring the sign, especially where the sign is obvious from the context. Note also that elasticity is a partial concept. It is evaluating the responsiveness of demand due to a change in one independent variable holding all the others constant. Strictly speaking, the derivative in the elasticity definition is a partial derivative. If we were to hold both prices constant and write demand as depending on income only, then we could calculate the elasticity of demand with respect to income. This idea generalises to all economic relationships.

Suppose that some economic variable Z is determined by the independent variables X and Y according to $Z = F(X, Y)$. We define the two elasticities, viz. elasticity of Z with respect to X and elasticity of Z with respect to Y as

$$\xi_{Z,X} = (F_X)(X/Z) \quad \text{and} \quad \xi_{Z,y} = (F_Y)(Y/Z),$$

where F_X and F_Y are the partial derivatives of Z with respect to X and Y, respectively. This concept will be exploited throughout the rest of this book.

2.6 Summary

- The consumer's optimum bundle will always lie on the budget line.
- In all cases, at an optimum, an IC will not "cross" the budget line.
- With strictly convex ICs (averages strictly preferred to extremes), the optimum will always lie on the interior of the budget line at a tangency between budget line and IC. Clearly, there is no "crossing" at the optimum.
- In the case of perfect complements, there is an interior solution characterised by a "quasi-tangent". Clearly, there is no "crossing" at the optimum.
- In the case of perfect substitutes, a corner solution prevails. There is complete specialisation (except in the case where slope of IC and budget line are equal). Clearly, there is no "crossing" at the optimum.
- In the case of concave preferences, a corner solution prevails. There is complete specialisation. Clearly, there is no "crossing" at the optimum.
- The consumers' optimum choices lead directly to the demand functions for X and Y. The demand function for X depends on price of X, price of Y and consumer income.
- The impact of a price change on consumer demand can be decomposed into a substitution effect and income effect.

- The substitution effect of a price change measures what would have happened to demand if price changed but the consumer was compensated to remain on the same indifference curve before and after the price change. Substitution effects are always negative (for convex indifference curves).
- The income effect of a price change measures the change in demand due to having a different level of purchasing power but implicitly holding price constant. Income effects are generally positive but there is a class of goods for which income effects are negative. Such goods are inferior goods.
- Giffen goods are a subset of inferior goods with such strong income effects that they outweigh the substitution effect. Giffen goods have upward-sloping demand curves.
- Income and substitution effects allow for a proper measure of compensation policy.
- The responsiveness of quantity demanded to a price change is formally measured by price elasticity of demand. This concept is generalisable to the relationship between any two economic variables.

Chapter 3

Generalisations, Applications and Extensions of the Choice Model

In the analysis of consumer choice, we focused a lot on the tangency solution. Our analysis was restricted to the two good cases, and the "derivation" of the tangency condition was essentially geometric intuition. Furthermore, in all the examples so far, the constraint was essentially linear. Before looking at further applications and extensions, it would be helpful to sketch a general solution method which works with more than two variables and also can encompass nonlinear constraints. The treatment of this important problem is heuristic rather than rigorous. We focus on how to use the method.

The standard problem in consumer theory as described earlier is of a consumer trying to reach the highest level of utility but being constrained by prices of the two goods and income. Formally, if $U(x, y)$ is his utility function and his income is m, and prices are p and q respectively, then his problem may be stated as

"Choose x and y so as to maximise $U(x, y)$ subject to $px + qy = m$". The solution provided the ICs corresponding to $U(x, y)$ are strictly convex is the familiar tangency solution together with the budget constraint.

The full solution as earlier is given by

$$\mathrm{MU}_x/\mathrm{MU}_y = p/q, \tag{2.2a}$$

and

$$px + qy = m. \tag{2.2b}$$

A more direct mathematical approach is to use the **Lagrangian method**. This is a method for solving constrained optimisation problems where we are required to find maxima (or minima) of a function of several variables subject to constraints on the choice of the variables. We proceed by defining a new function called the Lagrangian function which is given by

$$L(x, y, \lambda) = U(x, y) - \lambda[px + qy - m]. \tag{3.1}$$

Note that we have introduced another variable, $\lambda > 0$, into the problem. What purpose does this serve? If the constraint binds so that $px + qy = m$, then the value of L and U is the same as the term in square parentheses is zero. Thus, if we can find an (x^*, y^*) that simultaneously maximises L and satisfies the constraint, we will have solved our problem.

Treating L as a function of two variables x and y, the first-order conditions (FOC) for maximising L are given by

$$L_x = U_x - \lambda p = 0, \tag{3.2a}$$

$$L_y = U_y - \lambda q = 0. \tag{3.2b}$$

Equations (3.2a) and (3.2b) imply that $U_x = \lambda p$ and that $Uy = \lambda q$; and hence $(U_x/U_y) = [\lambda p/\lambda q]$. Cancelling λ and recalling that U_x is MU_x and Uy is MU_y, we get the familiar result of (2.2a), viz. that the optimum choice (x^*, y^*) must satisfy

$$MU_x/MU_y = p/q. \tag{2.2a}$$

And in order to make sure the constraint is satisfied, (x^*, y^*) must also satisfy (2.2b),

$$px + qy = m. \tag{2.2b}$$

These conditions are exactly what we had earlier. But the method of Lagrange can extend to more than two variable problems and also to cases where the constraint is nonlinear so long as the **feasible set** defined by the constraint is also convex and the indifference curves (or equivalent) are convex. In the linear case, the feasible set is defined by $px + qy \leq m$, which being a triangle in (x, y) space is obviously convex.

3.1 Labour Supply

A special case of some practical importance is concerned with the analysis of **work time**. Work and leisure are opposite sides of the same coin. Each hour of leisure is one hour less of work. The hourly wage is the opportunity cost of leisure. In effect, if an individual is "consuming" one hour of leisure, he is in effect "buying" it by paying a price equal to the hourly wage. And everyone values leisure. If we denote leisure by H (measured in fractions of a day) and the composite good whose price is 1 is denoted by C, we can think of an individual having a utility function given by $U = F(H, C)$ with the standard properties. For convenience, we assume strict convexity of ICs so that tangency solutions are valid.

Example 3.1: Ari has utility function given by $U = HC$. The wage is £W per full day and in addition Ari has a non-labour income of £K per day. How much will Ari work?

Denote work by L so that $L = 1 - H$ is the fraction of the day worked. Hence, his total income = £$(K + WL)$ or equivalently, £$[K + W(1 - H)]$ and since the price of the composite good is unity, the budget constraint is

$$C = K + W(1 - H), \tag{3.3}$$

which can be rewritten in a more familiar form as

$$WH + C = K + W. \tag{3.4}$$

The budget constraint (3.4) is in standard form where the prices of the two goods, leisure and the composite good, are W and 1 respectively and income is $K + W$.

Since the utility function has strictly convex indifference curves, we can apply the tangency solution. Since $MU_H = C$ and $MU_C = H$, then $MRS = C/H$ and relative price ratio $= W/1$. Hence, we get $C/H = W$ or $C = WH$. Substituting WH for C on the left-hand side of (3.3) yields the answer as $H^* = (K/2W) + 1/2$ and hence $L^* = 1 - H^* = 1/2 - (K/2W)$. As W rises, $(K/2W)$ falls so that leisure consumption H^* falls and labour supply L^* increases. This is the result that most people might expect. Rising wage is an incentive to work more. However, as the following example shows, this result is not universal.

Example 3.2: Rani has utility function given by $U = -H^{-1} - C^{-1}$. If daily wage is £W and non-labour income is £K, find her labour supply function and comment.

Despite the negative signs, the utility function has standard properties of positive marginal utilities and declining MRS. $MU_H = H^{-2}$ and $MU_C = C^{-2}$. Hence, $MRS = (C/H)^2$ which declines as H increases and C falls as we move down the IC. Hence, the tangency solution is valid.

Thus, $(C/H)^2 = W$ and by substituting into the budget constraint (3.3), we get $H^* = [(W + K)/(W + \sqrt{W})]$ and hence $L^* = [\{1 - (K/\sqrt{W})\}/\{1 + \sqrt{W}\}]$ and hence if $K = 0$ (or is sufficiently small), then L^* is decreasing in W.

Examples 3.1 and 3.2 show that the impact of wage on labour supply is uncertain. Depending on the utility function, labour supply may rise as wage rises (as in Example 3.1) or it may fall (as in Example 3.2). This ambiguity can best be understood by reference to income and substitution effects. Leisure may be presumed to be a normal good and *not* an inferior good. With no change in wage, a rise in non-labour income will induce greater leisure (and more consumption). When the wage rate rises, there are two effects. First, leisure gets more expensive and hence by the substitution effect consumption of leisure should fall. But a rise in the wage also increases the budget set thereby generating a positive income effect which increases leisure. Thus, in this case, even though leisure is a normal good, the substitution and income effects are in conflict and the overall outcome depends on the strength of each. In Example 3.1, the substitution effect outweighs the income effect and conversely in Example 3.2.

The peculiarity of the labour/leisure choice arises because in other cases, a rise in price of one good causes relative price increase and real income decline. If the good is normal, the real income decline will tend to lower consumption. Hence, substitution and income effects work together for normal goods. With leisure, price rise (wage rise) raises relative price of leisure BUT also raises real income. Hence, when leisure is normal, a wage rise produces conflict between the substitution effect (buy less leisure because it's got expensive) and the income effect (buy more leisure because you are richer). If leisure is a normal good — which it surely must be — the only safe prediction is that an increase in non-labour income (K) will increase demand for leisure and lower labour supply.

Example 3.3: Ann has utility function given by $U = U(H, C)$ where C is consumption of the composite good and H is hours of leisure per week. The ICs derived from U are strictly convex. The hourly wage rate is £W and her weekly non-labour income is £K. Total time available in the week is T. For what values of W will she definitely choose to work a positive number of hours?

Ann will want to maximise U subject to the budget constraint $C = K + W(T - H)$. The Lagrangian is

$$L(H, C, \lambda) = U(H, C) - \lambda[C - K - W(T - H)]. \tag{3.5}$$

The FOCs are $U_H/U_C = W$ and together with the budget constraint $C = K + W(T - H)$ will solve for H^* and C^*. But what if the proposed solution H^* exceeds total time available T? Clearly, then H^* is not a solution and Ann would choose the nearest H she can get which is $H = T$. Figure 3.1 illustrates participation in work.

In Figure 3.1, the budget line ABD has slope equal to the wage W. Non-labour income H is represented by BT. Three ICs are shown. At D, IC_1 cuts the budget line and Ann will move down the budget line towards B thereby moving onto a higher indifference curve. But even at B, Ann has an incentive to consume more leisure and move to the highest possible IC at A where the tangency occurs. But this move is infeasible — A is not in the budget set. Hence, Ann will end up at B with zero hours of work

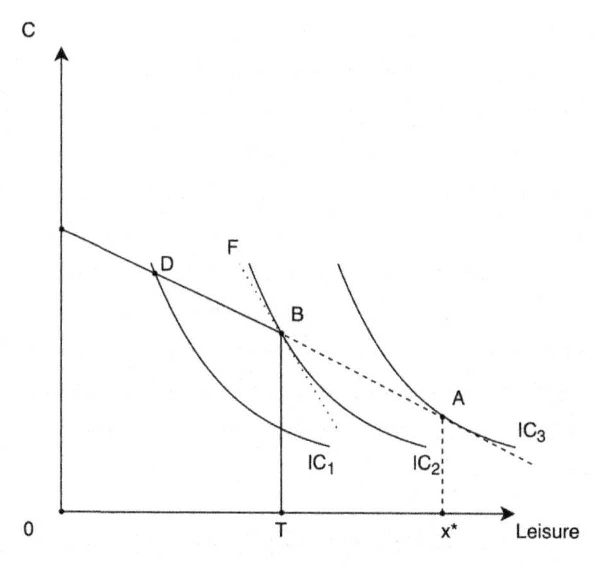

Fig. 3.1 Participation in Work

and T hours of leisure. She will NOT participate in the labour market. Note that at B, the budget line FB is a tangent to IC_2. Suppose the slope of FB is W_R. For any wage lower than W_R, the budget line will be flatter than FB and Ann would choose B. Conversely, for all wages exceeding W_R, Ann would move away from B towards less leisure (more work). W_R is called the **reservation wage**, the minimum wage required to persuade Ann to work. At lower wages, she "reserves" her labour.

Example 3.4: Ann has utility function given by $U = a \ln H + C$ where C is consumption of the composite good and H is hours of leisure per week. The hourly wage rate is £W and her weekly non-labour income is £K. Total time available in the week is T. For what values of W will she definitely choose to work a positive number of hours?

The ICs are convex. The tangency solution requires MRS = W or $a/H = W$ or $H^* = a/W$. To be meaningful, this must be less than T, i.e., $(a/W) < T$ or $W > a/T$, which means the reservation wage $W_R = a/T$.

For all wages exceeding this, she will work a positive number of hours. Intuitively, this makes sense. The higher the coefficient a, the higher Ann's MU of leisure. Hence, the higher the wage required to compensate Ann for giving up highly valuable leisure. In terms of Figure 3.1, the reservation wage (a/T) is the slope of FB. There is always some IC passing through B — IC_2 as shown in Figure 3.1. And the reservation wage is simply the slope of that IC at B.

3.2 Endogenous Income

In all of the examples up to now, non-labour income has been assumed to be given. In this section, we relax this assumption and assume instead that non-labour income is obtained from the sale of goods that the consumer has inherited before coming to market. We refer to this "inheritance" as an **endowment**.

Example 3.5: Ari has a utility function given by $U = xy$ where x is quantity of apples consumed and y is quantity of oranges consumed. The prices of apples and oranges are £p and £q per unit, respectively. Ari has an (inherited) endowment of $X^{\sim}$ and $Y^{\sim}$ respectively of apples and oranges. Describe his optimum. What happens if p rises?

Ari obtains an income M by selling his endowment. Therefore, $M = pX^{\sim} + qY^{\sim}$. He then maximises utility subject to the usual budget constraint to arrive at his optimal consumption levels given by

$$x^* = M/2p \quad \text{and} \quad y^* = M/2q \quad \text{which, given the value of } M\text{, implies,}$$

$$x^* = (pX^{\sim} + qY^{\sim})/2p \quad \text{and} \quad y^* = (pX^{\sim} + qY^{\sim})/2q.$$

Note that it follows directly from the budget constraint (and independently of the utility function) that if $x^* < X^{\sim}$, then $y^* > Y^{\sim}$ and vice versa. The quantity $(x^* - X^{\sim})$ is Ari's net purchase of X and $(y^* - Y^{\sim})$ is his net purchase of Y. One of these net purchases must be positive and the other negative (except in the fluke case when both are zero and Ari simply consumes his endowment!)

With a fixed income that does not depend on prices, a rise in price of X would lower X consumption (since both X and Y are normal if $U = xy$). Suppose $x^* < X^{\sim}$ so that Ari is a big seller of X. Then, the rise in p will raise his income. As X is normal and rise in p raises income, the income effect suggests rise in X consumption, thus going against the substitution effect which implies fall in X consumption because of a rise in p. Which effect is stronger? From $x^* = (pX^{\sim} + qY^{\sim})/2p$, we can see that as p rises, x^* falls. The positive income effect of a price rise is submerged by the negative substitution effect of a price rise. We can also see from $y^* = (pX^{\sim} + qY^{\sim})/2q$ that an increase in p increases y^* for two reasons. First, the rise in p raises Ari's income and so the income effect raises y^*; and second, the fact that q/p has fallen implies a substitution effect in favour of y^*. Figure 3.2 illustrates price change effects with given endowments.

In Figure 3.2, E is the endowment point. All budget lines must pass through E since E is always affordable at any set of prices. AEB is the original budget line. Ari's optimum choice is at G which is (x^*, y^*). As drawn, $x^* < X^{\sim}$ which implies Ari sells X (to buy Y). Hence, a rise in

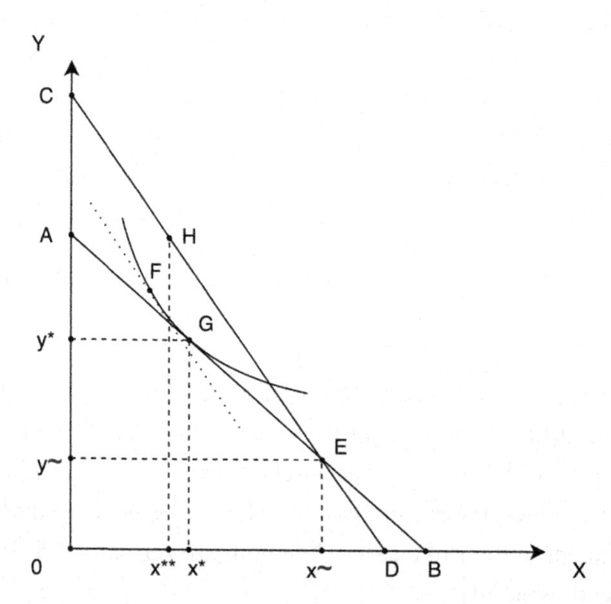

Fig. 3.2 Price Change Effects with Given Endowments

p reflected in the budget line CED increases his income as shown by the fact that CHE lies entirely above AGE. The rise in p leads to a pure substitution effect to F where X consumption is much lower than at G. But from here, the positive income effect kicks in and takes Ari from F to H. But in this case, the rise in X consumption from F to H is not enough to offset the fall in X consumption from G to F. Hence, overall, X consumption declines to x^{**}. The substitution effect has dominated the income effect. In the case of Y consumption, both income and substitution effects reinforce each other and Y consumption rises to y^{**}.

But what if Ari buys X rather than sells it? This means $x^* > X^{\sim}$ and Ari's optimum is on the segment EB. As can be seen, a rise in price of X in this case makes Ari poorer with the budget line now being ED. Again, the substitution effect pushes Ari towards lower consumption of X. But now, the income effect does the same. Income has fallen, so by the income effect, X consumption will tend to fall. Hence, his consumption of X falls as the price rises.

But these are by no means universal results. The fact that as p rises Ari may get richer (when he is a large seller of X) does imply that because of income effect, there is a force pulling towards increased X consumption. This force may or not overcome the substitution effect pulling in the opposite direction of lowering X consumption. It is possible in the case of some utility functions for the income effect to dominate the substitution effect.

Example 3.6: Rani has the utility function $U = xy$ where x is quantity of bread consumed and y is quantity of wine. Her initial endowment is (9, 3). Prices are £4 and £36 per unit of X and Y. Find her optimal bread/wine consumption bundle. If the government lowers the tariff on wine, the price of wine drops to £18. Find her new optimum. Is she better off? Describe the income and substitution effects. How much would Rani be willing to bribe the government not to lower the tariff?

Rani's income is the value of her endowment = $(9 \times 4 + 3 \times 36) =$ £144. Optimal consumption for this utility function is equal shares of expenditure. Thus, expenditure on X equals expenditure on $Y =$ £72.

Therefore, $x^* = 18$, $y^* = 2$ and $U^* = 18 \times 2 = 36$ utils. Note that Rani is selling wine. The fall in the price of wine lowers the value of her endowment to $[(9 \times 4) + (3 \times 18)] = £90$. Equal shares imply expenditure of £45 on each good. Hence, at the new prices, $x^{**} = 45/4$ and $y^{**} = 45/18 = 5/2$ and hence $U^{**} = (45/4) \times (5/2) = 225/8 = 28.125$. Rani is worse off because the value of her endowment has fallen.

To calculate income and substitution effects, note that at the new prices, we must have $y/x = 4/18$ or $9y = 2x$ or $x = (9/2)y$. Substituting in U, we get $U = (9/2)y^2$; and to keep Rani on the original indifference curve, we must have $(9/2)y^2 = 36$ or $y^+ = \sqrt{8} \approx 2.83$ and hence $x^+ \approx 12.74$ where (x^+, y^+) is the consumption bundle at the NEW prices giving the old utility of 36. Hence, the substitution effect on y is $y^+ - y^* = 2.83 - 2 = +0.83$. A lower price of y will raise y consumption due to substitution effect. But the total change in y consumption is $2.5 - 2 = +0.5$. Hence, the income effect is $+0.5 - (+0.83) = -0.33$, a fall. This shows that wine is a normal good whose consumption falls as income falls (once the substitution effect is netted out). Figure 3.3 illustrates endowments and income and substitution effect.

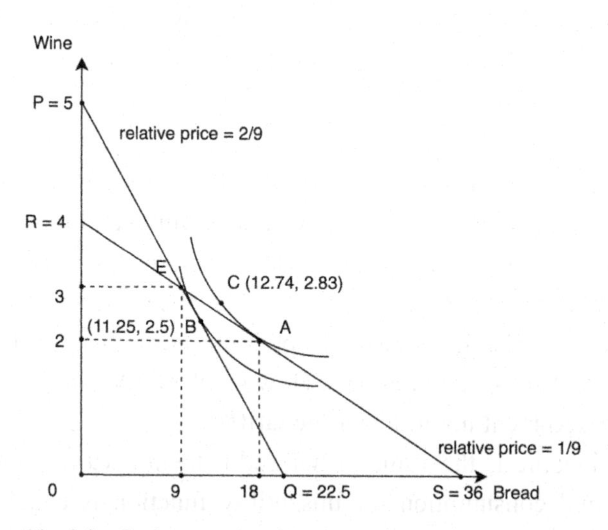

Fig. 3.3 Endowments and Income and Substitution Effect

In Figure 3.3, E is the endowment (9, 3). RES is the initial budget line reflecting relative price of X as 1/9. And PEQ is the new budget line reflecting the relative price 2/9. Initial optimum is at A which is (18, 2) and new optimum is at B (11.25, 2.5). The fall in price of y generates a substitution effect which lowers x consumption and £90 increases y consumption to C (12.74, 2.83). The subsequent movement from C to B is the income effect. As income has fallen, income effect should lower consumption of all normal goods. Since in this case income effect lowers X consumption from 12.74 to 11.25, and lowers Y consumption from 2.83 to 2.5, both X and Y are normal goods.

To compute the "bribe", note that the utility level in the new situation is 225/8. So, the most Rani will bribe is the amount which leaves her at least 225/8 utils at the original prices. At the original prices, we have $y/x = 1/9$ and hence $U = xy = 9y^2 = 225/8$ which implies $y^{***} = [5/(2\sqrt{2})]$ and $x^{***} = [45/(2\sqrt{2})]$ and hence expenditure at the original prices $= 90\sqrt{2} \approx 128$. So, Rani must have income of £128 to maintain the same utility with the original prices as she would have with an income of £90 at the new prices. But in the original situation, her income was £144. So, the most she will bribe is £144 – £128 = £16.

3.3 Summary

- Lagrange's method is a general procedure for solving optimisation problems that frequently arise in economic analysis.
- The consumer choice model can easily be extended to the study of labour market participation and hours worked.
- From the study of labour–leisure choice, it follows that labour supply can fall when wage rises provided leisure is a normal good with strong income effect.
- The labour–leisure choice model allows the calculation of a reservation wage below which the worker will choose not to work.
- Non-labour income is determined by the prices of the endowment goods. This approach is fully exploited in later chapters on intertemporal economics and general equilibrium theory.

Chapter 4

The Firm: Technology, Costs and Supply

In this chapter, we begin our analysis of the behaviour of another major player: the business **firm**.

4.1 Technology

The identity of a firm is its technology which converts the inputs into output. The inputs are typically envisaged as land, labour and capital. But of course, there are many others. The firm is assumed to possess what is called a **production function** which describes how the inputs combine to produce the output. For the most part, we will assume two inputs and one output and thus we could write the production function as $Y = F(L, K)$ where L is the labour, K stands for the capital good (machines) and Y is the output. Typically, we conceive of L and K as being a flow of services from labour and capital respectively measured in suitable units and Y as being the flow of output which corresponds to L and K.

There are many different ways to describe the properties of a production function. One important description is the **returns to scale** of a production function. Suppose the level of ALL inputs is doubled, will the output double, more than double or less than double? These three cases are described as constant returns to scale, increasing returns to scale or decreasing returns to scale. More formally, suppose the initial situation involves $L = L_0$, $K = K_0$ and $Y = Y_0$ so that $Y_0 = F(L_0, K_0)$. Now, let both inputs increase by a factor $t > 1$ so that $L_1 = tL_0$ and $K_1 = tK_0$. Let $Y_1 = F(L_1, K_1)$ be the corresponding level of output in the new situation. Now, compare Y_1 with tY_0. If Y_1 exceeds tY_0, returns to scale are increasing, if Y_1 equals tY_0, then returns to scale are constant, and if Y_1 is less than tY_0, then returns to scale are decreasing.

Example 4.1: For each of the following production functions, check the returns to scale: (a) $Y = LK$, (b) $Y = \sqrt{(LK)}$, (c) $Y = L^{\alpha}K^{\beta}$, (d) $Y = [\sqrt{L} + \sqrt{K}]^2$ and (e) $Y = AK + B\sqrt{(LK)}$.

In each case, we start from $L = L_0$ and $K = K_0$ and then multiply $L = L_0$ and $K = K_0$ by t to get L_1 and K_1.

(a) $Y_1 = L_1K_1 = (tL_0)(tK_0) = t^2L_0K_0 = t^2Y_0$ and since $t^2 > t$, we have $Y_1 > tY_0$ and hence increasing returns to scale.
(b) $Y_1 = \sqrt{(tL_0tK_0)} = t\sqrt{(L_0K_0)} = tY_0$ and hence constant returns to scale.
(c) $Y_1 = (tL_0)^{\alpha}(tK_0)^{\beta} = t^{\alpha+\beta}(L_0^{\alpha}K_0^{\beta}) = t^{\alpha+\beta}Y_0$. So, we have increasing, constant or decreasing returns to scale according as $(\alpha + \beta) > 1$, $= 1$ or < 1.
(d) $Y_1 = [\sqrt{tL_0} + \sqrt{tK_0}]^2 = t[\sqrt{L_0} + \sqrt{K_0}]^2 = tY_0$ and hence constant returns to scale.
(e) $Y_1 = AtK_0 + B\sqrt{(tL_0tK_0)} = AtK_0 + Bt\sqrt{(L_0K_0)} = tY_0$ and hence constant returns to scale.

Returns to scale is about what happens to output when all the inputs are simultaneously scaled up by the same factor. But production functions may also differ in the impact on output of increasing one factor, holding all the others constant. This impact is called the **marginal product** of the input. In particular, if $Y = F(L, K)$, then the partial derivative of Y with respect to L is the marginal product of labour. It is the response of output to a small change in the quantity of labour input. Similarly for capital.

Example 4.2: For each of the following production functions, calculate the marginal product of labour (MPL) and of capital (MPK): (a) $Y = LK$, (b) $Y = \sqrt{(LK)}$, (c) $Y = L^{\alpha}K^{\beta}$, (d) $Y = [\sqrt{L} + \sqrt{K}]^2$ and (e) $Y = AK + B\sqrt{(LK)}$.

Since MPL = partial derivative of Y with respect to L and since MPK = partial derivative of Y with respect to K, we calculate these by finding $\partial Y/\partial L$ and $\partial Y/\partial K$. We use the simpler notation $F_L \equiv \partial Y/\partial L$ and $F_K \equiv \partial Y/\partial K$.

(a) MPL $\equiv F_L = K$ and MPK $\equiv F_K = L$,
(b) MPL $\equiv F_L = \sqrt{(K)}/(2\sqrt{L})$ and MPK $\equiv F_K = \sqrt{(L)}/(2\sqrt{K})$,
(c) MPL $\equiv F_L = \alpha L^{\alpha-1}K^{\beta}$ and MPK $\equiv F_K = \beta K^{\beta-1}L^{\alpha}$,
(d) MPL $\equiv F_L = [\sqrt{L} + \sqrt{K}]/\sqrt{L}$ and MPK $\equiv F_K = [\sqrt{L} + \sqrt{K}]/\sqrt{K}$,
(e) MPL $= B\sqrt{K}/2\sqrt{L}$ and MPK $= A + B\sqrt{L}/2\sqrt{K}$.

Note that MPL and MPK are themselves functions of L and K. For the most part, we assume that MPL is a decreasing function of L and MPK is a decreasing function of K. In the example above, all the production functions have this property except (a) in which marginal products are constant. This is known as **diminishing marginal products** and is quite different from the phenomenon of decreasing returns to scale.

Production functions can be described graphically in much the same way as utility functions as illustrated by the examples in Section 2.3. Consider the production function $Y = F(L, K)$. If we fix the output level at say $Y = 1$, then the equation $F(L, K) = 1$ defines a level curve in (L, K) space which is called an **isoquant**. It shows all combinations of L and K which yield the same value of output, which in this case is 1. The slope of the isoquant is called the **Technical Rate of Substitution** (analogous to the marginal rate of substitution for indifference curves). Its calculation is similar too. In Example 1.10, let us redefine U to be output rather than utility and x and y to be labour and capital input, respectively. The partial derivatives of $F(x, y)$ now measure marginal product of production rather than marginal utility of consumption. Hence, the TRS is the slope of the isoquant and is measured by MPL/MPK. Once again, the convex shape of the isoquant implies decreasing (in absolute value) TRS as L increases.

4.2 Costs and Technology

The **cost** to a firm will depend on how much output it produces and what the price of its inputs is. More formally, we define the cost function of a firm as the minimum cost of producing a given output Y hiring inputs which cost w and r per unit respectively and write this as $C = C(Y, w, r)$. How is this cost function derived from the firm's production function? See the following examples.

Example 4.3: For the production function $Y = \sqrt{(LK)}$, find the cost function if wage w = £4 and capital rental r = £1 per unit.

The cost of production is simply the cost of the inputs required. So, if the firm hires L units of labour and K units of capital, then its cost $C = wL + rK$. In L, K space, this is a straight line with slope (w/r) and intercept (C/r). Everywhere on this straight line, the cost is the same, viz. C, and hence the line is described as an **iso-cost line**. As C changes (all else constant), this line shifts parallel to itself. In this example, since $w = 4$ and $r = 1$, the equation of the iso-cost line is given by

$$4L + K = C, \tag{4.1}$$

or equivalently,

$$K = C - 4L. \tag{4.1a}$$

In Figure 4.1, the parallel straight lines all correspond to $w = 4$ and $r = 1$ but with different levels of C. The nearer the straight line is to the origin, the lower the C and the better off the firm — all else equal. On this family of iso-cost lines, we impose the isoquant corresponding to Y units of output. The firm will want to get onto the lowest iso-cost line consistent with also being on the isoquant so that Y units are produced. Consider points like A and B at which the isoquant cuts an iso-cost line. These cannot be a cost-minimising optimum for the firm. Starting at A, the firm will lower costs and still produce Y by travelling down the isoquant towards D. Every such movement lowers costs till D is reached. Further movement

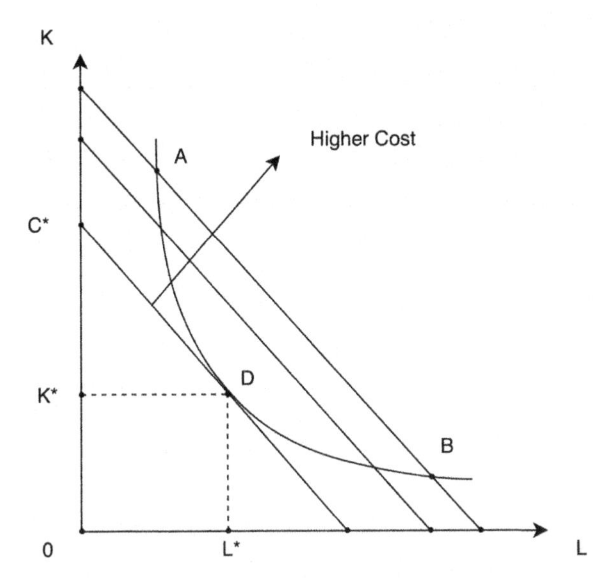

Fig. 4.1 Firm's Optimum Input Choice

down the isoquant increases costs once more. The same is true at B — travelling up the isoquant towards D lowers the cost of producing Y but once D is passed, costs rise again. The only point on the isoquant where such cost-lowering movements are not possible is at D itself where the isoquant is tangential to an iso-cost line. This means that the optimum is where slope of isoquant (TRS) equals the slope of the iso-cost line which is (w/r). The analogy with consumer choice is complete. The value of C corresponding to such a tangency is the minimum cost of producing Y given w and r. The optimum values are shown as L^*, K^* and C^*.

To find these values, we must solve the equation TRS = w/r. Since $Y = \sqrt{LK}$, MPL = $\sqrt{(K)}/(2\sqrt{L})$ and MPK = $\sqrt{(L)}/(2\sqrt{K})$ and hence TRS = MPL/MPK = K/L and hence $K/L = w/r = 4$ or $K = 4L$. Substituting this in the production function, we have $Y = \sqrt{LK} = \sqrt{L(4L)} = 2L$. Thus, $L = Y/2$ and $K = 4L = 2Y$ and $C(Y) = 4L + K = 4(Y/2) + 2Y = 4Y$.

This is what we set out to find, the minimum cost of producing Y units of output denoted by $C(Y)$. For $w = 4$, $r = 1$ and $Y = \sqrt{LK}$, $c(Y) = 4Y$.

The lessons from this example generalise. With convex isoquants, a tangency condition is the **cost-minimising** configuration. However, one subtle difference with consumer theory is that for the consumer, the budget line (iso-cost line) is fixed and the consumer selects the highest IC compatible with his budget, but in the case of the firm, the convex isoquant is fixed and the firm selects the lowest iso-cost line compatible with that isoquant.

Example 4.4: For each of the following production functions, find the associated cost function when the price hiring of labour is £w per unit and capital is £r per unit. (a) $Y = LK$, (b) $Y = \sqrt{(LK)}$ and (c) $Y = L^{\alpha}K^{\beta}$, $\alpha > 0$, $\beta > 0$.

(a) For $Y = LK$, MPL $= K$, MPK $= L$ and hence TRS $= K/L$ which must equal w/r at the optimum. So, $rK = wL$ is the tangency condition. Hence, $Y = LK = [L(w/r)L] = (w/r)L^2$ and so $L^* = \sqrt{(r/w)}\sqrt{Y}$ and from the tangency condition, $K^* = \sqrt{(w/r)}\sqrt{Y}$ and thus $C^* = \sqrt{rw}\sqrt{Y} + \sqrt{rw}\sqrt{Y}$ $= 2\sqrt{Y}(\sqrt{rw})$. If $W = 4$ and $r = 1$, then $C = 4\sqrt{Y}$.

(b) Here, TRS $= K/L$ (from Example 4.3) so $rK = wL$ is the tangency condition. And $Y = \sqrt{KL} = \sqrt{[(w/r)L]L} = [\sqrt{(w/r)}]L$ so that $L^* = [\sqrt{(r/w)}]Y$. From $rK = wL$, we get $K^* = [\sqrt{(w/r)Y}]$ and hence $C^* = (\sqrt{rw})Y + (\sqrt{rw})$ $Y = 2Y(\sqrt{rw})$. In Example 4.3, $w = 4$ and $r = 1$. Substituting in $C^* =$ $2Y(\sqrt{rw})$, we get $C^* = 4Y$ as before.

(c) The algebra of this problem is a bit tedious but it is instructive. Here, MPL $= \alpha Y/L$ and MPK $= \beta Y/K$. Hence, TRS $=$ MPL/MPK $= \alpha K/\beta L =$ $w/r \rightarrow (K/L) = (\beta w/\alpha r)$. Substitute in $Y = L^{\alpha}K^{\beta}$ to get $Y = L^{\alpha}L^{\beta}(\beta w/\alpha r)^{\beta}$ which solves for L as $L^* = Y^{(1/\alpha+\beta)}\ (\alpha r/\beta w)^{\beta/\alpha+\beta}$. Substituting L^* in $K = L(\beta w/\alpha r)$, we get $K^* = Y^{(1/(\alpha+\beta)}\ (\beta w/\alpha r)^{\alpha/\alpha+\beta}$. Hence, we get $C = wL^* + rK^* = Y^{(1/\alpha+\beta)}[w(\alpha r/\beta w)^{\beta/\alpha+\beta} + r(\beta w/\alpha r)^{\alpha/\alpha+\beta}]$ where the term in square parentheses is a constant so long as **factor prices** w and r are constant. In this case, we can write the cost function as $C = \lambda Y^{\Upsilon}$ where $\lambda = [w(\alpha r/\beta w)^{\beta/\alpha+\beta} + r(\beta w/\alpha r)^{\alpha/\alpha+\beta}]$ and $\Upsilon = 1/(\alpha + \beta)$ which is the reciprocal of the returns to scale parameter $(\alpha + \beta)$. If $(\alpha + \beta) = 1$ (constant returns to scale), then $\Upsilon = 1$ and we have $C = \lambda Y$

so that **average cost** AC $= C/Y = \lambda$ is constant. If $(\alpha + \beta) > 1$ (increasing returns to scale), then $\Upsilon = 1/(\alpha + \beta) < 1$ so that AC $= \lambda Y^{\Upsilon - 1}$ is decreasing in Y: we say the cost function is decreasing — as output expands average cost falls. Finally, if $(\alpha + \beta) < 1$ (decreasing returns to scale), then $\Upsilon = (1/\alpha + \beta) > 1$ so that AC $= \lambda Y^{\Upsilon - 1}$ is increasing in Y: we say the cost function is increasing — as output expands average cost rises. These results are intuitive. If we double the inputs, we double the cost. But if output increases by more than double, then the average cost has fallen.

Example 4.5: Show that average cost is decreasing/constant/increasing with output accordingly as the production function has increasing/constant/decreasing returns to scale.

Let $Y = F(L, K)$ be the production function. Suppose initial L, K and Y are given by L_0, K_0 and Y_0 respectively so that $Y_0 = F(L_0, K_0)$. Multiply both inputs by $t > 1$ so that the new input levels are $L_1 = tL_0$, $K_1 = tK_0$, and suppose the consequent value of output is $Y_1 = \lambda Y_0$. If $\lambda > t$, we have increasing returns to scale, if $\lambda = t$, we have constant returns to scale and if $\lambda < t$, we have decreasing returns to scale. Let C_0 be initial cost so that $C_0 = wL_0 + rK_0$. The new cost is $C_1 = wL_1 + rK_1 = t(wL_0 + rK_0) = tC_0$. The new output is $Y_1 = \lambda Y_0$. Denote the new and old average costs by AC_1 and AC_0. Then, $\text{AC}_1 = C_1/Y_1 = tC_0/\lambda Y_0 = (t/\lambda)\text{AC}_0$. Hence, AC falls if $\lambda > t$, is constant if $\lambda = t$ and rises if $\lambda < t$.

4.3 Costs: Total, Average and Margin Functions

In the previous section, we showed how the total cost of a firm varied with the output level. Given the production function parameters and factor prices w and r, we obtained total costs C as $C = C(Y)$. From this, we obtained the average cost function as AC $= A(Y) = (C(Y)/Y)$. There is yet another way to describe costs which is **marginal cost**. If output increases by a small amount, the consequent increase in cost per unit change in output is the marginal cost. It is measured as the derivative of the total cost so that marginal cost MC = $M(Y) = C'(Y)$. These three concepts are intimately linked. Once the total cost function $C(Y)$ is known, then both $A(Y)$ and $M(Y)$ are immediately determined. It should be emphasised that all three cost concepts are functions of output. The next example examines the relationship between the average and marginal cost functions.

Example 4.6: If $A(Y)$ is the average cost function and $M(Y)$ is the marginal cost function, show that $\boldsymbol{A'(Y) = [M(Y) - A(Y)]/Y}$ and discuss its significance.

Since $C(Y) = Y.\, A(Y)$, we can differentiate both sides using the product rule. Then, we get

$C'(Y) = A(Y) + YA'(Y)$ or $M(Y) = A(Y) + YA'(Y)$ or $[M(Y) - A(Y)]/Y = A'(Y)$ as required.

What this important result says is that if $A'(Y) > 0$ — which means that AC is increasing in Y — then MC exceeds AC and vice versa. If $A'(Y) < 0$ — which means that AC is decreasing in Y — then MC < AC and vice versa. When $A'(Y) = 0$ so that AC is neither increasing nor decreasing, then AC = MC. There is strong intuition behind this result. Consider a set of numbers which has an average of A, and then we add another number M to it. M is the marginal number. Suppose M exceeds A, then the average of the new set must exceed A. In other words, the average is increasing. Conversely, if M is less than A, then the average of the new set must be less than A; ergo, the average is falling. This result is so important and of such wide applicability that we will refer to it as the **Theorem of Margin and Average**.

Example 4.7: If AC is U-shaped with a minimum at $\boldsymbol{Y_{min}}$, sketch the AC and MC curves.

Since AC has a minimum at $Y = \boldsymbol{Y_{min}}$, we know that AC must be decreasing up to $Y = \boldsymbol{Y_{min}}$ and increasing thereafter. Thus, the derivative of AC must be negative for $Y < \boldsymbol{Y_{min}}$, zero at $Y = \boldsymbol{Y_{min}}$ and positive thereafter. Using the Theorem of Margin and Average, we know that for

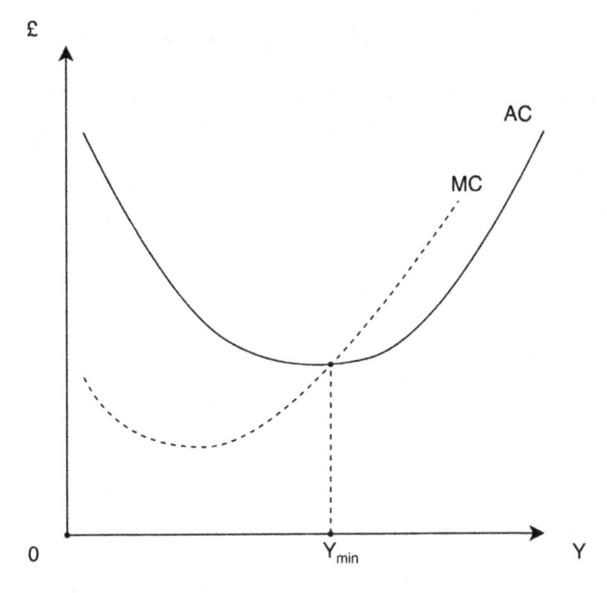

Fig. 4.2 Average and Marginal Cost

$Y < \boldsymbol{Y}_{\mathbf{min}}$, MC < AC, and for $Y > \boldsymbol{Y}_{\mathbf{min}}$, MC > AC and when $Y = \boldsymbol{Y}_{\mathbf{min}}$, then MC = AC. This is illustrated in Figure 4.2 — which is a familiar diagram from many elementary textbooks.

In Figure 4.2, the Y space is divided into two zones: one to the left of $\boldsymbol{Y}_{\mathbf{min}}$ where MC < AC and AC is decreasing and the other to the right of $Y_{\min}$ where MC > AC and AC is increasing. At $\boldsymbol{Y}_{\mathbf{min}}$, the two are of course equal as AC is stationary.

Example 4.8: If AC is given by $A(Y) = a - bY + cY^2$, find MC and sketch both curves.

Since $A(Y) = a - bY + cY^2$, then $C(Y) = Y.\ A(Y) = aY - bY^2 + cY^3$. As MC $= M(Y) = C'(Y)$, we get $M(Y) = a - 2bY + 3cY^2$. Thus, we have $M(Y) - A(Y) = Y(2cY - \mathrm{b})$; and since $Y > 0$, we have $M(Y) > A(Y)$ if $Y > (b/2c)$ and $M(Y) < A(Y)$ if $Y < (b/2c)$. Obviously, when $M(Y) = A(Y)$, then $Y = (b/2c)$. By differentiation of $A(Y)$, we also can show that AC is U-shaped and has a minimum at $Y = (b/2c)$. This is reflected in Figure 4.2 with $\boldsymbol{Y}_{\mathbf{min}} = (b/2c)$.

4.4 Costs in the Short and Long Run

In all the examples so far, the firm has been free to choose the level of both inputs. Situations where this is possible are called **long-run** situations. By contrast, **short-run** situations are where the level of at least one input, say capital, is fixed, perhaps by history. In the long run, there is full flexibility but in the short run, flexibility is limited. The importance of the distinction is illustrated in Example 4.9.

Example 4.9: The production function is given by $Y = (LK)^a$. Find the cost function when K is freely chosen and when K is fixed at $K = K_0$.

Note that the production function is a special case of the one in Example 4.4(c) with $\beta = \alpha = a$. Clearly, we have increasing/constant and decreasing returns to scale accordingly as $a > ½$, $a = 1/2$ and $a < ½$.

To solve the long-run cost minimisation problem, we recall from Example 4.4 that TRS = MPL/MPK = $\alpha K/\beta L = w/r \rightarrow (K/L) = (\beta w/\alpha r)$. With $\beta = \alpha$, this reduces to $K/L = (w/r)$. Substituting into the production function we get

$$L^* = (Y^{1/a}r/w)^{1/2}, \quad K^* = (Y^{1/a}w/r)^{1/2} \quad \text{and} \quad C^* = 2(wr)^{1/2}Y^{1/2a}.$$

But in the short run, K is fixed at K_0, and then the amount of L is just determined straight off by the short-run production function $Y = (K_0L)^a$. Hence, in the short run, the labour input requirement is given by $L^{**} = Y^{1/a}/K_0$ which means the short-run cost function $C^{**} = w[Y^{1/a}/K_0] + rK_0$.

Computing the marginal cost functions for the long- and short-run cost functions yields

$$\text{MC}^* = dC^*/dY = (wr)^{1/2}(1/a)Y^{(1/2a)-1} \quad \text{and}$$
$$\text{MC}^{**} = dC^{**}/dY = (w/K_0)((1/a)Y^{(1/a)-1}.$$

If the value of K_0 happens to equal the optimal long-run value of K which is given by $K^* = (Y^{1/a}w/r)^{1/2}$, then MC* and MC** will be equal. This can be shown by substituting $(Y^{1/a}w/r)^{1/2}$ for K_0 in the equation for MC**.

To reinforce the intuition of the argument in Example 4.9, we consider a special case in Example 4.10.

Example 4.10: The production function is given by $Y = (LK)^{1/2}$. Find the cost function when K is freely chosen and when K is fixed at $K = K_0$. Assume $w = 4$ and $r = 1$.

From Example 4.4(b), $TRS = K/L$ so $rK = wL$ is the tangency condition. Hence by substitution, we get that $L^* = [\sqrt{(r/w)}]Y$ and $K^* = [\sqrt{(w/r)Y}]$ and hence $C^* = (\sqrt{rw})\ Y + (\sqrt{rw})Y = 2Y(\sqrt{rw})$. Since $w = 4$ and $r = 1$, we get $L^* = Y/2$, $K^* = 2Y$ and $C^* = 4Y$ as before. If $Y = 100$, then $K^* = 200$, $L^* = 50$ and $C^* = 400$.

Suppose now that the target value of Y is still 100 but K is "stuck" at $K_0 = 100$ or $\sqrt{K} = 10$. Then, since $Y = \sqrt{KL}$, we get $L = Y^2/K = 100$. Thus, $C^{**} = [(4 \times 100) + (1 \times 100) = 500$, which is higher than the optimum long-run cost of 400. This is because in the short run, K^{**} is too low at 100 and consequently, L^{**} is too high at 100. The optimal L, K combination for $w = 4$ and $r = 1$ can't be used because K is "stuck" at $K = 100$! Only if by fluke K was stuck at $K_0 = 200$ (the long-run optimum value for $w = 4$, $r = 1$) would $L^{**} = Y^2/K_0 = 100^2/200 = 50$ and hence $C^{**} = 400 = C^*$.

The short-run cost function is given by $C^{**}(Y, K_0) = wY^2/K_0 + rK_0$. To minimise C^{**} by appropriate choice of K, we differentiate C^{**} with respect to K_0 and set it equal to 0. Thus, $(\partial C^{**}/\partial K_0) = -wY^2/K_0^2 + r = 0$ which solves to give $K_0^* = \sqrt{(w/r)}Y$ — which is of course K^{**} — the value of the optimal long-term value of K. Second-order conditions are easily verified. Thus, in general, short-run costs are always higher than long-run costs — EXCEPT when K_0, the short-run predetermined value of K, happens to coincide with K^{**} — the value of the optimal long-term value of K. The loss of flexibility that the short run entails implies cost minimising can never be as good as in the long run except in one fluke case!

4.5 The Significance of Fixed Costs

Another important issue in thinking about costs is the prevalence of what economists call **fixed costs**. These are costs which do not depend on the output level at all. For instance, suppose a firm rents premises at a fixed rental F per annum. The firm must pay F regardless of the level of output. This is an example of a fixed cost. Any long-term contract which is not dependent on output is a fixed cost to the firm. Naturally, such fixed costs are more prevalent in the short run. Most contracts can be nullified in the long run. By contrast to fixed costs, those costs which directly depend on output are sometimes **variable costs**. The sum of fixed and variable costs is total cost. In the simple examples discussed in Section 4.4, the presence of fixed costs does not materially affect the derivation of the cost function. We think of the cost functions derived in Section 4.4 as just variable cost functions. Adding F to this gives the overall cost function. However, there are cases where the fixed cost matters. See the contrast between Examples 4.11 and 4.12.

Example 4.11: A firm has two plants A and B. The cost function for plant A is given by $C^A = (Y^A)^2/5$ and that for plant B is $C^B = 5Y^B$ where Y^A and Y^B are the output produced in A and B, respectively. Derive the firm's cost function if (1) it can run only either A or B and (2) if it can run both plants simultaneously.

Note that in this example, there are no fixed costs at all.

If firm can only use one plant or the other, then it uses A when $C^A \leq C^B$. If Y is total output produced, then $C^A \leq C^B$ if $Y^2/5 \leq 5Y$ or $Y \leq 25$. Hence, the cost function C is given by

$$C(Y) = Y^2/5 \quad \text{for } Y \leq 25,$$
$$C(Y) = 5Y \quad \text{for } Y \geq 25.$$

The cost function is $Y^2/5$ (the convex curve) till $Y = 25$ and then switches to the straight line when Y exceeds 25. The cost function is continuous but has a kink at $Y = 25$.

With the prospect of being able to use both plants, the situation changes dramatically. Suppose the firm is actually using both plants and suppose the marginal cost in plant A exceeds that in plant B. The firm can lower its cost of production by raising production level in plant B while lowering an equal amount in plant A. Hence, if both plants are to be used, the optimal allocation of production between the two plants must be when the marginal cost in both plants is equal, i.e., $MC^A = MC^B$. But $MC^A = 2Y^A/5$ and $MC^B = 5$ and of course, $Y^A + Y^B =$ total output Y. Equating MC^A to MC^B, we get $Y^A = 25/2$ and thus $Y^B = Y - 25/2$. Hence, the cost-minimising strategy is to produce first 12.5 units on A and then switch on B to produce the remainder of output.

Thus, $C(Y)$ is now given by

$$C(Y) = Y^2/5, \quad \text{for } Y \leq 12.5 \quad \text{and}$$
$$C(Y) = 31.25 + 5(Y - 12.5), \quad \text{for } Y \geq 12.5.$$

Note that plant A is now only used by itself till Y reaches 12.5. Thereafter, both plants are used. If Y exceeds 12.5, then $C(Y) = 31.25 + 5(Y - 12.5) = 5Y - 31.25$.

Figure 4.3 illustrates the difference in the two calculations.

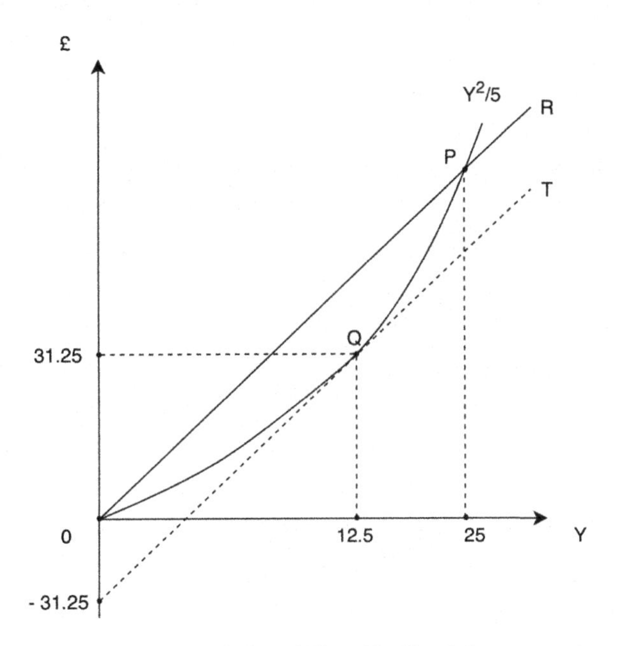

Fig. 4.3 Choice of Plant, No Fixed Cost

In Figure 4.3, the curve $C = Y^2/5$ is drawn along with the parallel straight lines $C = 5Y$ (the line OR) and $C = 5Y - 31.25$ (the broken line parallel to OR). At point P, where $Y = 25$, the curve $Y^2/5$ cuts the straight line 5Y. If only one plant can be used, then it is the switchover point from "Use Plant A only" to "Use Plant B only". The cost function is 0QPR. Beyond P, only plant B is used.

When both plants can be used, the calculations are different. 0QP is still the cost for using plant A only while the dashed line TQ represents the cost of using both machines in optimal combination. At point Q where $Y = 12.5$, $C = Y^2/5$ is tangent to $C = 5Y - 31.25$ (since both have a slope of 5 when $Y = 12.5$). Beyond Q, $(Y - 12.5)$ units are produced in plant B in addition to the 12.5 units produced in plant A. Hence, the cost function is 0QT. The cost saving from using both plants in an optimal way is the difference between QPR and QT. With fixed costs, the solution changes again. See Example 4.12.

Example 4.12: A firm has two plants A and B. The cost function for plant A is given by $C^A = (Y^A)^2/5$ and that for plant B is $C^B = 5Y^B + 20$ where Y^A and Y^B are the output produced in A and B, respectively. Derive the firm's cost function if it can run both plants simultaneously.

Note the fixed cost of £20 in C^B. If both plants are used, it must be the case that marginal cost in A and B is the same or else a reallocation would be optimal. This will still occur after $Y = 12.5$. In the "mixed regime", both machines are used optimally, then the total cost $C(Y)$ is given by

$C(Y)$ = cost on A + cost on B = $(12.5)^2/5 + 5(Y - 12.5) + 20 = 5Y - 31.25 + 20 = 5Y - 11.25$. This cost must be less than the cost of using just A. That is to say, the mixed regime (where by 12.5 units are made in A and the remaining $(Y - 12.5)$ units are made in B) is used whenever $5Y - 31.25 + 20 \leq (Y)^2/5$. The cut-off value of Y satisfies $Y^2/5 - 5Y + 11.25 = 0$. This is a quadratic with two roots, viz. $Y = 22.5$ and $Y = 2.5$. Hence, we can write the inequality $5Y - 31.25 + 20 \leq (Y)^2/5$ as $(Y - 2.5)(Y - 22.5) > 0$. This requires either Y to be less than 2.5 or Y to be greater than 22.5. Obviously, we can rule out $Y < 2.5$ since Y has to be bigger than 12.5 to even consider the mixed regime. Thus, we use the mixed regime when Y exceeds 22.5. Hence, we can write the cost function as

$$C(Y) = Y/5 \quad \text{for } Y \leq 22.5 \quad \text{and}$$
$$C(Y) = 5\text{Y} - 11.25 \quad \text{for } Y \geq 22.5.$$

Once again, the cost function is continuous but with a kink at $Y = 22.5$. Figure 4.4 illustrates choice of plant, with fixed costs.

The cost function for the mixed regime is the straight line $5Y - 11.25$. It pays to switch over to the mixed regime only if output level exceeds $Y = 22.5$. Note that the higher level of output before introducing the mixed regime is optimal is because of the fixed cost associated with switching on plant B. So, the firm will use only plant A till $Y = 22.5$. For higher output levels, the firm will CUT production in A to 12.5 and produce the remaining ($Y - 12.5$) units of output on B at a marginal cost of 5 per unit plus a fixed cost of 20.

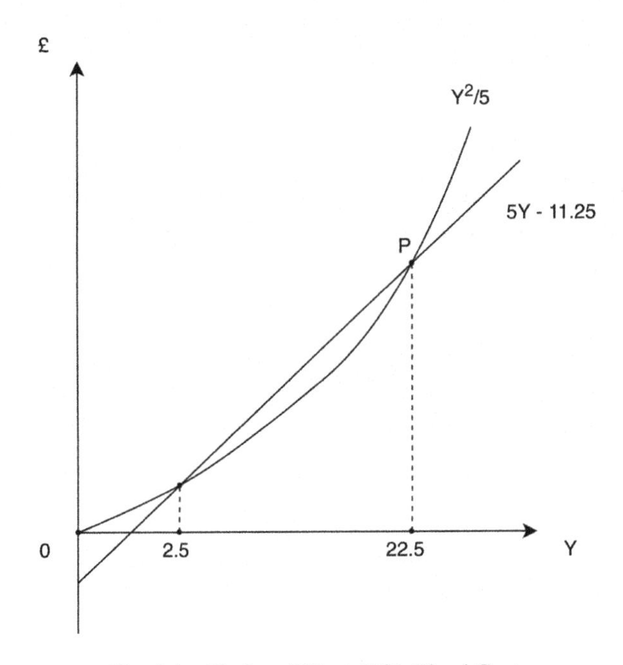

Fig. 4.4 Choice of Plant, With Fixed Costs

4.6 The Supply Curve of the Firm

So far, we have analysed how the firm combines inputs and plants in order to produce a given output at the lowest possible cost. But what determines the output the firm will produce? Throughout this book, we will assume that the firm seeks to maximise its **profits**. This motivation mirrors the utility-maximising motivation of consumers in Chapter 2. As with consumers, we assume that firms have no power to influence the price — they are **price takers**. This price-taking assumption limits the analysis to a particular type of **market structure** known as **perfect competition**. Later, we will study the actions of profit-maximising firms in other market environments. For now, we stick with the price-taking idea.

Suppose a firm has a cost function $C(Y)$ and faces a given price p. How much output will it produce and put on the market? The profits of the firm are given by total revenue less total costs. Thus, profits $\prod = pY - C(Y)$, where Y is the output. In choosing its optimal output Y^*, the firm will maximise $\prod$ by setting the first derivative $d\prod/dY = 0$ and checking that the second derivative $d^2\prod/dY^2 < 0$.

Example 4.13: A firm has a cost function given by $C(Y) = 10 + Y^2$. It faces a price of 8. (a) How much should it produce? (b)How much profit does it make? (c) How does maximum profit vary as price changes?

(a) Profit = Revenue – Costs $\rightarrow \prod(Y) = PY - C(y) \rightarrow \prod(Y) = 8Y - 10 - Y^2$.

Differentiating with respect to Y, we get

$d\prod/dY = 8 - 2Y = 0 \rightarrow 8 = 2Y$ which is interpreted as saying $p = \text{MC}$ is the first-order condition for maximising profit.

But is this sufficient to yield a maximum? To check, obtain $d^2\prod/dY^2$ as $d^2\prod/dY^2 = -2 < 0$ and hence a maximum is obtained. Solving $p = \text{MC}$ or $8 = 2Y$, we get $Y^* = 4$. This is the profit-maximising level of output and it will be produced so long as the value of profits at $Y = 4$ is greater than the value of profits at $Y = 0$.

(b) At $Y^* = 4$, $\prod^* = 8.4 - 10 - 4^2 = 6$ which certainly exceeds $\prod(0)$ which is -10.

(c) Suppose the price is p. Then, from $p = \text{MC}$, we get $Y^* = (p/2)$ and $\Pi^* = (p)(p/2) - 10 - [(p/2)^2] = (p^2/4) - 10$. Hence, $\Pi^* > 0$ so long as $p^2 > 40 \rightarrow p > 6.3$. If $p < 6.3$, maximum profits are negative and the firm would be better off **shutting down** IF by so doing it can escape the fixed costs of 10. So, in the long run, it would shut down although in the short run, it may continue despite making a loss. For $p > 6.3$, the firm will increase output and profits as p rises. Note that at $p = 6.3$, $Y^* = 3.15$ and $\text{MC} = 6.3$ and $\text{AC} = [10/Y + Y]$ also equals 6.3. In terms of Figure 4.2, 3.15 is $Y_{\min}$. Beyond $Y_{\min}$, the MC curve is higher than AC, so since $p = \text{MC}$, p will exceed AC and therefore positive profits will be earned.

The crucial result is $p = \text{MC}$ which implies that the firm will supply along its MC curve subject to the caveat that profits must be positive if fixed costs are escapable. In terms of Figure 4.2, 3.15 is $Y_{\min}$ and the firm's response to rising prices is shown by the MC curve from $Y_{\min}$ onwards. We have found the **firm's supply curve** which shows how much the firm will produce and sell at every conceivable price. In this example, the supply curve is $Y^* = p/2$ for $p > 6.3$, $Y = 0$ for $p \leq 6.3$ or in inverse form as $p = 2Y$ for $Y > 3.15$.

If fixed costs are NOT escapable, then the condition for staying in business is weaker — it merely requires that p (or MC) should exceed average variable costs. In this example, variable costs are Y^2 and hence average variable cost is Y. But $p = 2Y$ which always exceeds Y and hence the firm will never shut down. However small p is, the firm makes revenue higher than variable costs and so it stays in business making a loss because this loss is less than -10 which is the loss that would be made if output was zero.

The legal structure surrounding bankruptcy laws has a role to play in determining the shutdown condition.

4.7 Summary

- Technology is summarised in a production function.
- When discussing technology, a clear distinction between returns to scale (the impact of a uniform increase in all factor inputs) and

marginal productivity (returns to one factor — all others constant) is crucial.

- In deriving the cost function, we need factor input prices as well as the production function.
- There is a simple relationship between the shape of long-run average costs and returns to scale.
- In deriving the short-run cost function, we need to specify the level at which one of the factors is fixed. Short-run costs can never be lower than long-run costs.
- The relationship between average, marginal and total costs is determined entirely by their mathematical definitions.
- The supply curve of a price-taking firm is that part of the marginal cost curve which enables the firm to make a maximum profit which is larger than the profits made if output is zero. This depends on whether fixed costs are avoidable in the long run.

Chapter 5

Demand, Supply and the Competitive Market

In Chapter 3, we saw how to derive an individual's demand curve for a commodity starting from their preferences, their income and the market price. Holding all else constant, the demand curve for a price-taking utility maximising individual shows the quantity demanded by the individual at every conceivable market price. The inverse demand curve expresses the same relationship with price as the dependent variable and quantity as the independent variable. Similarly, in Chapter 4, we saw how to derive an individual firm's supply curve for a commodity starting from their technology, factor prices and the market price of the commodity. Holding all else constant, the supply curve for a price-taking firm relates the quantity supplied by the profit-maximising firm at every conceivable market price. The inverse supply curve expresses the same relationship with price as the dependent variable and quantity as the independent variable. In this chapter, we use these ideas to discuss the configurations that arise when we consider many price-taking consumers and many price-taking firms to arrive at market demand and supply. We will study the market equilibrium and how it changes in both the short and the long run.

5.1 The Market Demand and Supply Curves

Consider a market of two individuals Ann and Bill whose inverse demand curves are known. What will the market demand curve — the relationship between given market price and quantity demanded by all consumers in the market taken together — look like? See Example 5.1.

Example 5.1: Ann's demand curve for pizza is given by $QD_A = 100 - 2P$ while Bill's demand curve for pizza is given by $QD_B = 200 - 4P$. Find the market demand curve and the market inverse demand curve. Compare with the individual demand curves. Illustrate diagrammatically.

Let QD_m denote market demand. Then, by definition, $QD_m = QD_A + QD_B = 300 - 6P$. Hence, the inverse demand curve is given by $P = 50 - (1/6)QD_m$. The inverse demand curves for Ann and Bill are $P = 50 - (1/2)QD_A$ and $P = 50 - (1/4)QD_B$, respectively. Note that in the conventional (P, Q) space, the market demand curve is much flatter than either Ann's or Bill's. This reflects the fact that a small price cut has a much bigger effect on the market than on any individual. Figure 5.1 illustrates individual and market demands.

In Figure 5.1, the three inverse demand curves — Ann, Bill and market — are marked as A, B and M. The slopes of each are shown as 1/2, 1/4 and 1/6, respectively. Consider a trial price of $P = 40$. Then, as shown, $QD_A = 20$, $QD_B = 40$ and $QD_m = 60$. The inverse market demand curve is obtained by the "lateral summation" of the individual inverse demand curves. For any price, we travel horizontally till we locate QD_A on Ann's demand curve A, then continue till we locate QD_B on Bill's demand curve B and then continue till we get to $QD_A + QD_B$. This point lies on the market demand curve. Repeat this procedure for every price and we get the inverse market demand curve, *M*, which reflects the demands of all consumers taken together.

The market supply curve is obtained in exactly the same way from individual supply curves of individual firms or **producers**. The only difference is of course that supply curves slope upwards. This in no way alters the lateral summation principle. See Example 5.2.

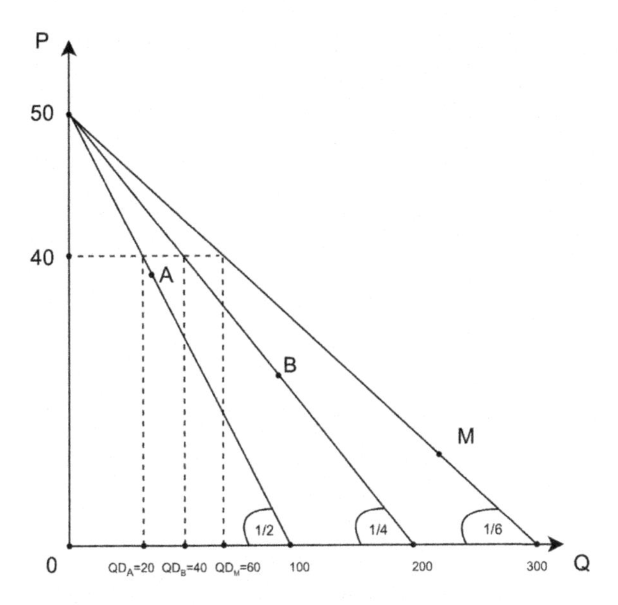

Fig. 5.1 Individual and Market Demands

Example 5.2: Amble's supply curve of pizza is given by $Q\Sigma_A = 2P$ while Bumble's supply curve of pizza is given by $Q\Sigma_B = 4P$. Find the market supply curve and the market inverse supply curve. Compare with the individual firm supply curves.

Let $Q\Sigma_m$ denote market supply. Then, by definition, $Q\Sigma_m = Q\Sigma_A + Q\Sigma_B = 6P$ or in inverse form as $P = (1/6)Q\Sigma_m$. Again, we see that the slope of the inverse market supply is much less than the slope of the inverse individual supply curves.

5.2 Elasticity: Alternate Measures and Applications

In the previous section, we noted that the responsiveness of quantity to a change in price was significantly greater for the market than for the individual. As we saw in Chapter 2, the concept economists use for measuring responsiveness is elasticity.

Denoting elasticity by ϵ and letting δ denote "a small change", recall that we define elasticity as follows:

$$\epsilon = (\delta Q/Q)/(\delta P/P). \tag{5.1}$$

In the above definition, the numerator is the proportional quantity response ("the outcome") and the denominator is the proportional price change ("the stimulus"). We can rewrite Eq. (5.1) more conveniently as

$$\epsilon = (\delta Q/\delta P) \times (P/Q). \tag{5.1a}$$

And when the changes are small enough, we can replace $(\delta Q/\delta P)$ by the derivative dQ/dP and write elasticity as

$$\epsilon = (dQ/dP) \times (P/Q). \tag{5.1b}$$

which shows how elasticity is linked to the slope. The higher the (dQ/dP), the lower its inverse $[dP/dQ]$ and hence the flatter the (inverse) demand or supply curve. The following example illustrates the use of the concept.

Example 5.3: The demand curve for pizza is given by $Q = a - bP$. Find the price elasticity of demand.

Using (5.1b), we get $\epsilon = -b(P/Q) = -[bP]/[a - bP]$. We should note two points about this calculation. First, note that ϵ is negative as we are looking at a normal demand curve. For convenience, we drop the sign when talking of elasticity and use absolute value of the slope in measurement. The context will make it clear whether an increase in the stimulus variable leads to an increase or decrease in the outcome variable. Note also that the elasticity changes as P changes. In other words, elasticity is a function, not a number! Its actual value will depend on the initial value of P. For a normal demand curve, the ratio (P/Q) falls as P gets smaller and we move down the demand curve. Hence, price elasticity gets numerically smaller as P gets smaller, and conversely.

Example 5.4: Show that an alternative calculation of elasticity is given by $\epsilon = \{d \log Q\}/\{d \log P\}$.

Since $d \log Q = (1/Q)dQ$ and $d \log P = (1/P)dP$, the result follows by substituting these into $\{d \log Q\}/\{d \log P\}$. Hence, we get

$$\epsilon = \{d \log Q\}/\{d \log P\}. \quad (5.1c)$$

Example 5.5: Find the price elasticity of demand for the demand curve $P = AQ^{-1/\beta}$.

To use (5.1b), rewrite the demand curve as $Q = [P/A]^{-\beta}$ then differentiate and substitute into (5.1b) to get the answer. This is tedious. It is far simpler to use (5.1c).

Since $P = AQ^{-1/\beta}$, take logs on both sides to get $\log P = \log A - (1/\beta) \log Q$ which on multiplying throughout by β can be rewritten as $\log Q = -\beta \log P + \beta \log A$. Now, think of $\log Q$ and $\log P$ as two variables, say Y and X. Differentiating Y (or $\log Q$) with respect to X (or $\log P$), we get $dY/dX = \{d \log Q\}/\{d \log P\} = -\beta$. Thus, $\epsilon = -\beta$ or ignoring sign, $\epsilon = \beta$. Note that in this special case, elasticity is a constant. It does not depend on the starting value of P. This is the only demand function which has this property. Some special cases of interest are when $\beta = 0$, $\beta = 1$ or $\beta \to \infty$. If $\beta = 0$, then there is no change in quantity as price changes so Q is constant at say $Q = Q_0$ — the demand curve is vertical at $Q = Q_0$. If $\beta = 1$, then $PQ = A$, i.e., **total revenue** is constant and the demand curve is a rectangular hyperbola. And if $\beta \to \infty$, then price is constant at $P = A$ and the demand curve is horizontal at this price.

The concept of elasticity can be generalised far beyond price elasticity of demand and supply. Consider any economic relationship of the form $Y = F(X, Z)$, where Y is the dependent (outcome) variable and X and Z are both independent (stimulus) variables. We can define the elasticity of Y with respect to X holding Z constant as $\epsilon(X) = (\delta Y/\delta X)\,[X/Y]$, where $(\delta Y/\delta X)$ is the partial derivative of Y with respect to X holding Z constant. Similarly, we can define the elasticity of Y with respect to Z holding X constant as $\epsilon(Z) = (\delta Y/\delta Z)[Z/Y]$, where $(\delta Y/\delta Z)$ is the partial derivative of Y with respect to Z holding X constant. For example, we have seen that an individual's demand for any commodity depends on both price and income. So, if Y is demand, X is price and Z is income, then we have two elasticity concepts. The price elasticity of demand is $\epsilon(X)$ while $\epsilon(Z)$ is the **income elasticity of demand**. The method of calculation remains the same.

Example 5.6: Find the price and income elasticities of demand for the demand curve given by $Q = AP^{\beta}Y^{\Upsilon}$.

We would normally expect β to be negative and Υ to be positive, but as we will ignore the sign anyway, it makes no difference to the calculation.

Taking logs of $Q = AP^{\beta}Y^{\Upsilon}$, we get $\log Q = \log A + \beta \log P + \Upsilon \log Y$. To get $\epsilon(P)$, we simply treat Y as constant (like A) and thus get $\epsilon(P) = \beta$. Now, treat P as constant and we get $\epsilon(Y) = \Upsilon$. All that has happened is that derivatives are replaced by partial derivatives.

Example 5.7: Find the relationship between price, marginal revenue and price elasticity of demand.

Let $P = f(Q)$ be a downward-sloping inverse demand curve. Then, total revenue TR is given by $\text{TR} = PQ = [f(Q)][Q]$. Elasticity is defined to be positive so that we define it as $\epsilon = -[dQ/dP][P/Q]$ or $(-1/\epsilon) = (dP/dQ)(Q/P)$.

Hence, marginal revenue (MR) is given by

$$\begin{aligned} \text{MR} &= d(\text{TR})/dQ \\ &= Qf'(Q) + f(Q) \\ &= f(Q)[\{f'(Q)\}\{Q/f(Q)\} + 1] \\ &= P[1 + (dP/dQ)(Q/P)] \\ &= P[1 - 1/\epsilon]. \end{aligned}$$

Thus,

$$\text{MR} = P[1 - 1/\epsilon]. \tag{5.2}$$

Two points to note. For downward-sloping demand curves, MR is always less than P as ϵ is positive. It raises the possibility that at some stage for low enough ϵ, MR will become negative so that increasing output leads to a fall in total revenue. Obviously, from (5.2), MR is positive only if $1 - 1/\epsilon$ exceeds zero which implies $\epsilon > 1$, numerically. Thus, if and only if $\epsilon > 1$ numerically, then an increase in output (fall in price) increases total revenue. The intuition behind this result stems from noting that because total revenue equals price times quantity, the percentage change in total revenue is the sum of the percentage change in price plus the percentage change in quantity. Since, along the demand curve, price and quantity move in opposite directions, the effect on total revenue depends on the magnitude of the price effect and the quantity effect. When price elasticity is bigger than 1 (numerically), this means that the quantity effect dominates. The increase in output raises total revenue while the accompanying fall in price lowers total revenue. When price elasticity exceeds 1, the former effect is bigger than the latter and hence total revenue rises.

5.3 Short-Run Equilibrium Price

We now can combine the market demand and supply curves to study the determination of **equilibrium market price** in a competitive market. Throughout, we maintain the assumption that every consumer and every firm behaves as if they are a price taker, choosing only optimum quantity for any given price. In other words, no economic agent has any **market power** to influence price. This is the fundamental assumption of perfect competition. We also assume that the number of firms and consumers is fixed so the analysis is short run.

We define an equilibrium price as one in which the quantity demanded by the totality of consumers is equal to the quantity supplied by the totality of firms, i.e., market demand equals market supply. In a graphical framework, this requires the intersection of the market demand and supply curves.

Example 5.8: The market supply curve in a competitive market is given by $Q\Sigma_m = 6P$ while the market demand curve is given by $\text{QD}_m = 300 - 6P$. What is the equilibrium market price and quantity traded?

By definition, equilibrium requires $Q\Sigma_m = \text{QD}_m$ and hence $6P = 300 - 6P$ whose solution is $P^* = 25$ and by substitution in either $Q\Sigma_m$ or QD_m, we get $Q^* = 150$. These starred values are the equilibrium market configurations. If the market price happens to be 25, then the quantity demanded

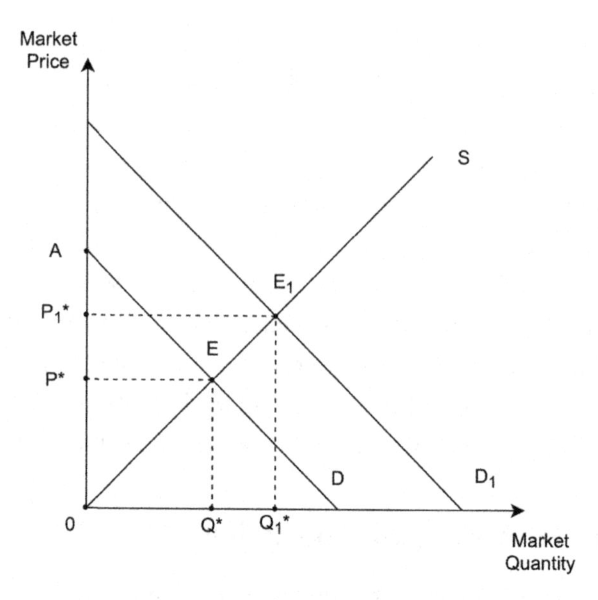

Fig. 5.2 Competitive Equilibrium

and quantity supplied will be exactly equal to 150. All consumers and all firms will be able to carry out their optimum choices. That is what makes $P^* = 25$ an equilibrium price. In this simple example, the equilibrium is unique. Figure 5.2 illustrates competitive equilibrium.

In drawing the market demand and supply curves, we must remember that we normally put price on the vertical axis and quantity on the horizontal axis. In order to do this, we need to convert the market demand and supply curves to their "inverse" form. For simplicity, we call $Q\Sigma_m$ the market supply S and QD_m the market demand D. Then, we get inverse supply curve as $P(s) = (1/6)S$ and inverse demand as $P(d) = 50 - (1/6)D$, where $P(s)$ and $P(d)$ are the **supply price** and **demand price**, respectively. For any supply quantity S, the supply price $P(s)$ is the minimum price required by producers to supply S units of the good. For any demand quantity D, the demand price $P(d)$ is the maximum price consumers as a whole will pay to buy D units of the good.

In Figure 5.2, S is the inverse market supply curve while D is the inverse market demand curve. They intersect at E which is the position of market equilibrium with a price of P^* and a corresponding quantity of Q^*. Thus, (P^*, Q^*) is the equilibrium configuration.

Suppose now that consumer preferences for this good increase so that market demand curve shifts to D_1 in Figure 5.2. The new equilibrium is at E_1 with price–quantity configuration (P_1*, Q_1*). The narrative that is customarily told is that at P* (the original equilibrium price), there is excess demand for the good, so the market adjusts by raising price till the new equilibrium is reached at P_1*. Similarly, we can calculate the impact of a shift in market supply curve. Simultaneous shifts in both curves can also be analysed in similar fashion. In Example 5.9, we analyse a more general specification of the demand/supply curves studied in Example 5.8.

Example 5.9: The market supply curve in a competitive market is given by $S = \beta P$ while the market demand curve is given by $D = a - bP$. In inverse form, these are $P(s) = (1/\beta)S$ and $P(d) = (a/b) - D/b$. What is the equilibrium market price and quantity traded? How does the equilibrium change if the parameters of the supply curve (β) and/or those of the demand curve (a, b) change?

Since equilibrium requires $S = D$, it follows that $\beta P = a - bP$ or

$$P^* = [a]/[b + \beta], \tag{5.3a}$$

$$Q^* = [a\beta]/[b + \beta]. \tag{5.3b}$$

From (5.3a) and (5.3b), we can immediately see the impact of changes. Figure 5.3 illustrates changes to the equilibrium.

In Figure 5.3, the downward-sloping (inverse) demand curve has slope $(1/b)$ and intercept at A which has a height (a/b) while the inverse supply curve has slope $(1/\beta)$. A rise in a shifts the demand curve parallel to itself to the NE raising P* and Q* (exactly as in Figure 5.2). A fall in β raises $(1/\beta)$ and hence swivels the supply curve in the direction of the arrow. The effect is a rise in P* but a fall in Q*.

5.4. Consumer and Producer Surplus

One consequence of using inverse demand and supply curves is that it is easier to identify the **surplus** going to consumers and producers. If a consumer is willing to pay a maximum of £10 for a good but actually pays

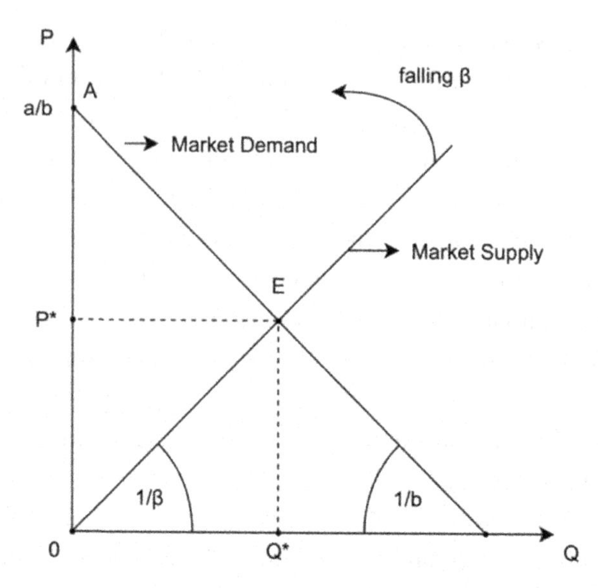

Fig. 5.3 Changes to the Equilibrium

only £7, then it is natural to think of his "surplus" as £(10 – 7) = £3. Similarly, if the minimum price a producer requires to produce a good is £6 but in fact, he receives £10 for it, it is natural to think of his surplus as £(10 – 6) = £4. For any agent, surplus is a measure of the **net benefit**. In other words, it is the total benefit (value) received from an activity less what must be paid to realise that benefit.

In Figure 5.3, consider the quantity Q^*. The market price P^* equals both the maximum consumers will pay and the minimum that producers must receive. Hence, the marginal unit Q^* produces no surplus. But all intra-marginal units do produce a surplus. Consider producers first. The rising supply curve 0E measures the minimum price $P(s)$ required for each successive unit to be produced. But the actual price is P^*. Hence, the difference $P(s) - P^*$ is the producer surplus for each intra-marginal unit, $s = 1, 2, 3, 4,\ldots, Q^*$. So, the total producer surplus is the sum of these producer surpluses for each individual unit. Geometrically, it is the area of the triangle $0EP^*$. By exactly similar reasoning, the total consumer surplus is the sum of $[P^* - P(d)]$ for each individual intra-marginal unit consumed, i.e., for $d = 1, 2, 3,\ldots, Q^*$. Clearly, this is the area of triangle AEP^*. Hence, the total surplus generated by the market is sometimes referred to as the sum of producer and consumer surplus which is the triangle AE0. Note that in order to justify adding the two surpluses, we must assume that both parties (consumers and producers) are equally important in some sense.

5.5 Taxation and Competitive Markets

Many **commodities** — petrol, alcohol, etc. — are subject to **taxation**. We analyse how such taxation affects the equilibrium. We consider quantity taxes, i.e., those which are fixed per unit of output. This contrasts with taxes levied on a percentage basis but this does not materially affect the analysis. The essence of taxation is that the tax drives a wedge between the price paid by consumers $P(d)$ and the price received by suppliers $P(s)$. For example, in the UK, in 2021, the tax on petrol was 58 pence per litre. The price the consumer pays was around 128 pence per litre. The difference in the two is 70 pence, which is what the producer gets. This example illustrates the principle that if a tax of t per unit is levied, then it follows that

$$P(d) = P(s) + t. \tag{5.4}$$

This simple equation forms the basis for analysing the tax impact.

Example 5.10: The market supply curve in a competitive market is given by

$$S = -\alpha + \beta P(s),$$

while the market demand curve is given by $D = a - bP(d)$. In inverse form, these are $P(s) = (1/\beta)S + (\alpha/\beta)$ and $P(d) = (a/b) - D/b$. If a tax of t per unit is levied, what is the equilibrium market price and quantity traded?

Directly from Equation (5.4) and noting that in equilibrium $S = D = Q$, we have that $P(d) = (a/b) - Q/b = (1/\beta)Q + (\alpha/\beta) + t$ which immediately solves for Q^* and then P^* as

$$P^*(s) = [a + \alpha - bt]/[b + \beta], \tag{5.5a}$$

$$Q^* = [(a\beta - \alpha b - b\beta t)]/[b + \beta], \tag{5.5b}$$

$$P^*(d) = [a + \alpha + \beta t]/[b + \beta]. \tag{5.5c}$$

In previous examples, we had for convenience assumed $\alpha = 0$. If we insert $\alpha = 0$ in Eq. (5.5), the results are a generalisation of Eq. (5.3). When $t = 0$ (and $\alpha = 0$), we get back exactly the results of (5.3a) and (5.3b) with $P^*(s) = P^*(d) = P^* = a/[b + \beta]$. Clearly, a rise in t will lower Q^*, and raise $P^*(d)$ and lower $P^*(s)$. The final player in this market is the government who gets tax revenue $T = tQ^*$. Figure 5.4 illustrates the impact of tax.

In Figure 5.4, AB is the inverse demand showing $P(d)$ for every Q while CD is the inverse supply curve showing $P(s)$ for every Q. The initial equilibrium with zero tax is at E. Introduction of the tax shifts the supply curve to FG showing $[P(s) + t]$ for every Q. Note that FG is a vertical displacement of the original supply curve by the amount t. It is parallel to CD. The new equilibrium is at $E(t)$. The quantity traded is Q^* (lower than before), the consumers pay $P^*(d)$ (higher than before) while producers receive $P^*(s)$ (less than before) and government **tax revenue** is tQ^* which is the shaded rectangle.

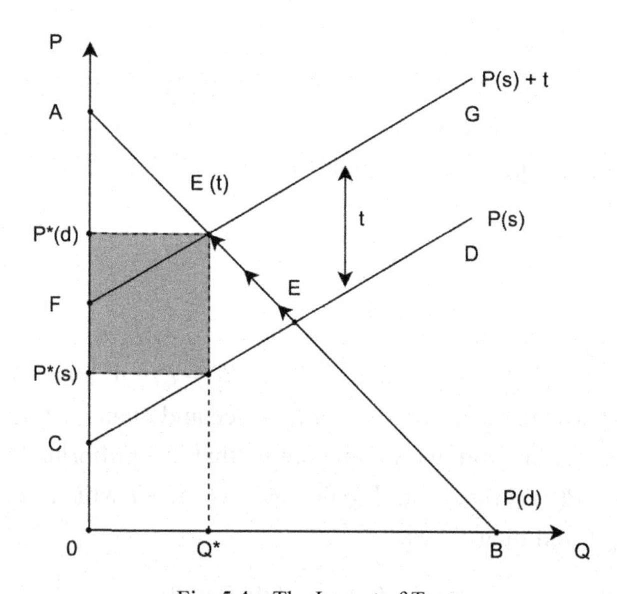

Fig. 5.4 The Impact of Tax

The following example examines the so-called "deadweight loss" from taxation. This is simply the value of the reduction in total surplus post tax. In other words,

Deadweight loss = loss in consumer surplus
+ loss in producer surplus – gain in tax revenue.

Note that by its very construction, deadweight loss assumes that all three elements of surplus are equally weighted.

Example 5.11: The market supply curve in a competitive market is given by $S = -\alpha + \beta P(s)$ while the market demand curve is given by $D = a - bP(d)$. In inverse form, these are $P(s) = (1/\beta)S + (\alpha/\beta)$ and $P(d) = (a/b) - D/b$. If a tax of t per unit is levied, what is the equilibrium market price and quantity traded? Is the change for the better?

This adds the deadweight loss calculation to Example 5.10. Figure 5.5 illustrates the deadweight loss.

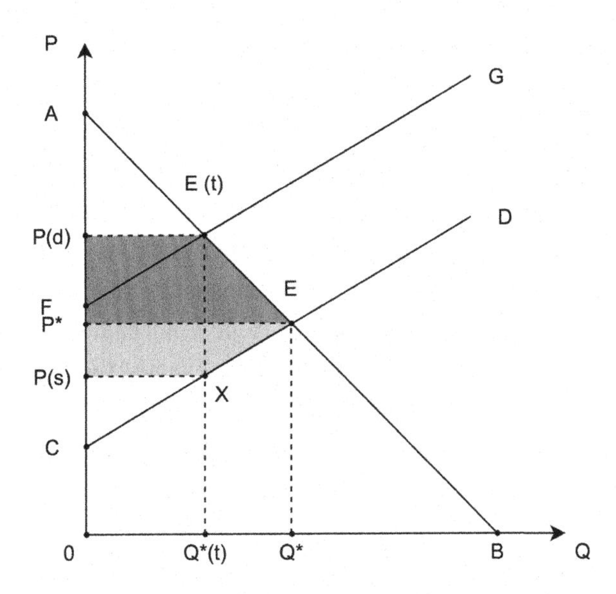

Fig. 5.5 The Deadweight Loss

Figure 5.5 replicates Figure 5.4 but with different emphasis. The pre-tax equilibrium is at E, while the post-tax equilibrium is at $E(t)$. Initially (at E), the consumer surplus is the triangle AP^*E and producer surplus is the triangle CP^*E. Post tax, these are the triangle $AP(d)E(t)$ and the triangle $P(s)XC$. By subtraction, the loss in consumers surplus is the trapezoid shape (with dark shading) $P(d)E(t)EP^*$ while the loss in producer surplus is $P^*EXP(s)$ (light shaded area). The total loss of consumer plus producer surplus is thus the area $P(d)E(t)EXP(s)$. Against that, we offset the gain in government tax revenue which is the rectangle $P(d)E(t)XP(s)$ which is just the tax rate t $(=E(t)X)$ multiplied by equilibrium quantity $(=P(d)E(t))$. Hence, the deadweight loss is the triangle $E(t)EX$ which has a height of $(Q(t) - Q^*)$ and a base of t. Thus, its area is $0.5t\{Q^* - Q(t)\}$ which measures the deadweight loss (which we denote DWL). This shows the source of the DWL as arising because of the output fall due to the tax imposition. From Eq. (5.5b), we obtain both $Q(t)$ and Q^* (which is $Q(t)$ when $t = 0$). Substituting into $DWL = 0.5t\{Q^* - Q(t)\}$, we get $DWL = [0.5(b\beta)t^2]/[b + \beta)]$. This result shows that the deadweight loss increases as the square of the tax rate.

Note also from $DWL = \{[0.5\ (b\beta)t^2]/[b + \beta]\}$ that $DWL = 0$ if $\beta = 0$. Now, β is a measure of the price elasticity of the supply curve. Hence, we can conclude that the lower the supply elasticity, the less the deadweight loss from a tax. Intuitively, the lower the supply elasticity, the smaller the impact of tax on equilibrium output. In the limiting case when supply elasticity is zero (the supply cure is vertical), the deadweight loss is zero as the output change due to tax is zero! When the supply curve is vertical, consumers pay the same price before and after tax and the quantity sold is the same. Hence, no change in consumer surplus. However, producer surplus falls by exactly the amount of tax times the constant quantity sold. But this last is also the tax revenue of the government. Hence, loss of producer surplus is exactly offset by the increase in government revenue and there is no deadweight loss. If the supply curve is perfectly elastic (horizontal), then the opposite happens. The entire burden of the tax is borne by consumers and there is significant deadweight loss.

5.6 Long-Run Equilibrium in Competitive Markets

In Section 5.3, we showed how to derive market supply and demand curves starting from the individual ones which are themselves based on profit and utility maximisation. An essential part of the derivation was lateral summation with a fixed number of firms and consumers. While this is perfectly valid in the short run, we need to consider what happens in the long run — a period of time in which the number of market participants can change. Every change in the number of participating agents will cause shifts in the short-run supply and demand cures because the lateral sum is being done over a different number of agents.

In the case of market demand, a once-for-all increase in consumers simply means a once-for-all outward shift in demand. There is no continuing dynamic on the demand side. The supply side is both more complex and more interesting. Recall Figure 5.2. The shift in demand causes a price rise and a quantity rise. But the number of firms is fixed. Hence, output of each firm is higher in the new equilibrium at E_1. Profits of each individual firm must be higher too or else they would not have produced the additional output. What is the consequence of this rise in profits? If there were N firms in the market initially each making the minimum profit required for survival at E, then the larger profits of each firm at E_1 will surely be an incentive for other firms to enter the market. In the perfect competition model, we assume **free entry** (and exit) of firms. There are no barriers to this process. How much entry will choke off the profit signal? The following examples illustrate the issues at stake.

Example 5.12: The cost function of a firm in a competitive market is given by $C = 16 - 4x + x^2$, where x is the output produced in tons and C is the cost in £. Discuss the conditions under which the firm will stay in the market in the long run. Find its long-run supply curve.

The firm will stay in the market in the long run if and only if its maximised profits in the long run are positive. If not, it will declare itself bankrupt and leave the market. The firms' average and marginal costs (denoted A and M, respectively) are given by

$$A(x) = 16/x - 4 + x, \tag{5.6a}$$

$$M(x) = -4 + 2x. \tag{5.6b}$$

For profit maximisation, we set price $p = M(x)$ and this is sufficient since we can see from Eq. (5.6b) that $M(x)$ is upward sloping so that the second-order condition for maximisation is satisfied. Thus, the profit maximising output x^* is given by

$$x^* = (p + 4)/2. \tag{5.6c}$$

But before we can claim this is the long-run supply curve, we need to be sure about the positivity of the maximum profits obtained from choosing $x^* = (p + 4)/2$. The value of the maximum profits is given by

$$\prod^* = Px^* - A(x^*)x^*. \tag{5.6d}$$

Clearly, for positive profits, we require $p > A(x^*)$. But since we know $p = M(x^*)$, it follows that positive profits require $M(x^*) > A(x^*)$.

The simplest way to check this out is to examine the shapes of $A(x)$ and $M(x)$. Differentiating $A(x)$ to get $A'(x) = 1 - (16/x^2)$, we can show that $A(x)$ is U-shaped with a minimum at $x_{\text{min}} = 4$. $M(x)$ is linear. At $X = 4$, both M and A are equal to 4. For $x < 4$, $M(x)$ is less than $A(x)$ and thus profits will be negative. For $x > 4$, $M(x)$ exceeds $A(x)$ and profits are positive. At $x = 4$, profits are zero. From Eq. (5.6c), we can see that $x = 4$ is an optimum when $p = 4$. For higher p, x^* will exceed 4 and $M(x^*)$ will exceed $A(x^*)$ so that positive profits are earned and the firm stays in the market. The meaningful part of the long-run supply curve is that part of the marginal cost curve when $p > 4$. Equivalently, it's that part of marginal cost curve where marginal cost exceeds average cost. Formally, we may write this as

$$\begin{aligned} S &= (p + 4)/2, \quad \text{for } p \geq 4 \\ &= 0, \quad \text{for } p < 4. \end{aligned} \tag{5.7}$$

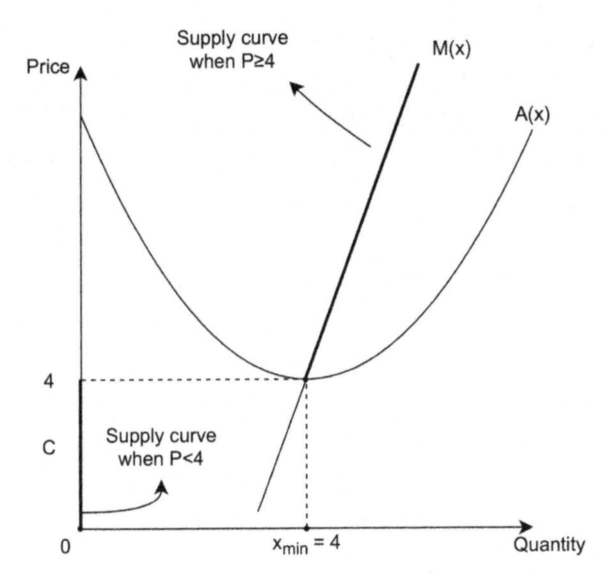

Fig. 5.6 The Long-Run Supply Curve

Figure 5.6 illustrates the long-run supply curve.

In Figure 5.6, the U-shaped $A(x)$ curve has a minimum at $x = 4$ where it cuts the $M(x)$ curve which is an upward-sloping straight line. For price below 4, the maximised profits are negative and so the firm shuts down and output is zero. For prices in excess of 4, the maximised profits are positive and the firm stays in the market producing an optimum (profit maximising) level of output read off the marginal cost curve.

Example 5.13: All firms (actual and potential) in a competitive market have identical cost functions given by $C = 16 - 4x + x^2$, where x is the output produced by a firm (in tons) and C is the cost in £. All firms behave as price takers so that the market is competitive. The market demand curve is given by $p = 100 - 4X$, where X is the market output (as opposed to x which is the output of a single firm). How many firms are there in long run equilibrium? What happens if market demand shifts to $p = 132 - 4X$?

The cost includes an allowance for **"normal profit"**. Economic or supernormal profit is the profit over and above "normal profit". So, if market price exceeds average cost, then supernormal profits are made. In this case, in the long run, firms currently not in the market enter. Conversely, if losses are being made, firms currently in the market will exit. So, in long-run equilibrium, the firm will make zero profit, which implies market price = average cost. But profit maximising implies price = marginal cost. Thus, in long-run equilibrium, we must have price = marginal cost = average cost. From Example 5.12, we know that at $x^* = 4$ tons, average and marginal costs are equal and average cost is minimised and both equal £4. Hence, the long-run equilibrium price is £4. And each firm produces $x^* = 4$ tons. Note that these calculations on long run firm size and long run equilibrium price are independent of the demand curve and depend only on the cost function.

From the demand curve $p = 100 - 4X$, we get $X^* = 24$ tons when $p = £4$. But each firm is producing 4 tons at $p = £4$. Hence, the number of firms is 24/4 = 6. If demand shifts, this has no impact on long run equilibrium price. Thus, we now solve for X from $4 = 132 - 4X$ which yields $X^* = 32$ tons as equilibrium market output. Hence, the number of firms is now 32/4 = 8. Entry of 2 firms has occurred.

This example was solved under the probably unrealistic assumption that firms act as strict price takers. With only 6 or 8 firms, it is likely that firms will not behave this way but will take into account how their actions may affect the market price. This is discussed in later chapters.

Example 5.14: In a perfectly competitive industry (with free entry/exit in the long run), all existing firms as well as all potential entrants have identical U-shaped average cost curves. A change in consumer tastes shifts the market demand curve to the right so that at every price, market demand is now higher than before. Show, using suitable diagrams, the impact of this shift in both short and long runs.

Figure 5.7 illustrates dynamics of perfect competition.

In Figure 5.7, the left panel shows the firm's optimum as price changes while the right panel shows market equilibrium as market demand and supply shift. In the right panel, the initial market demand curve is at D while the initial market supply curve based on N firms is S.

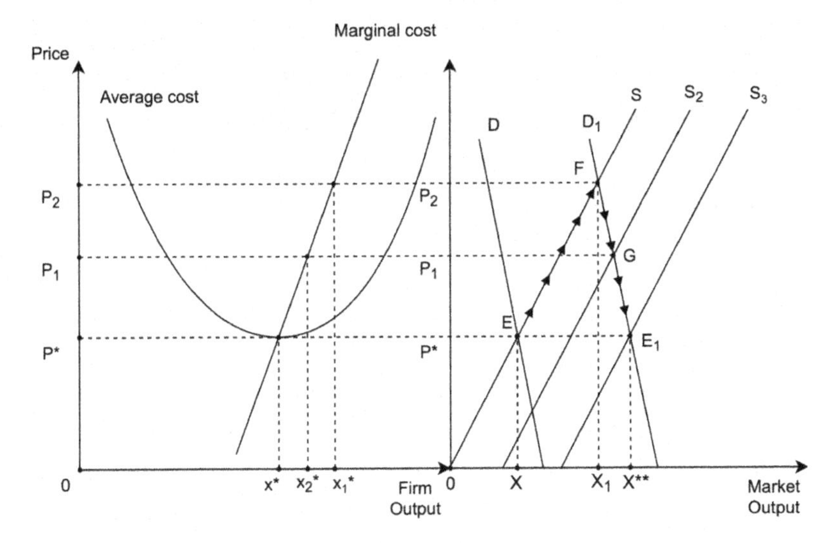

Fig. 5.7 Dynamics of Perfect Competition

The equilibrium is at E with price P^* and market quantity X^*. Suppose the initial equilibrium is a stable long-run equilibrium with zero (supernormal) profits for each firm as shown in the left panel where at P^*, the firm produces x^* and earns zero profit since P^* equals average cost. Now, suppose market demand shifts to the right to D_1 as shown in the right panel. In the short run, the number of firms is fixed at N so that the supply curve does not shift. The intersection of D_1 and S at F is the new short-run equilibrium. Price is now P_1 and market quantity is X_1. In the left panel, we see that at P_1, each firm produces a bigger amount x_1^* and N times x_1^* is X_1. Note also that at P_1, the firm is making a (supernormal) profit since price exceeds average cost. This is what induces entry of some firms. Hence, in the right panel, supply curve shifts to S_2. Equilibrium is at G with market price P_2. Note that P_2 is less than P_1. However, P_2 is still larger than P^*; firms (as shown in the left panel) are still making profits. Hence, entry occurs again and the supply shifts further to the right. Eventually, the supply curve will shift to S_3 and the equilibrium will be at E_1 with price P^* and quantity X^{**}. Now, entry stops as firms are making zero profits. The arrows in the right panel show how the economy moves.

Initially, price rises but then falls steadily till the original long-run price P^* is reached. Quantity increases at every stage until X^{**} is reached. Each firm is now producing at x^* and earning zero profit.

5.7 Summary

- Inverse market demand and supply curves are obtained by lateral summation of individual demand and supply curves. They are more elastic than their constituent individual counterparts.
- In the short run with a fixed number of firms (and consumers), the competitive market equilibrium configuration (price and quantity) is obtained by the intersection of market demand and supply curves.
- Commodity taxation drives a wedge between the price consumers pay and the price producers receive. This wedge alters the quantity produced and sold as well as the surplus going to consumers and producers.
- In the long run with free entry and exit of (identical) firms, each firm in the market earns zero super-normal profit. All firms in the market are producing where minimum average cost equals marginal cost equals price.
- Any exogenous shift in demand will eventually induce change in the number of (identical) firms but this has no impact on long-run price which is entirely determined by long-run minimum average cost.

Chapter 6

Market Power and Imperfect Competition

In the previous chapter, we analysed equilibrium price–quantity configurations in a competitive market. The essence of such a market is that each agent — firm and consumer — takes market price as given and reacts to it by choosing a quantity to sell or buy. In effect, this means no agent has any market power to influence the price. In this chapter, we look at situations where at least one agent has market power and can directly influence the price. We will focus on firms as the agents possessing market power. Examples of consumer market power (through consumer associations, etc.) are rare. There are many different ways in which economists have conceived the market power of firms. We shall look at the most common forms in this chapter.

6.1 Monopoly

Consider a market in which there is a sole producer/supplier of a good. This firm is a **monopolist**. The monopolist faces the entire market demand curve and chooses a price/quantity configuration. Note that the monopolist cannot choose both price and quantity independently. He has to respect the demand curve. His problem boils down to asking which of the infinitely many price–quantity configurations represented by the demand curve is profit maximising for him. Obviously, the firm's cost function will play a part in the decision too. See Example 6.1.

Example 6.1: The market demand curve is given by $Q = 100 - 2P$ while the monopolist firm's cost function is given by $C(Q) = 10Q \cdot P$ is measured in £ and Q in units of the good. What price will the monopolist charge? How much will he produce and sell? What are his profits?

In solving this problem, it is easier to think of the monopolist as choosing a quantity and allowing the demand curve to "determine" the price. We proceed in steps as follows:

- **Step 1**: Obtain the inverse demand curve as $P = 50 - (Q/2)$.
- **Step 2**: Obtain the total revenue function as $R = PQ = 50Q - (Q^2/2)$.
- **Step 3**: Obtain profits' function as $\prod = R - \text{C} = 50Q - (Q^2/2) - 10Q$.
- **Step 4**: Obtain FOC for maximising $\prod$ as $(d\prod/dQ) = 50 - Q - 10 = 0$.
- **Step 5**: Solve to get $Q^* = 40$.
- **Step 6**: Confirm $Q^* = 40$ as firms' optimum output by checking SOC $(d^2\prod/dQ^2) = -1 < 0$.
- **Step 7**: Substitute optimum output $Q^* = 40$ into the demand curve to obtain $P^* = £30$.
- **Step 8**: Substitute P^* and Q^* into profit function to obtain maximised value of profits $\prod^* = P^*Q^* - C(Q^*) = £800$.

We generalise Example 6.2 to enable a fuller discussion of the principles involved.

Example 6.2: The market demand curve is given by $Q = a - bP$ while the monopolist firm's cost function is given by $C(Q) = cQ$. P is measured in £ and Q in units of the good. What price will the monopolist charge? How much will he produce and sell? What are his profits? Illustrate diagrammatically.

Here, $R = (aQ/b) - (Q^2/b)$ and hence $(dR/dQ) = (a/b) - 2(Q/b)$. The term dR/dQ is the marginal revenue (MR) function. The demand curve by definition is the average revenue function. Note that because inverse demand is linear, so is MR and indeed has a slope exactly twice as large (numerically) as the demand curve. Note also that as discussed in Chapter 4, $dC/dQ = c$ is the marginal cost. Hence, the first-order condition for maximising profits which is $(d\prod/dQ) = 0$ can be restated as $dR/dQ = dC/dQ$ or MR = MC which amounts to setting $(dR/dQ) = (a/b) - 2(Q/b) = c$ to yield optimum quantity as $Q^* = (a - bc)/2$. Note that if $a = 100$, $b = 2$ and $c = 10$ as in Example 6.1, $Q^*= 40$ as before. P^* and $\prod^*$ are then obtained by direct substitution. Figure 6.1 illustrates monopoly optimum.

The bold downward-sloping line HF is the demand curve and the dashed downward-sloping line HG is the **marginal revenue curve** corresponding to HF. Note that because the inverse demand curve is linear, the marginal revenue curve is also linear but with twice its slope (numerically). Since $C = cQ$, total cost is proportional to output and both average and marginal costs are constant at c. This is shown as the dashed horizontal line ST. The MR line cuts MC at T which corresponds to output level Q^*. Drawing a vertical line upwards from Q^* to meet HF at E and then

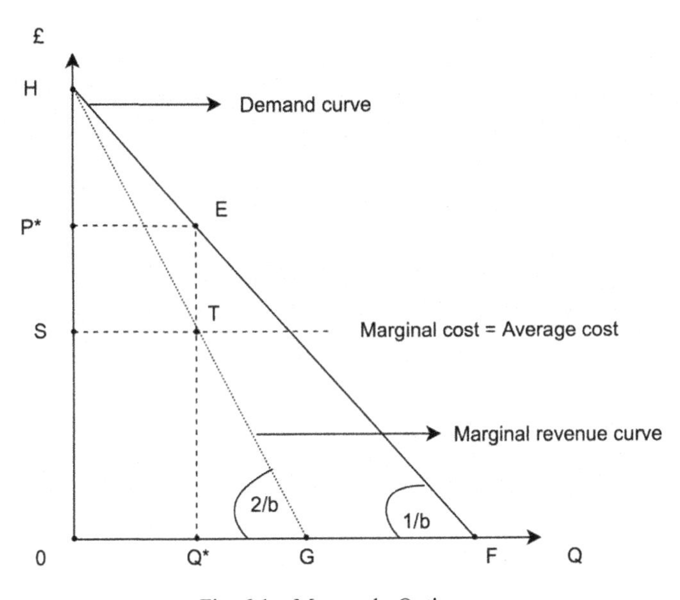

Fig. 6.1 Monopoly Optimum

drawing a horizontal line from E to the vertical axis locate the optimum price at P^*. Since $0Q^*$TS is total cost and $0Q^*$EP* is total revenue, the rectangle STEP* is total profit. The simple monopoly problem is solved. By assumption, there is only one firm. Market power resides with this firm because other firms cannot enter to try and prise away some of the large economic profits being made.

Note some simple extensions. First, suppose there is a tax of t per unit sold levied on the monopolist. What changes? In effect, the marginal cost of the monopolist is now $c + t$ and so in Figure 6.1, the dashed line ST moves upwards and thus Q^* falls, P^* rises and maximised profits, $\prod^*$, also fall. Second, suppose in addition to the constant marginal cost c, the firm has a fixed cost of K. The true profits of the firm are now $(\prod^* - K)$. If $\prod^* < K$, then the firm is making negative profits. It will seek to shut down in the long run since in the long run, the firm can avoid K and thus earn zero rather than negative profit. The following example generalises the problem.

Example 6.3: The inverse demand curve in the market is $P = F(Q)$, where $dF/dQ < 0$ as demand curve slopes downwards. The cost function is $C = C(Q)$, where $dC/dQ > 0$ so that MC is everywhere positive. What restrictions must be placed on $F(Q)$ and $C(Q)$ to guarantee a solution to the monopolist's problem?

$$\prod = QF(Q) - C(Q) = R(Q) - C(Q), \quad \text{where } R \text{ is the revenue.}$$

The first- and second-order conditions for Q^*, the value of Q that maximises profits' maximum, are given by

FOC: $dR/dQ - dC/dQ = 0$ or $\text{MR}(Q^*) = \text{MC}(Q^*)$,

SOC: $(d^2R/dQ^2) - (d^2C/dQ^2) < 0$ at Q^*.

The FOC is standard, but SOC needs interpretation. Note that (d^2R/dQ^2) is the slope of MR which is negative so long as $F''(Q) \leq 0$. This condition is always true for linear downward sloping demand curves as then $F''(Q) = 0$. Also, (d^2C/dQ^2) is the slope of MC which can be positive, zero or negative. If the slope of MC is either zero (as in Examples 6.1 and 6.2) or positive, then the SOC is always satisfied. The only complicated case is if the slope of MC is negative. In that case, the SOC requires that in numerical terms, the slope of MR is *bigger* than the slope of MC. Equivalently, at Q^*, the MR curve must be steeper than the MC curve. Figure 6.2 illustrates monopoly optimum with decreasing marginal cost.

In Figure 6.2, HF is the (inverse) demand curve, HG is the corresponding MR curve and ST is the marginal cost curve. Note that ST is downward sloping. ST meets HG at Q^*. The difference (MR – MC) is marginal profits. Prior to Q^*, at points like Q_1, MR exceeds MC and so the firm will expand production as marginal profits are positive. Beyond Q^*, at points like Q_2, the opposite is true and the firm will contract production as marginal profits are negative. Hence, the optimum is at Q^*. If the slopes of ST and HG were reversed, then their intersection would no longer represent maximised profit. Rather it would be a point of maximum loss.

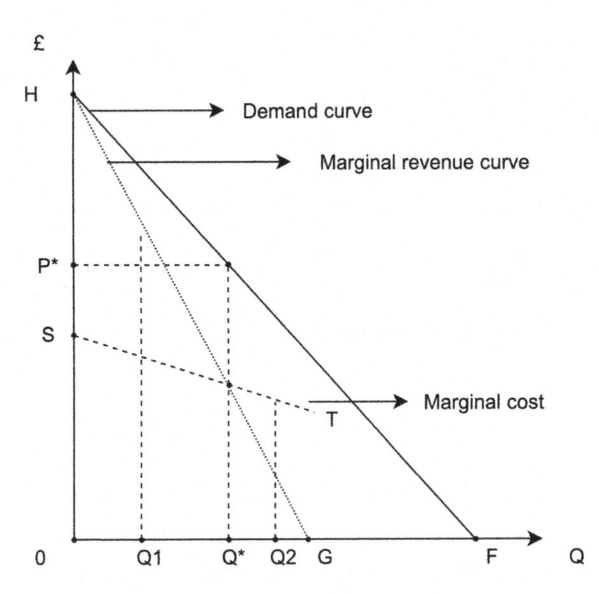

Fig. 6.2 Monopoly Optimum with Decreasing Marginal Cost

Note that from Eq. (5.2), MR $= p[1 - 1/\epsilon]$, where ϵ is the numerical value of elasticity, and also that at FOC, MR = MC. But clearly, MC is strictly positive and hence so is MR. Given that MR $= p[1 - 1/\epsilon]$, positive MR implies $\epsilon > 1$. The monopolist will only produce at a point on the demand curve where elasticity is bigger than 1. In fact, since MR = $p[1 - 1/\epsilon]$ = MC, it follows that defining $k = 1/[1 - 1/\epsilon]$, we have $p = k$ MC, where k is called the "**markup**" and is bigger than 1. The bigger the elasticity, the smaller the markup. In the limiting case of perfect competition, price elasticity tends to infinity and hence markup is unity and p = MC. We return to this theme in Section 6.2.

6.2 Duopoly and Oligopoly

If perfect competition is one extreme characterisation of market structure, then monopoly is the opposite extreme. In this section, we look at some intermediate cases where market power is shared between two or more firms. The simplest of these structures in which we assume two firms is called **duopoly**. We assume the firms are rivals and there is no collusion. Each firm acts quite independently of the other. In the following examples, we illustrate the basic tools of analysis before combining them to analyse the whole market situation.

Example 6.4: One good is produced by two competing firms who both have constant AC = MC but at different levels, viz. c_1 and c_2 with $c_1 > c_2$. Firms are rivals — there is no collusion. The market demand curve is given by $p = a - bq$. Each firm chooses its output on the basis of a guess about what the rival will produce and sell. This **conjecture**/expectation about rival strategy is denoted as q_i^e, $i = 1, 2$. Find the optimum output of each firm as a function of its conjecture. Illustrate diagrammatically.

Consider firm 1 first. Its conjecture about the rival is q_2^e and MC = AC is c_1. Firm 1 believes that firm 2 will produce q_2^e, and hence if he produces q_1, then market quantity will be $(q_2^e + q_1)$ and the market price will be $p = a - b(q_2^e + q_1)$. Thus, he perceives his local **residual demand curve** — which shows the price consequence of his decision given his conjecture — as

$$P = a - bq_2^e - bq_1. \tag{6.1}$$

This is in effect the perceived demand curve of firm 1. It is sometimes called the conjectural demand curve.

Hence, his MR curve, MR_1, is given by

$$MR_1 = a - bq_2^e - 2bq_1. \tag{6.2}$$

Note that both the residual/conjectural demand curve and the residual/conjectural marginal revenue curve will shift as the conjecture q_2^e changes. From Eq. (6.2), it is clear that if firm 1 conjectures that his rival is going to increase his output so that q_2^e is higher, then the conjectural MR curve, i.e., MR_1, will slide downwards towards the origin.

As MC is constant and MR_1 downward sloping, second-order conditions are satisfied, and firm 1 maximises profit by setting $MC_1 = MR$ and choosing output level q_1^* given by

$$q_1^* = (a - c_1)/2b - q_2^e/2. \tag{6.3}$$

Note that Eq. (6.3) shows the optimum output of firm 1 as a function of its conjecture (q_2^e) and its marginal cost (c_1) and parameters of the market demand curve (a and b). Figure 6.3 illustrates optimum with conjecture.

HF is the market demand curve and CD is firm 1's residual demand curve IF his conjecture is q_2^e. It is parallel to HF but has a lower intercept at $C = a - bq_2^e$. MR_1 is the marginal revenue of firm 1 derived from CD. It intersects MC at output level q_1^* which is firm 1's optimum relative to his conjecture q_2^e. As his conjecture changes, the point C will shift and thus MR_1 will shift and there will be a new optimum as shown in Eq. (6.3) which describes firm 1's optimum conditional on his conjecture. It is called firm 1's **reaction function**. It shows how firm 1's strategy reacts to any shift in firm 2's assumed strategy. Firm 1's Reaction Function (RF1) is a straight line in (q_2, q_1) space. If q_1 is on the horizontal axis, then it's easier to rewrite (6.3) as

$$q_2^e = (a - c_1)/b - 2q_1^*. \tag{6.4}$$

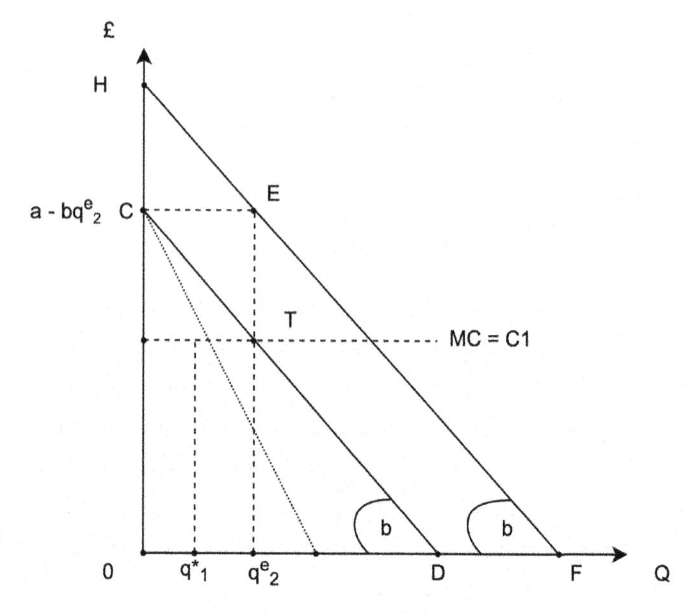

Fig. 6.3 Optimum with Conjecture

Hence, RF1 is downward sloping with a slope of -2 and intercept $(a - c_1)/b$.

By symmetry with (6.3), RF2 is given by

$$q_2^* = (a - c_2)/2b - q_1^e/2, \tag{6.5}$$

where q_1^e is firm 2's conjecture about firm 1's choice of output. Equation (6.5) is Firm 2's Reaction Function, RF2, and is also a downward-sloping straight line in (q_2, q_1) space with slope $-1/2$ and intercept $(a - c_2)/2b$.

Example 6.5: One good is produced by two competing firms who both have constant AC = MC but at different levels, viz. c_1 and c_2 with $c_1 > c_2$. Firms are rivals — there is no collusion. The market demand curve is given by $p = a - bq$. Each firm chooses its output on the basis of a guess about what the rival will produce and sell. This conjecture/expectation about rival strategy is denoted as q_i^e, $i = 1, 2$. Draw both reaction functions and find the equilibrium outputs and price.

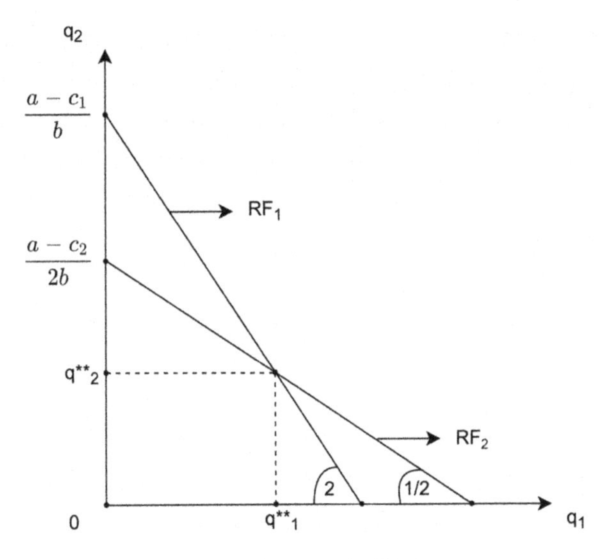

Fig. 6.4 Cournot Equilibrium

Suppose firm 1's conjecture is justified by firm 2's optimum choice and simultaneously, vice versa. Then, there is no force for change. Hence, we will conceive of the equilibrium as a situation where simultaneously $q_1{}^* = q_1{}^e$ and $q_2{}^* = q_2{}^e$. This type of equilibrium is called a **Cournot equilibrium**. Figure 6.4 illustrates Cournot equilibrium.

In Figure 6.4, the steep straight line is RF1 with slope 2 (in absolute value) — as in Eq. (6.4). The shallow straight line with slope 1/2 (in absolute value) is RF2 as in Eq. (6.5). So long as $(a - c_1)/b > (a - c_2)/2b$, then the two RFs intersect at $[q_1{}^{**}, q_2{}^{**}]$ given by

$$[q_1{}^{**}, q_2{}^{**}] = [a + c_2 - 2c_1/3b, a + c_1 - 2c_2/3b]. \tag{6.6}$$

These are the Cournot–Nash equilibrium values. At $[q_1{}^{**}, q_2{}^{**}]$, both firms' anticipation of the other's strategy is justified and both firms are simultaneously maximising profits. There is no force for change. Hence, it is an equilibrium. Note the following properties of the Cournot equilibrium.

Since $c_1 > c_2$, then $q_1{}^{**} < q_2{}^{**}$. Intuitively, this makes sense — the high-cost firm has lower market share. In the special case when both firms have identical costs so that $c_1 = c_2 = c$, then $q_1** = q_2** = q** = (a - c)/3b$ and hence market output is $Q** = 2(a - c)/3b$. Contrast this with a monopolist with the same costs whose optimum output is $Q_m = (a - c)/2b$ which is less than $Q**$. To solve the symmetry case of equal costs, one only needs to calculate one reaction function, then set $q_1* = q_2* = q**$ and solve for $q**$. Thus, if in Eq. (6.3), we set $q_1* = q_2* = q**$ and $c_1 = c$, we get $q** = (a - c)/3b$ as before.

Turning to prices, for the duopoly, the market price is $p** = a - bQ** = [a + 2c]/3$ while the monopoly price is $P_m = (a + c)/2$ which is higher than $p**$ because $a > c$.

Thus, even the introduction of modest competition (two firms) lowers market price and increases market output. What will happen with even more firms? See the following example.

Example 6.6: One good is produced by n competing firms which all have constant and equal MC = c. Firms are rivals — there is no collusion. The market demand curve is given by $p = a - bq$. Each firm chooses its output on the basis of a guess about what rivals will produce and sell. Find the optimum output of each firm and comment.

Let there be n firms all with equal unit cost = c.

Firm 1 conjectures that all other firms produce q^e each so that total output produced by rivals is $(n - 1)q^e$ and hence the residual demand curve for firm 1 is given by

$$p = a - b(q_1 + (n - 1)q^e) \text{ and hence } \mathrm{MR}_1 = a - b(n - 1)q^e - 2bq_1.$$

Since profit maximising by firm 1 requires $\mathrm{MR}_1 = \mathrm{MC}$,

$$\mathrm{MR}_1 = a - b(n - 1)q^e - 2bq_1* = c. \tag{6.7}$$

But since all firms are the same, they will all produce the same amount in equilibrium, i.e., $q_1* = q^e = q**$.

Thus, from (6.7), we have

$$q** = (a - c)/b(1 + n), \tag{6.8}$$

$$Q** = nq* = [(a - c)/b][n/(1 + n)]. \tag{6.9}$$

By substituting Q^{**} into the demand curve, we get

$$p^{**} = a/(1 + n) + c\,[n/(1 + n)]. \tag{6.10}$$

Note that as $n = 1$, we get monopoly price ($p^{**} = [a + c]/2$) and as n goes to infinity, we get p^{**} tending to c — the perfectly competitive price.

Thus, our intuition is confirmed. Oligopoly — a market with several firms — will degenerate into monopoly when there is only one firm and will approach perfect competition as the number of firms gets large.

6.3 Discriminating Monopoly

In the previous sections, it was implicitly assumed that every consumer was charged the same price. But this need not necessarily be the case. Suppose a monopolist was able to "**segregate**" or segment the market so that some consumers could be treated differently from others. For instance, a rail company could charge students/senior citizens (with documentary proof of status) a different price from other regular customers. The markets are fully segregated with no seepage between them. The monopolist would surely wish to exploit this situation by charging different prices to different properly segregated consumers. Example 6.6 illustrates the issues.

Example 6.7: A monopolist has constant average and marginal cost 10. The monopolist faces two demand curves from segregated consumers. These are given by $p_1 = 20 - 4q_1$ and $p_2 = 30 - 2q_2$, respectively. Discuss the monopolist's pricing strategy.

The monopolist has two choice variables: q_1 and q_2. Suppose he chooses (q_1^*, q_2^*). The monopolist can compute $MR_1\,(q_1^*)$ and $MR_2\,(q_2^*)$ from each demand curve. Suppose he finds that $MR_1\,(q_1^*)$ exceeds $MR_2\,(q_2^*)$. Then, the pair (q_1^*, q_2^*) cannot be an optimum because the firm can keep total output (and hence total cost) constant but reallocate one unit of output towards market 1 and reduce the sale in market 2 by one. Profits will rise by the amount $[MR_1\,(q_1^*) — MR_2(q_2^*)]$. The same argument holds in reverse if $MR_2\,(q_2^*)$ exceeds $MR_1\,(q_1^*)$. Thus, at an optimum, we must have $MR_1(q_1^*) = MR_2(q_2^*)$. But how large must this common MR be? Once again, by a familiar argument, we must have MR = MC. Thus, the conditions for an optimum must be

$$\mathbf{MR_1(q_1^*) = MR_2(q_2^*) = MC(q_1^* + q_2^*).}$$

Of course, in this example, calculations are much easier because of the assumption that MC does not depend on the level of output produced but is a constant. In this example, both demand curves are linear and hence the two MR equations are given by

$$MR_1 = 20 - 8q_1, \tag{6.11}$$

$$MR_2 = 30 - 4q_2. \tag{6.12}$$

Since the optimum must satisfy $MR_1 = MR_2$ which implies

$$20 - 8q_1 = 30 - 4q_2. \tag{6.13}$$

Also, since both values of MR must equal MC, we have using market 1, that

$$20 - 8q_1 = 10. \tag{6.14}$$

Solving (6.13) and (6.14), we get $(q_1^*, q_2^*) = (5/4, 5)$ and hence by substituting these into the two demand curves, we get $(p_1^*, p_2^*) = (15, 20)$. We can further calculate both elasticities of demand at the optimum. These are $(\epsilon_1, \epsilon_2) = (3, 2)$. Note that market 2 has higher price and lower elasticity than market 1. This result is quite general. It does not depend on linear demand curves but follows directly from the fact that $MR = p[1 - 1/\epsilon]$ and that at an optimum $MR_1 = MR_2$ which implies that $p_1^*/p_2^* = [(1 - 1/\epsilon_2)/(1 - 1/\epsilon_1)]$ which implies $p_1^* < p_2^*$ if $\epsilon_1 > \epsilon_2$.

An alternative method of solution is to use the technique of maximising a function of two variables.

$$\Pi(q_1, q_2) = p_1 q_1 + p_2 q_2 - c(q_1 + q_2). \tag{6.15}$$

Equation (6.15) defines the profits made by the monopolist which he seeks to maximise. The first-order conditions are as follows:

$$\prod_1 = \partial\prod(q_1, q_2)/\partial q_1 = 0, \tag{6.16a}$$

$$\prod_2 = \partial\prod(q_1, q_2)/\partial q_2 = 0. \tag{6.16 b}$$

Carrying out the partial differentiation required in (6.16a), we get $MR_1 = c$ and in (6.16b), we get $MR_2 = c$ — which collectively gives us back

$$\mathbf{MR_1\ (q_1^*) = MR_2\ (q_2^*) = MC\ (q_1^* + q_2^*).}$$

To check the second-order conditions, we need the higher-order partial derivatives of $\prod(q_1, q_2)$. Denoting these by $\prod_{ij}$ where $i, j = 1, 2$, the SOC conditions require $\Delta = [(\prod_{11})\ (\prod_{22}) - (\prod_{12})^2] > 0$ AND $\prod_{11} < 0$ as can be verified from any book on intermediate calculus. In this example, we have

$$\prod_1 = \partial\prod(q_1, q_2)/\partial q_1 = 20 - 8q_1, \tag{6.17a}$$

$$\prod_2 = \partial\prod(q_1, q_2)/\partial q_2 = 30 - 4q_2. \tag{6.17b}$$

And hence, the higher-order partial derivatives are

$\prod_{11} = -8$, $\prod_{22} = -4$ and $\prod_{12} = 0$ so that $\Delta = +32$ and since $\prod_{11}$ is obviously negative, the SOC are satisfied. In the final example of this section, we look at a more extreme case of discrimination.

Example 6.8: A monopolist has constant average and marginal cost of c per unit. The demand curve is given by $p = a - bq$. The demand curve reflects the maximum price that each individual would pay. If the monopolist is able to charge a different price for each unit sold (sometimes known as **perfect discrimination**), discuss the monopolist's optimal pricing strategy.

Suppose each consumer buys only one unit of the good. When $q = 1$, the maximum price payable is $a - b$; for $q = 2$, the maximum price payable is smaller at $a - 2b$, etc. If each person (unit) is sold the good at their maximum price, then the marginal revenue curve becomes the demand curve! Thus, the monopolist maximises profit by solving as ever MR = MC which means $a - bq^* = c$ which is the same $q^* = (a - c)/b$ that would be produced under perfect competition but the distribution of surplus is completely different. Under perfect competition, equilibrium price is c and output is $q^* = [(a - c)/b]$ and the entire surplus goes to consumers. Under perfectly discriminating monopoly, the same output $q^* = [(a - c)/b]$ generates the same total surplus BUT it all goes to the producer; consumers get nothing!

It is sometimes argued that perfect price discrimination by a monopolist which results in the competitive output being produced does represent an efficient outcome. The fact that the distribution of surplus is completely different is deemed not to matter because a suitable redistributive scheme can be designed to allocate surplus in a way that is deemed socially just. While this may be true in principle, it is hard to see the practical importance of the argument.

6.4 Summary

- A monopolist faces the whole market demand curve and chooses price and quantity of the market demand curve.
- Profit maximising requires MR = MC provided MC is either upward sloping or if sloping downwards is flatter than the MR curve.
- The monopolist's optimum position will always be at a point where price elasticity of demand exceeds one.
- The monopolist's markup over marginal cost decreases as price elasticity increases.
- Under duopoly, each firm starts from a conjecture about rival output which then allows calculation of the residual demand curve for each.
- Each firm then sets MC = MR obtained from the residual demand curve to obtain optimal output.
- As conjecture changes, so does optimal output; the relationship between the two is called the reaction function.
- Equilibrium is where both reaction functions intersect.
- If both firms have the same marginal cost, then each firm produces the same output.

- With n firms, we have a market structure called oligopoly. A symmetric oligopoly equilibrium will reduce to perfect competition as n gets large and reduce to monopoly if $n = 1$. Total surplus is smallest under monopoly.
- If the monopolist is able to discriminate between consumers, he can increase profits by exploiting different elasticities of demand.
- In the case of perfect discrimination, when it is possible to charge each consumer a different price, the quantity outcome is the same as in perfect competition but monopolist gets the entire surplus.

Chapter 7

Inter-temporal Economics

In the previous chapters, we assumed that decision-making never involved commodities beyond a single period, i.e., today. However, there are very important decisions which by their nature are spread over time. Examples include how to balance present with future consumption. One strategy is to **save** (consume less than current income) today and invest the savings to generate income for future consumption. We start by assuming that the decisions to save and invest are carried out by the same agent. We further imagine that there are only two periods of time which we call the "current" or "today" (period 0) and the "future" or "tomorrow" (period 1). In reality, the future consists of many periods but nothing conceptually important is lost by the simplicity of the two-period model. We assume there is only one good called corn which can be consumed today or tomorrow.

7.1 Discounting, Interest Rate and Budget Line

The fundamental price which links the present and the future is the **interest rate**. In working with present and future commodities and incomes, it is important to note that corn today and corn tomorrow are effectively different commodities which cannot be aggregated without the use of prices. See Example 7.1.

Example 7.1: Robinson can lend or borrow as much as he likes at an interest rate of 10% per period. He expects to receive an income of £110 in period 1. How much is his future income worth today?

Suppose £110 in period 1 is worth £x today. Then, equivalently, it must be possible to convert x today into 110 tomorrow. This can be achieved by **lending** £x at a rate of 10%. In period 1, Robinson will get back the interest which is 10% of £x plus the principal lent which was £x. This adds up to £$(x + 10\% x)$ = £$1.1x$. But if £$1.1x$ = £110, then £$x = 100$. This is the **present value** of his future income. Note the present value is smaller. This process of conversion from future to present using interest rate is called **discounting**.

Example 7.2: Any agent can **borrow** or **lend** as much as they like at an interest rate of r per period. He expects to receive an income of £Y in period 1. If £X is the present value of £Y, what is the relationship between X, Y and r?

Following the same logic as above, $X = [Y/(1 + r)]$ is the present value of Y in the future. Another way to look at this problem is to compute the *future* value of £X now. By lending £X at rate r, the lender will acquire £$X(1 + r)$ in the future. Hence, Y, the future value of X, is given by £Y = £$X(1 + r)$.

Example 7.3: Any agent can borrow or lend as much as they like at an interest rate of r per period. Robinson has an income of m_0 today and m_1 tomorrow. What is the value of his **wealth**?

The present value of m_1 is $[m_1/(1 + r)]$ and the present value of m_0 is just m_0. Hence, wealth W which is defined as the sum of the present value of all income streams is just $W = m_0 + [m_1/(1 + r)]$.

Example 7.4: Any agent can borrow or lend as much as they like at an interest rate of r per period. Robinson has an income of m_0 today and m_1 tomorrow. If he consumes c_0 and c_1 corn in present and future, what is his budget constraint, assuming that the unit price of corn is unity in both periods?

Suppose $c_0 < m_0$ so that Robinson saves $s = (m_0 - c_0)$ today and lends it out at rate r. In period 1, this saving has grown to $s(1 + r) = (m_0 - c_0)(1 + r)$ which augments his period 1 income of m_1. Hence, the maximum value of c_1 is given by $(m_0 - c_0)(1 + r) + m_1$. Thus, $c_1 \leq [(m_0 - c_0)(1 + r) + m_1]$ which dividing by $(1 + r)$ can be rewritten as

$$c_0 + c_1/(1 + r) \leq m_0 + m_1/(1 + r), \tag{7.1}$$

which can be neatly summarised as follows: present value of consumption must be no greater than present value of income. Note the greater flexibility that borrowing/lending permits. Without the financial market, Robinson's budget constraint would be much tighter at $c_0 \leq m_0$ and $c_1 \leq m_1$. If in (7.1), the weak inequality is replaced by strict equality, then (7.1) represents the boundary of the budget set. Figure 7.1 illustrates inter-temporal budget constraint.

In Figure 7.1, we measure present consumption c_0 and present income y_0 on the horizontal axis. This is valid because of the assumption that the

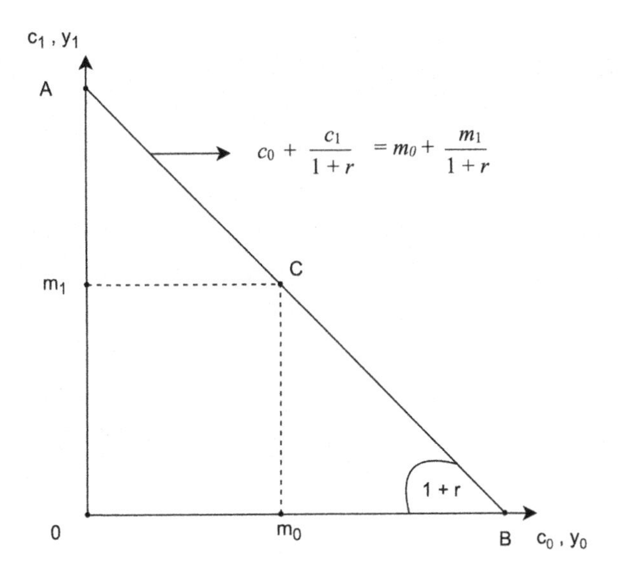

Fig. 7.1 Inter-Temporal Budget Constraint

price of corn is unity. In effect, we are measuring income in real terms, i.e., in corn units. On the vertical axis, we measure corn consumption and corn income in period 1. The consumer's two-period endowment is (m_0, m_1) at point C. The equation of the straight line ACB is given by

$$c_0 + c_1/(1 + r) = m_0 + m_1/(1 + r), \tag{7.2}$$

which can be rewritten as

$$c_1 = [(1 + r)m_0 + m_1 - (1 + r)c_0]. \tag{7.2a}$$

Thus, ACB has a slope of $(1 + r)$ and an intercept at A of $(1 + r)m_0 + m_1$. The intercept is just the future value of the endowment. It represents how much corn he could consume in the future if his present consumption was zero.

Without borrowing/lending, the budget set is the rectangle $0m_0Cm_1$. With borrowing/lending, the budget set expands to include the whole triangle 0AB. Since every option open to the consumer without borrowing/lending is also available with borrowing/lending but NOT conversely, the consumer is clearly better off with the ability to lend and borrow. Finally, note that if consumption in both periods has positive marginal utility (non-satiation), then the consumer will always locate his/her optimum on the budget line ACB.

Example 7.5: Any agent can borrow or lend as much as they like at an interest rate of r per period. The unit price of corn is unity in both periods. Robinson has an income of m_0 today and m_1 tomorrow. How does his budget line change if the interest rate r increases?

Since the (absolute) slope of the budget line is $(1 + r)$, a rise in r will make the budget line steeper. But it must still pass through C in Figure 7.1 since C is always feasible. In other words, the budget line will swivel with C being the swivel point. The new intercept will be higher. Thus, all budget lines must pass through C for any interest rate as Robinson can always just consume his endowment. These budget lines are sometimes called the **trading line** or the market line. It shows the consumption possibilities that arise from the existence of a **financial market**.

7.2 Discounting and Preferences

At the simplest level, consumer preferences over present and future consumption are summarised for any two goods as $U(c_0, c_1)$. However, the time dimension is usually captured in a rather special way. If we let $V(c)$ be the period-specific utility from consuming c units of corn in that period, then $V(c_0)$ is the utility in period 0 from consuming c_0 in period 0 while $V(c_1)$ is the utility in period 1 from consuming c_1 in period 1. But as the $V(c_1)$ utils arrive one period, hence, their present value to the consumer may be written as $\beta V(c_1)$, where β is the **discount factor**, which typically is assumed less than 1. Another way of thinking about this is that β is a measure of "impatience". The lower the β, the more consumer wants instant gratification and treats the future as less valuable. Thus, it is common to think of the utility of intertemporal consumption as valued in the present being given by $U(c_0, c_1) = V(c_0) + \beta V(c_1)$. It is common to refer to β as the discount factor and $\delta > 0$ as the discount rate where $\beta = [1/(1 + \delta)]$. Example 7.6 illustrates the trade-offs.

Example 7.6: Rani has **inter-temporal utility function** given by $U = \ln c_0 + \beta \ln c_1$. Find the marginal utility of current and future consumption and the MRS between them. Is MRS diminishing (in absolute value)?

By partial differentiation, we obtain the marginal utilities as

$$\text{MU}_{c0} = 1/c_0 \quad \text{and} \quad \text{MU}_{c1} = \beta/c_1.$$

Hence (ignoring sign), the MRS along any indifference curve is given by MRS = $\text{MU}_{c0}/\text{MU}_{c1} = [c_1/\beta c_0]$. It is clear that as one moves down the indifference curve by increasing c_0 and reducing c_1, MRS diminishes since the ratio $[c_1/c_0]$ falls. The following example generalises this result.

Example 7.7: Ari has inter-temporal utility function given by $U = V(c_0) + \beta V(c_1)$. Find the MRS between them. What restrictions on $V(c)$ are sufficient to obtain MRS diminishing (in absolute value)?

By the same logic as in Example 7.6, we obtain MRS as $[V'(c_0)/\beta V'(c_1)]$. Now, if $V''(c) < 0$ then as Ari moves down the indifference curve by increasing c_0 and reducing c_1, $V'(c_0)$ must decrease and $V'(c_1)$ must rise so that the ratio $[V'(c_0)/V'(c_1)]$ must fall. Hence, MRS is diminishing. Note that the function $\ln(c)$ clearly satisfies $V''(c) < 0$. Hence, $V'(c) > 0$ and $V''(c) < 0$, are sufficient for diminishing MRS (in absolute value).

Having described both constraints and consumer preferences, it is time as in Chapter 2 to combine these to study consumer's optimum.

7.3 Inter-Temporal Consumer Optimum

In this section, we use the apparatus of consumer theory developed in Chapter 2. In the inter-temporal context, the relative price is the interest rate, so naturally, we would wish to study what happens when the interest rate changes. As we will see, income and substitution effects both play a part. Example 7.8 illustrates the basic problem.

Example 7.8: Ari has inter-temporal utility function given by $U = \ln(c_0) + \beta \ln(c_1)$. His endowment is the income stream (10, 100). Find his optimum consumption bundle (c_0^*, c_1^*) if the interest rate is r. Is Ari a saver/lender or a borrower? Illustrate on a diagram.

Since $\ln c$ has negative second derivative, we know that Ari's inter-temporal utility function has diminishing MRS or convex indifference curves. Hence, consumer optimum as in Chapter 3 will require MRS = slope of budget line. This relationship is often called the "Euler equation" and in this case amounts to

$$[c_1/\beta c_0] = (1 + r). \tag{7.3a}$$

The optimum choice must of course satisfy the budget constraint which states that present value of consumption must equal present value of income. This is given by

$$c_1/(1 + r) + c_0 = 10 + 100/(1 + r). \tag{7.3b}$$

Solving (7.3a) and (7.3b) as a pair of simultaneous equations yields the optimum as

$$c_0^* = [10 + 100/(1 + r)]/[1 + \beta], \tag{7.4a}$$

$$c_1^* = [10(1 + r) + 100][\beta/1 + \beta]. \tag{7.4b}$$

The higher is r (the relative price of c_0), the smaller is c_0^*. Ari is a saver/lender if his optimum current consumption is less than his period zero income. Otherwise, he is a borrower. For instance, if $\beta = 1$, then $c_0^* = 5 + 50/(1 + r)$. Now, $c_0^* > m_0$ if $5 + 50/(1 + r) > 10$ or $r < 9$. Figure 7.2 illustrates inter-temporal consumption optimum.

Figure 7.2 is an augmented version of Figure 7.1. The augmentation consists of an indifference curve tangent to AB at E and a straight line (0E) through the origin representing the Euler equation which has a slope of $\beta(1 + r)$. E is Ari's optimum position where the Euler equation (7.3a) cuts the budget constraint (7.3b). It is the highest indifference curve Ari can reach while remaining on the trading line. Note that $c_0^* > m_0$ as drawn. Ari borrows the positive amount $[c_0^* - m_0]$.

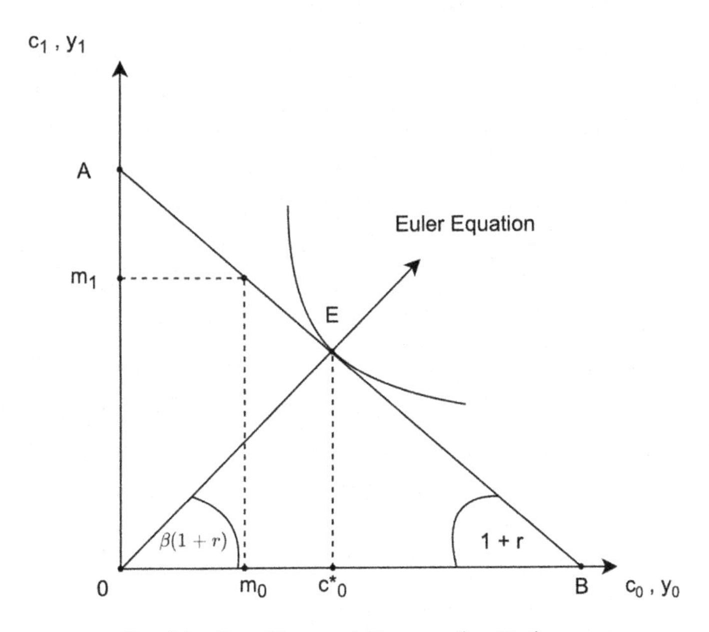

Fig. 7.2 Inter-Temporal Consumption Optimum

Example 7.9: Ari has inter-temporal utility function given by $U = \ln(c_0) + \beta \ln(c_1)$. His endowment is the income stream (m_0, m_1). Find his optimum consumption bundle (c_0^*, c_1^*) if the interest rate is r. Is Ari a saver/lender or a borrower? What is the impact of a rise in r? Illustrate on a diagram.

Proceeding as in the previous example, we get

$$c_0^* = [m_0 + \{m_1/(1 + r)\}]/[(1 + \beta)], \tag{7.5a}$$

$$c_1^* = [m_0(1 + r) + m_1][\beta/(1 + \beta)]. \tag{7.5b}$$

Here, the condition for Ari to be a saver/lender is that $[m_0 + \{m_1/(1 + r)\}]/[(1 + \beta)] < m_0$ which reduces to $r > \{[(m_1/m_0)/\beta] - 1\}$. In other words, he saves if the interest rate exceeds some critical value $r_c = \{[(m_1/m_0)/\beta] - 1\}$. This answer is intuitive. If Ari has high future income relative to current income, then this critical value rises and hence his incentive to save falls. This condition which states save if and only if r exceeds r_c also goes some way to answering the question of what happens if r rises. Clearly, r_c is unchanged. Therefore, it follows that if the old r exceeded r_c, then the current higher r will surely exceed r_c too. Once a saver/lender, Ari continues to save if r rises. But does he necessarily save/lend more? Figure 7.3 illustrates effect of interest rate of saver.

In Figure 7.3, ACB as before is the initial budget line reflecting an interest rate r. Ari's endowment is at C. Ari's initial optimum is at E where he consumes c_0^* saving $[m_0 - c_0^*]$. The rise in interest rate to $r+$ is shown by the budget line MCN which is steeper than ACB but passes through C since the endowment is always feasible. The dotted line through F is parallel to MCN and touches the original indifference at F. Hence, the movement from E to F is the pure substitution effect — c_0^* falls (and c_1^* rises). But this is not the end of the story. The budget line MCN lies to the north-east of the dotted line through F; hence, MCN reflects a higher wealth than the dotted line through F. The positive income effect (assuming both present and future consumption are normal goods) implies that the final equilibrium at G will involve more of c_0 and c_1 as compared to F. Therefore, overall c_1^* must rise but the impact on c_0^* is ambiguous. The substitution effect lowers present consumption (due to the price rise)

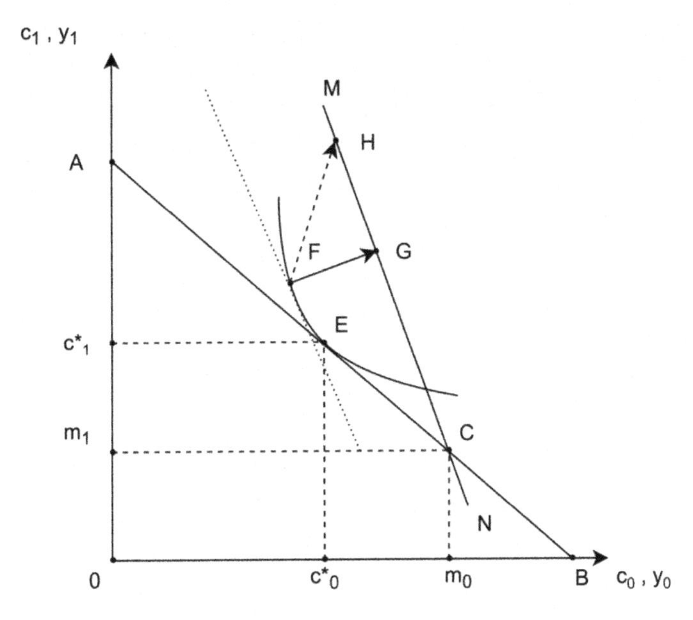

Fig. 7.3 Effect of Interest Rate on Saver

but the positive income effect raises present consumption. As drawn, at G, present consumption is higher than c_0* — savings have fallen due to a rise in r! This is because a large income effect dominates a smaller substitution effect. But this is not guaranteed. The income effect could easily have moved Ari from F to H rather than G. And in that case, savings would rise — the substitution effect would dominate the income effect.

What if Ari had been a borrower at the initial interest rate? The pure substitution effect is the same as before — c_0* falls (and c_1* rises). But the rise in interest rate hurts a borrower and the income effect is negative tending to lower both c_0* and c_1*. Thus overall, c_0* falls and his borrowing is diminished but the impact on c_1* is ambiguous.

Example 7.10: Ari and Rani both have inter-temporal utility functions given by $U = [\ln(c_0) + \beta \ln(c_1)]$ BUT each has a different value of β. Both have the same endowment which is the income stream (m_0, m_1). The interest rate for savers/lenders is r_s and for borrowers, it is r_b and $r_s < r_b$. It is known that Ari saves while Rani borrows. Who has the bigger value of β? What happens as the borrowing and lending rates converge?

In the previous example, we derived the condition for Ari to be a saver as

$$r > \{[(m_1/m_0)/\beta] - 1\}, \tag{7.6}$$

which rearranges to

$$\beta > [(m_1/m_0)/(1 + r_s)] = \beta^+, \tag{7.6a}$$

since Ari faces the rate r_s.

For Rani, the borrowing rate of interest is r_b and as a borrower, for her, $c_0^* > m_0$ which requires

$$r < \{[(m_1/m_0)/\beta] - 1\}, \tag{7.7}$$

or

$$\beta < [(m_1/m_0)/(1 + r_b)] = \beta^-. \tag{7.7a}$$

Comparing (7.6a) and (7.7a), we see that $\beta^+ > \beta^-$ because $r_s < r_b$. And since Ari has $\beta > \beta^+$ while Rani has $\beta < \beta^-$, it follows that

$$0 < \beta\,(\text{Rani}) < \beta^- < \beta^+ < \beta\,(\text{Ari}) < 1.$$

Other individuals whose β value lies between β^- and β^+ will need further analysis. If r_b falls to r_s, then β^- converges to β^+. Ari and Rani are unaffected in so far as Ari remains a saver/lender while Rani remains a borrower. However, those individuals with β in the middle range may change their borrowing/saving behaviour. Conversely, if r_s rises to r_b, then β^+ converges onto β^- with the same consequences.

7.4 Saving and Investment

In the previous section, we saw how individuals could rearrange the profile of their inter-temporal consumption by making use of the financial market where they could lend or borrow at a fixed rate of interest. By borrowing, they brought some consumption forward to the present from the future. By saving and lending, they did the opposite, i.e., increased future consumption by lowering present consumption. In this section, we examine another route by which individuals can increase future consumption by saving some of their current endowment. This route is by **direct investment** (as opposed to lending) For instance, an individual can invest part of current endowment on education which enhances future productivity and thus generates future income which augments future endowment, thus increasing future consumption. A farmer may save part of his current corn endowment to plant a seed of corn which produces corn in the future, thereby increasing future corn available for consumption. Where such productive investments are available, individuals have a choice of saving to invest for the future. How is this decision made? See Example 7.11.

Example 7.11: Ari has inter-temporal utility function given by $U = [\ln(c_0) + \ln(c_1)]$. His endowment is the income stream (m_0, m_1). Ari also has access to a production function $y_1 = F(h)$ which converts some current income h into future income y_1. If $F(h) = 10\sqrt{h}$ and $(m_0, m_1) = (12, 10)$, how much will Ari save and invest? Compare his welfare to a situation in which he cannot invest but can lend/borrow at $r = 0.25$.

Suppose Ari saves and invests h in the present. His present consumption is then $12 - h$ while his future consumption is $10 + 10\sqrt{h}$. Hence, his utility is given by

$$U = \ln(12 - h) + \ln(10 + 10\sqrt{h}). \tag{7.8}$$

The trade-off is clear. Increasing h lowers the utility from present consumption but increases that from future consumption. For ease of calculation, let $\sqrt{h} = x$ or $h = x^2$. Further noting that $\ln(c_0) + \ln(c_1) = \ln(c_0\, c_1)$, we can rewrite Eq. (7.8) in terms of x as

$$U = \ln[(12 - x^2)\,(10 + 10x)]. \tag{7.9}$$

And since $\ln x$ is an increasing function of x, we can simplify further by just maximising $(12 - x^2)(10 + 10x) = 10[(12 - x^2)(1 + x)]$ which is equivalent to maximising $V(x) = [(12 - x^2)(1 + x)]$.

To maximise $V(x)$, we use the standard FOC and SOC. These are as follows:

$$dV/dx = -3x^2 - 2x + 12 = 0, \tag{7.10a}$$

and

$$d^2V/dx^2 = -6x - 2 < 0. \tag{7.10b}$$

The quadratic equation in (7.10a) has two roots, viz. 1.69 and –2.36, of which 1.69 satisfies the SOC in (7.10b). Hence, $x^* = 1.69$ and $h^* = x^{*2} = 2.86$. Hence, Ari's optimal choices are to save and invest $h^* = 2.86$, hence consuming $c_0^* = 12 - 2.86 = 9.14$ in the present. In the future, his optimal consumption will be $10 + 10\ (1.69) = 26.9$. The maximised value of his utility is $\ln(9.14 \times 26.9) = \ln 246$.

If instead of investment opportunities Ari only has trading opportunities at an interest rate $r = 0.25$, then from Eqs. 7.5(a) and 7.5(b) and with $(m_0, m_1) = (12, 10)$, his optimal consumption plan (c_0^*, c_1^*) is (10, 12.5) which yields a total utility of $\ln(c_0^* c_1^*) = \ln(125)$ which is clearly lower than that obtained by investment. This result is not general but occurs because the technology is so productive. To better understand what is happening, consider the trade-off between output (consumption) today and tomorrow. Denote the output available as (x_0, x_1). Then, since $x_1 = 10 + 10\sqrt{h}$ and $x_0 = 12 - h$, it follows that the trade-off between x_1 and x_0 is given by

$$x_1 = 10 + 10\sqrt{(12 - x_0)}. \tag{7.11}$$

Equation (7.11) is what is called the **Production Possibility Frontier** (PPF). It represents the maximum amount of x_1 that can be obtained given any fixed level of x_0. Ari will seek to get on to the highest indifference curve consistent with being on the PPF. This can be contrasted with the situation in Figure 7.2 where Ari gets on to the highest indifference curve consistent with remaining on the trading line. Figure 7.4 illustrates trade or investment.

In Figure 7.4, the convex curve DC is the PPF. Starting at C, the initial endowment point with $x_0 = 12$ and $x_1 = 10$; it rises at a diminishing rate to

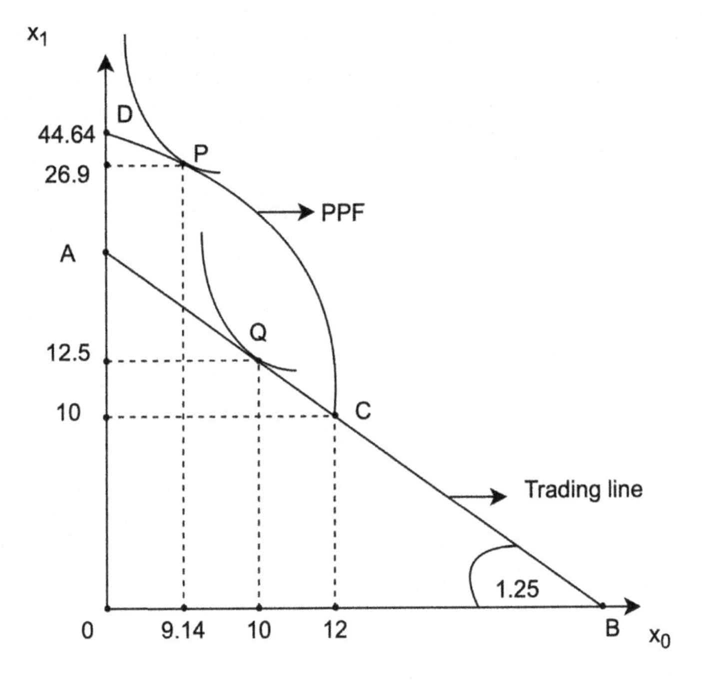

Fig. 7.4 Trade or Investment

reach its maximum of $x_1 = 44.64$ when $x_0 = 0$ which is point D. The consumer can choose any point on DC. As shown, the optimum is at P(9.14, 26.9) where $U^*(\text{inv}) = \ln 246$. If instead Ari could only trade, the trading line is ACB and his optimum position would be at Q(10, 12.5) and $U^*(\text{trade}) = \ln 125$. It is clear from the diagram that investment is the better option for this combination of production function and interest *rate*. But this is by no means a general result. The following example considers a situation where both trade and investment are simultaneously possible.

Example 7.12: Rani has inter-temporal utility function given by $U = \ln(c_0) + \ln(c_1)$. Her endowment is the income stream (m_0, m_1). Rani also has access to a diminishing returns production function $y_1 = F(h)$ which converts some current income h into future income y_1. She can borrow/lend at interest rate r. Describe her optimal strategy. Illustrate by a suitable diagram.

Rani can proceed in two steps. First, she maximises her wealth by investment. The present value of wealth is given by $W = m_0 - h + [m_1 + F(h)]/[1 + r]$. In order to maximise this, differentiate W with respect to h to obtain the FOC:

$$F'(h^*) = 1 + r. \tag{7.12}$$

The intuition is that if Rani invests h^*, then by sacrificing one extra unit of consumption now, Rani gets $F'(h)$ $(1 + r)$ in the future if she invests and $(1 + r)$ if she lends. At the optimum, these must be equal. This investment transforms her initial wealth $W = m_0 + [m_1/(1 + r)]$ into the higher number W^+ given by

$$W^+ = W = m_0 - h^* + [m_1 + F(h^*)]/[1 + r]. \tag{7.13}$$

Rani then uses her enhanced endowment and trades to obtain optimum consumption where MRS = $(1 + r)$. Figure 7.5 illustrates savings, investment and trade.

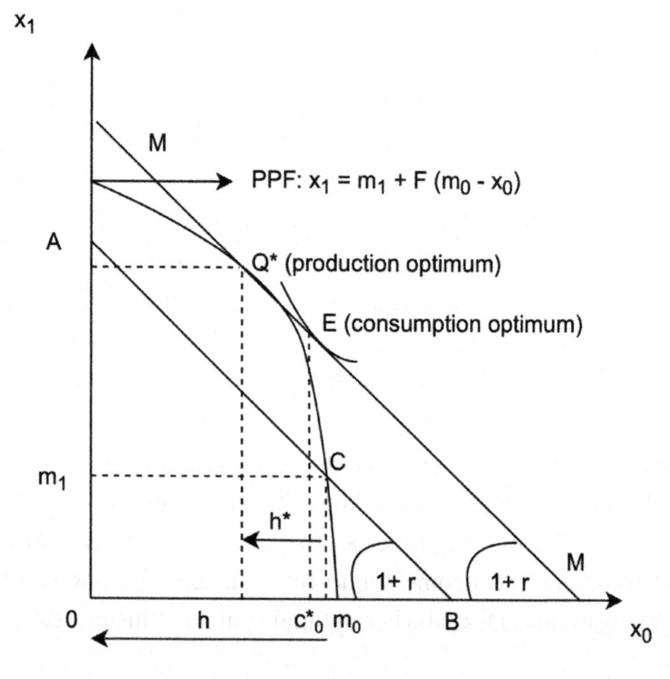

Fig. 7.5 Savings, Investment and Trade

In Figure 7.5, ACB is the trading line without investment possibilities. It has slope $(1 + r)$ and passes through the endowment point C. On the horizontal axis, we measure h as starting at m_0 and going towards the origin. The curved shape $Q^*C\ m_0$ is the PPF. In step 1, Rani maximises wealth by getting onto the highest possible trading line. For each possible trading line of slope $(1 + r)$, the horizontal intercept measures present value of wealth. Thus, initial wealth is given by point B. The straight line MM parallel to ACB is the highest attainable trading line given $F(h)$. The PPF $F(h)$ is tangent to MM at Q^*. This is Rani's production optimum. She invests h^* to achieve this. Starting from Q^*, she then trades to achieve her consumption optimum at E. Comparing Q^*, E and C show that Rani invests h^* but only saves $m_0 - c_0^*$ which is less than h^*. The balance of her investment, i.e., $\{h^* - [m_0 - c_0^*]\}$, is financed by borrowing. In the absence of a financial market, Rani could only invest what she saved. The additional source of investment makes her better off.

A crucial implication of the previous example is that an individual's optimum investment (h^*) and hence production is completely independent of her preferences. This **separation theorem** as it is called requires perfect markets and a convex production function for investment.

7.5 Summary

- When analysing inter-temporal decisions, all future quantities must be appropriately discounted.
- The inter-temporal budget line reflects the interest rate. Its slope is $(1 + r)$.
- Consumers' inter-temporal preferences depend on the discount factor.
- A perfect financial market enables consumers to borrow and lend at the going interest rate.
- With access only to a financial market, consumer optimum will equate MRS to the slope of the budget line which is $(1 + r)$.
- With access only to a production function for investment, consumer optimum will equate MRS to the slope of the PPF.

- With access to both a financial market and a production function, consumer optimum is obtained in two steps. First, by first equating slope of PPF to slope of budget line, consumer maximises wealth (which exceeds endowed wealth). She then trades along the trading line till MRS equals slope of the trading line.
- Consumer investment can exceed consumer saving because of borrowing possibility.

Chapter 8

Coordination of Exchange and Production

In all economies, there are many economic agents taking decisions simultaneously. Consumers are deciding what to buy, how much to save, etc. Firms are deciding what and how much to produce and sell, how much to invest, how many workers and machines to hire, etc. In this chapter, we study the issue of how such myriad decision-making is coordinated. Do we get order or chaos? We will analyse the role played by markets and a **planner** in **coordination**.

In the simplest case, we can imagine an economy with two economic agents and two goods. The two agents are Ari and Rani and the two goods are apples and oranges. Each agent has a stock of these goods (their endowments). Both derive utility from consumption of these goods. Will they just consume their endowments or will they seek to trade? We start with the simplest case of pure exchange before moving on to more complex examples where we consider the firm as an active agent hiring inputs and producing goods. The focus of the analysis is on whether consumers' decisions and firms' decisions are properly coordinated and on whether such coordination results in "good" outcomes.

8.1 Exchange

We start with what is called a **pure exchange economy**; there is no production. Each agent is a potential trader who owns a stock of both commodities. It is always open to them to consume their stock. What incentives do they have to trade in this economy?

Example 8.1: Ari and Rani have the same utility function $U(x, y) = xy$, where x is oranges and y is apples. Ari's endowment is 20 oranges and 10 apples while Rani's endowment is 10 oranges and 20 apples. Will they trade?

If Ari consumes his endowment, he will get $U_0 = 20 \times 10 = 200$ utils. Can he do better? Suppose Ari can exchange p apples for one orange. If Ari gives up one orange, he ends up with 19 oranges and $(10 + p)$ apples. Hence, his utility would be $U_1 = [19 \times (10 + p)] = 190 + 19p$ which exceeds U_0 provided p exceeds $10/19 = 0.53$. But Ari could also give up one apple and get $1/p$ oranges. Then, his utility would be $U_2 = [(20 + 1/p) \times 9]$ which exceeds U_0 if $p < 9/20 = 0.45$. Thus, there are many values for p in which Ari would be better off by exchange.

Essentially, the same is true for Rani. For clarity, denote her utility by $V = xy$. If she gives up one orange, her utility is $V_1 = [9 \times (20 + p)]$ which exceeds $V_0 = 200$ if $p > 20/9 = 2.22$. If she gives up one apple, her utility $V_2 = [(10 + 1/p) \times 19]$ which exceeds V_0 if $p < 1.9$. Once again, there are many values of p for which Rani would be better off by exchange. We can see that there are now three sub-intervals for p, i.e., $p < 0.53$, $p > 1.9$ and finally p lying in between 0.53 and 1.9. Only the last of these represents values of p which could lead to trade.

Consider any p between 0.53 and 1.9, say $p = 1$. Then, Ari would choose to give up one orange and get one more apple ending up with (19, 11) while Rani would give up one apple and get one more orange ending up with (11, 19). Both would now have utility of 209 rather than 200 with no trade and are thus better off. Note that p is nothing but the price of an orange (in terms of apples). Note also that the exchange when $p = 1$ is sustainable because Ari wants to sell oranges and buy apples at $p = 1$, while Rani wants to buy oranges and sell apples at $p = 1$. And Ari's demand for one apple is exactly matched by Rani's willingness to sell one apple. At the same time, Ari's willingness to sell one orange is exactly matched by Rani's willingness to buy one orange. The gains from trade go to both traders.

Example 8.2: Using the same information as in Example 8.1, show how Ari's willingness to sell oranges varies with the price p which is the price of an orange in terms of apples. Also, show Rani's willingness to buy oranges varies with p. If there is a market in which p is set, find the equilibrium value of p. Illustrate diagrammatically.

The value of Ari's endowment is $20p + 10$ (measured in apples). His optimisation problem is to maximise $U = xy$ subject to the constraint $px + y = 20p + 10$. The tangency solution is the familiar MRS equals price ratio, which implies $y/x = p$ or $y = px$ which substituted into the constraint gives $x^*_A = 10 + 5/p$. As this is Ari's optimal consumption of oranges, his offer to sell oranges is given by $20 - [10 + 5/p] = 10 - 5/p$ which is positive so long as $p > (1/2)$. As the price of oranges rises from (1/2), he will want to sell more oranges up to the limit of his endowment of 20 oranges. By similar logic, we find Rani's optimal consumption of oranges as $x^*_R = 5 + 10/p$. Hence, her willingness to buy oranges is given by $5 + (10/p) - 10 = 10/p - 5$ which is positive if $p < 2$. For an equilibrium, willingness to buy must equal offer to sell. Hence, we have $10 - 5/p = 10/p - 5$ or $p^* = 1$. At this price, Ari wants to sell 5 oranges and Rani wants to buy 5 oranges! The market "clears". Note that both Ari and Rani are maximising their utility and that their actions are mutually compatible at $p^* = 1$.

Another way to find the equilibrium price is to note that for the market as a whole, the total supply of oranges is 30. But total consumption demand is $x^*_A = 10 + 5/p$ plus $x^*_R = 5 + 10/p$, i.e., market demand is $15 + 15/p$. Hence, solving $30 = 15 + 15/p$, we get $p^* = 1$ as before.

Furthermore, note that by adding up the two budget constraints of Ari and Rani, we get

$$px_A + y_A + px_R + y_R = 30p + 30. \tag{8.1}$$

But since the market for X (Oranges) clears, we also know that

$$px_A + px_R = 30p. \tag{8.2}$$

Subtracting (8.2) from (8.1), we get

$$y_A + y_R = 30, \tag{8.3}$$

which asserts that the total demand for y (apples) equals 30, which is the market supply and hence the market for apples also clears. This result generalises and is called **Walras's law**. It can be stated thus: "If in a system of n markets, $n - 1$ of them clear, then so will the nth one". Figure 8.1 depicts the competitive equilibrium using the famous "Edgeworth box" diagram.

There are two origins: one in the southeast corner at A (for Ari) and the other in the opposite northwest corner at R (for Rani). Oranges are

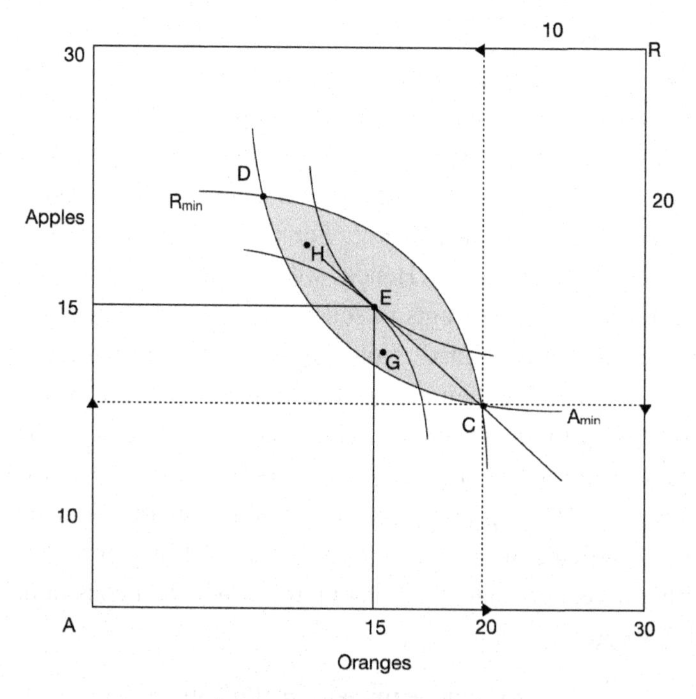

Fig. 8.1 Competitive Equilibrium with Trade

measured on the *x* axis and Apples on the *y* axis. The lengths of the sides of the box measure the total availability of oranges and apples. Thus, starting from A and going horizontally to the right, we measure oranges for Ari. Starting from R and going horizontally to the left, we measure oranges for Rani. Similarly, in measuring apples for Ari, we start at A and go vertically upwards while measuring apples for Rani, we start at R and go vertically downwards. The horizontal length of the box is the sum of the orange endowments of Ari and Rani, i.e., 30. It's the total availability of oranges in this economy. Similarly, the vertical length of the box is the sum of the apple endowments of Ari and Rani, i.e., 30. It's the total availability of apples in this economy. Any point in the box represents an allocation of oranges and apples to Ari and Rani which just exhausts the availability. The point C which is (20, 10) for Ari and (10, 20) for Rani is of special interest. It represents the initial endowments of both A and R.

There are two indifference curves through C: A_{min} for Ari and R_{min} for Rani. These measure the utility each would get if they consumed their endowments and did not trade. Feasible trades must offer a higher utility than these minimum values (which in this example is 200 utils for each). It is represented by the shaded cone-shaped area. Any straight line through C represents a potential price line. There are infinitely many of these. Given a price line through C of slope p (the price of oranges), both Ari and Rani choose their optimum consumption bundles represented by a tangency of their respective indifference curves with the price line. If this common price line produces a tangency for both at the same point within the cone, then this price is an equilibrium price and the resulting consumption choices are an equilibrium allocation. The point E is the competitive equilibrium. Note that at E, both the indifference curves have a **back-to-back tangency**. This follows because each is optimising and therefore the slope of their indifference curves must equal p (the price ratio). Hence, the slope of both indifference curves must be the same, i.e., there is a back-to-back tangency. From our earlier calculations, we know that the slope of the straight line CE is 1 and that the point E is (15, 15) for both Ari and Rani. At E, each gets a utility of 225 utils and is thus better off by trading.

Suppose we try a different price say 0.75 oranges per apple. The slope of the line through C will fall. Both Ari and Rani will seek to shift their consumption towards more oranges than 15 because they will now require MRS to equal 0.75. But the MRS can only fall if the ratio of oranges to apples consumed rises. Hence, for both, the tangency with price line will now occur at higher than 15 oranges at points like G and H, respectively. Thus, at $p = 0.75$, the total demand for orange consumption exceeds 30. Since the tangencies are now at different points and involve a total consumption of oranges which is not feasible, this lower price of 0.75 cannot be an equilibrium. Optimising trading decisions by both players are not mutually consistent. Only at a price of 1 does this mutual consistency of optimising decisions by both players occur at E. In this example, this equilibrium is unique but this is not a general result. But it does show how a market can properly coordinate the independent decisions of independent traders through the price mechanism.

8.2 Efficiency and Planning

As noted earlier, in all economies, there are many economic agents taking decisions simultaneously. We have seen how competitive markets can act as a coordination device which results in a **competitive allocation**, such as E (above). In this section, we will analyse the potential role played by a social planner in coordinating these myriad decisions. What criterion might the planner use in deciding how to allocate apples and oranges between Ari and Rani?

Economists conventionally assume that the planner uses a criterion known as the **Pareto criterion**. This states that a Pareto efficient allocation is one in which no individual can be made better off without at least one individual being made worse off. A planner using this criterion is called a Paretian planner. And allocations which satisfy the Pareto criterion are called *Pareto efficient allocations*. On the face of it, the Pareto criterion sounds like a reasonable criterion. But the Pareto criterion does in effect embody some quite strong and unpalatable assumptions. See the following example.

Example 8.3: A Paretian planner is trying to divide a cake between Ari and Rani. What shares might the Paretian planner give to each?

An equal division of the cake is Pareto efficient. If Ari is made better off by being given 60% of the cake, then Rani is necessarily made worse off because her allocation falls to 40%. But this same argument holds for any division which adds up to 100%. Consider, for example, a division of the cake which is 100% to Ari and hence 0% to Rani. This is also a Pareto efficient allocation. Rani cannot be made better off without Ari being made worse off. Thus, a Paretian planner's decision could result in extreme inequality! There is no Paretian basis for choosing between a 50–50 division and a 100–0 division as both are Pareto efficient.

The only Pareto INEFFICIENT allocations are those which do not exhaust the whole cake. For example, if the division is, say, Ari 45% and Rani 35%, then there is still 20% of the cake left. It can be given to either Ari or Rani, making the recipient better off without making the other worse off. This is clearly a Pareto improvement.

This example illustrates the limitations of the Pareto criterion. It is compatible with extreme inequality. The Pareto criterion does not imply a complete ranking in that there are many allocations which cannot be pairwise ranked. It is not unique. There are many Pareto efficient allocations.

Furthermore, a strictly egalitarian planner might wish to rank allocations by inequality. Thus, the allocation 45–45% would be preferred to 45–55% even though the latter is Pareto efficient allocation while the former is not! We should not assume that every movement from a non-Pareto efficient allocation to a Pareto efficient allocation is necessarily improving. It depends on societal preferences as embodied in the planner. The leap from a Pareto efficient allocation to claiming that this allocation is socially desirable (or just) is a giant one. The following example explores these ideas further.

Example 8.4: Ari has utility function $U(x, y)$, where x is oranges and y is apples, while Rani has utility function $V(x, y)$. The total available supply of oranges and apples is X^+ and Y^+, respectively. Describe the set of all Pareto efficient allocations.

Denote Ari's allocation as (x^A, y^A) and Rani's as (x^R, y^R), where $x^A + x^R = X^+$ and $y^A + y^R = Y^+$. In other words, we only consider "no wastage" allocations. If $x^A + x^R < X^+$ or $y^A + y^R < Y^+$, then some X or Y could be arbitrarily given to Ari or Rani without making the other worse off. A necessary condition for Pareto efficient allocation is that there should be "no wastage" of resources. In terms of Figure 8.1, any allocation in the Edgeworth box is a "no wastage" allocation. The entire stock of oranges and apples is being utilised. To illustrate the set of Pareto efficient allocations, consider the Edgeworth box diagram in Figure 8.2.

Consider a point like G. Ari's indifference curve U^1 passes through G. Rani's indifference curve V^1 also passes through G. The "cone-shaped" shaded area enclosed by these indifference curves represents allocations in which at least one person is better off without the other person being worse off. The arrows from U^1 (pointing towards A) and from V^1 (pointing towards R) show the direction of increased utility for Ari and Rani. At H,

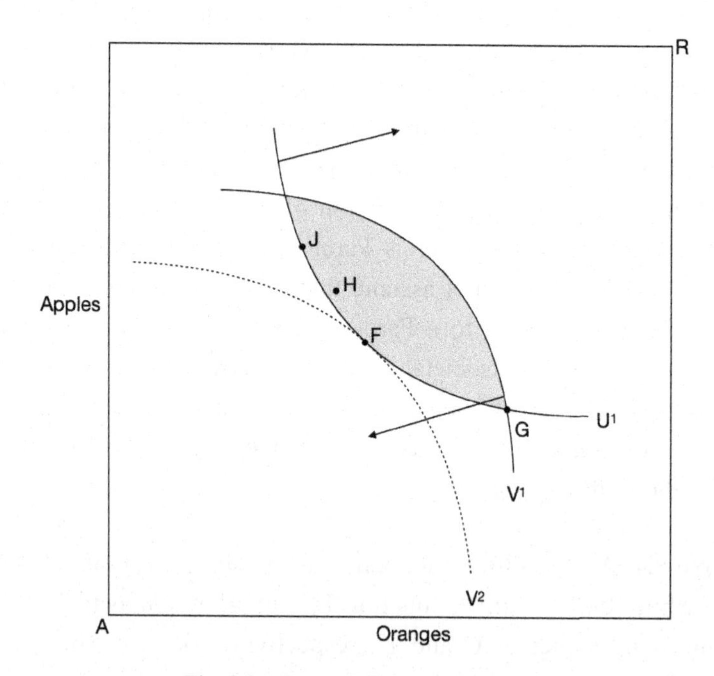

Fig. 8.2 Pareto Efficient Allocations

both are better off compared to G. At J, Ari is no worse off (still on U^1) but Rani is better off compared to G. Therefore, G is NOT a Pareto efficient allocation.

Consider now a point like F where the indifference curves U^1 and V^2 have a "back-to-back" tangency. The cone-shaped area associated with G has disappeared. Any movement from F to make either Ari or Rani better off necessarily makes the other worse off by pushing them onto a lower indifference curve. F is a Pareto efficient allocation. Only "back-to-back" tangency points are Pareto efficient. Thus, H which is not a "back-to-back" tangency is NOT Pareto efficient. Note that at H, both Ari and Rani are better off than at G and H is then said to **Pareto dominate** G. Comparing F and G, Ari is equally well off but Rani is better off at F. Hence, we say that F **weakly Pareto dominates** G. But there is no way using only the Pareto principle that we can compare H and F. At H, Ari is better off (compared to F) but Rani is worse off. The Pareto criterion simply fails in situations like this.

8.3 The Contract Curve and Welfare Theorems

The "back-to-back" tangency condition means that a common tangent to both indifference curves can be drawn through the point F. But the slope of each indifference curve is MRS. Thus, at points like F, the MRS of both Ari and Rani are equal and equal to the slope of the common tangent. In principle, there will be many such "back-to-back" tangency points within the Edgeworth box. The set of all such "back-to-back" tangency points is called the **contract curve**. See Example 8.5.

Example 8.5: Ari and Rani have the same utility function $U = xy$, where, as before, x is oranges and y is apples. There are 20 oranges and 20 apples in this economy. Find the equation of the contract curve and illustrate graphically.

Every point on the contract curve involves back-to-back tangency. In other words, MRS (Ari) = MRS (Rani). For both, MRS = y/x. Also, $x^R = 20 - x^A$ and $y^R = 20 - y^A$. Hence, MRS (Ari) = (y^A/x^A) and

MRS (Rani) = $[(20 - y^A)/(20 - x^A)]$ and hence equal MRS requires $(y^A/x^A) = (20 - y^A)/(20 - x^A)$ which solves on multiplying out to yield $y^A = x^A$ which is the equation of the contract curve. Figure 8.3 illustrates the contract curve.

In Figure 8.3, the 45-degree straight line through A is the contract curve CC. Its equation is $y^A = x^A$. Every point on the straight line is a "back-to-back" tangency of indifference curves. P and Q are examples. Ari would prefer Q but Rani would prefer P. There is no way using Pareto only that P and Q can be compared. Consider also a point like H which is off the contract curve. The indifference curves through H must enclose a "cone" as shown since there is no back-to-back tangency at H. The section of the "cone" on the contract curve is MN. Clearly, every point on MN at least weakly Pareto dominates H. Nonetheless, a strongly egalitarian planner may prefer H to either P or Q. Not all points off the contract curve (e.g., H) are Pareto dominated by all points on the contract curve. But every point off the contract curve is dominated by some point on the contract curve.

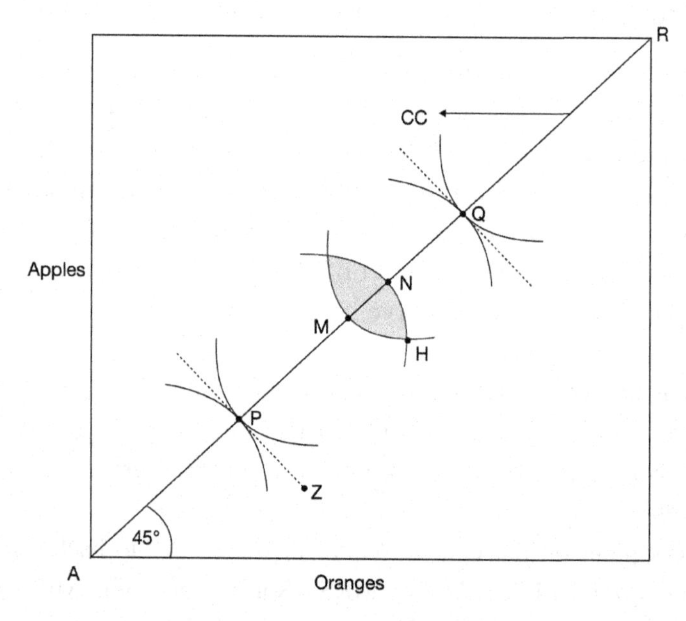

Fig. 8.3 The Contract Curve

This feature of "back-to-back" tangency has important implications. We saw in Section 8.1 that a competitive equilibrium is characterised by this feature. But so is the set of Pareto efficient points. This immediately opens up the relationship between these two quite distinct ideas which are connected through the contract curve. Since competitive equilibrium requires MRS (Ari) = MRS (Rani) = price ratio, then it follows that all competitive equilibria must lie on the contract curve. But every Pareto efficient allocation also lies on the contract curve. This implies that the set of Pareto efficient allocations (as would be chosen by a Paretian planner) is the same as the set of competitive equilibrium allocations as determined by the market. This is the basis of the two so-called fundamental theorems of welfare economics. **The first theorem of welfare economics** states that every competitive allocation is Pareto efficient. The **second theorem** is more subtle. It states that any Pareto efficient allocation (as determined by the social planner) can be attained through using the competitive market but requires initial endowments to be transferable.

Figure 8.3 illustrates the second theorem. Suppose the planner's preferred allocation is Q. But the present endowments at Z are such that the only competitive equilibrium is at P. How does the planner go from P to Q? What he must do is redistribute endowments to lie on the dashed line through Q, then the competitive equilibrium will be at Q. In this way, transferability of endowments allows the planner to achieve any Pareto efficient outcome using the market mechanism rather than direct control.

8.4 Production and Planning: The Robinson Crusoe Economy

The previous section focused on exchange only. There was no production. Effectively, we were looking just at traders, not firms. While useful for understanding the concepts of market clearing and Pareto efficiency and the relationship between them, ignoring production has obvious limitations. In this section, we remedy this shortcoming.

Consider a simple economy with one production unit called the firm and one **worker-consumer** called Robinson Crusoe. Hence, the name the

Robinson Crusoe economy. The firm is characterised by its production function and Robinson by his utility function. The firm uses labour to produce corn according to the production function:

$$\mathrm{C} = F(L). \tag{8.4}$$

In Eq. (8.4), C is corn produced using L units of labour time. It is further assumed that $F(L)$ exhibits positive diminishing marginal product of labour so that the feasible production set is convex as described in Chapter 3. In calculus terms, this amounts to $F'(L) > 0$ (positive marginal product) and $F''(L) < 0$ (diminishing marginal product). The maximum amount of time available (for labour or leisure) is normalised to unity. Robinson derives utility from corn consumption C and leisure time H (which is obverse of labour time) where $L + H = 1$. Robinson's utility function is given by

$$U = U(\mathrm{C}, H). \tag{8.5}$$

It is assumed that the indifference curves obtained from the utility function are convex in the conventional way. The partial derivatives of U are U_C the marginal utility of consumption and U_H the marginal utility of leisure.

We start with the planner (who is a Paretian) with objective to maximise U, i.e., to put Robinson on his highest possible indifference curve. In achieving this objective, the planner has to respect the constraint imposed by the production function, namely that total corn produced C cannot exceed $F(L)$. Obviously, all Pareto efficient solutions must have $\mathrm{C} = F(L)$. Formally, we write this planning problem as

$$\text{Max } U(\mathrm{C}, H) \quad \text{subject to } \mathrm{C} = F(L) \quad \text{and} \quad H = 1 - L.$$

To solve this diagrammatically, note that Robinson's indifference curves, which are of the usual downward sloping variety in (C, H) space, are UPWARD sloping in (C, L) space because $L = 1 - H$. Figure 8.4 illustrates the solution.

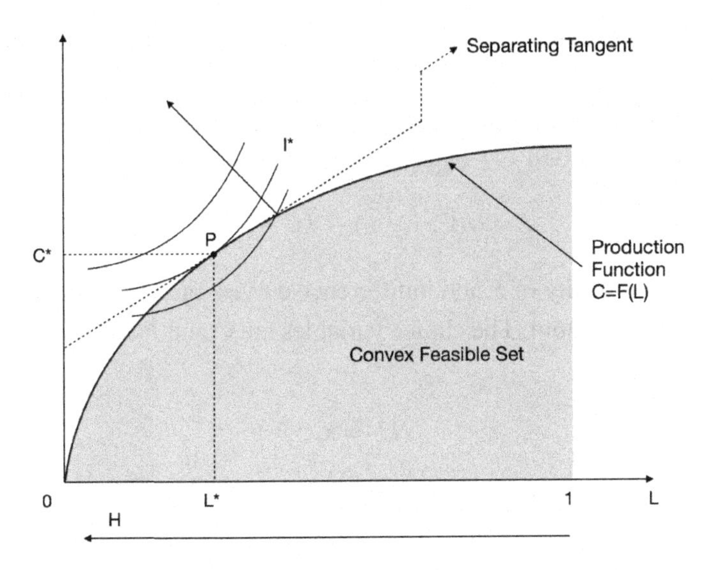

Fig. 8.4 Pareto Efficiency with Production

In Figure 8.4, labour time L is measured on the horizontal axis going left to right and leisure time H is measured on the same axis going right to left. The maximum time available is unity. The area below the production function and bounded by $L = 1$ is the feasible set. It is clearly convex. The indifference curves slope upwards and are convex too. The planner wants to get to the highest indifference curve possible. Outcomes in the northwest direction (shown by the arrow) are preferred. The planner's optimum is at P which is on the boundary of the feasible set and also on the indifference curve labelled I^*. Planner chooses labour time L^* and corn production and consumption is C^*. It is clearly Pareto efficient as there is no other feasible allocation that can yield a higher utility for Robinson. Note the common tangent through P is a **separating line**. All points on or below the separating line give a lower utility to Robinson, except at P. All points on or above the separating line are infeasible except P. The slope of the indifference curve I^* is $\text{MRS} = \text{MU}_H/\text{MU}_C$ while the slope of the production function is $\text{MPL} = F'(L)$. Only at P are these equal.

Hence, P represents the maximum utility subject to the production constraint.

The Lagrangian corresponding to the problem Max $U(C, H)$ subject to $C = F(L)$ and $H = 1 - L$ can (following 3.1) be written as

$$Ł = U(C, 1 - L) - \lambda(C - F(L)). \quad (8.6)$$

Given convexity of F and indifference curves, the FOCs are sufficient for a utility maximum. The choice variables are C and L and the FOCs are as follows:

$$U_C = \lambda, \quad (8.7a)$$

$$-U_H = -\lambda F'(L). \quad (8.7b)$$

Eliminating λ, by dividing Eq. (8.7b) by (8.7a), yields the same result as in Figure 8.4, viz. $[U_H/U_C] = F'(L)$ or slope of IC = MRS = slope of production function = MPL. If the economy was organised by a social planner, they would ask Robinson to work L^* units of labour time and deliver C* units of corn to Robinson. There would be no reference to a "price mechanism" or prices. This is direct control by the planner. The following examples illustrate these rather abstract ideas.

Example 8.6: Robinson has the utility function $U = \alpha \ln H + C$ and $\alpha < 1$. The production function is $C = F(L) \equiv \ln(1 + L)$. Find the Pareto efficient allocation and illustrate graphically.

As $U_C = 1$ and $U_H = \alpha/(1 - L)$, and $F'(L) = 1/(1 + L)$, the FOC implies $\alpha/(1 - L) = 1/(1 + L)$, which yields $L^* = [(1 - \alpha)/(1 + \alpha)]$ which lies between 0 and 1 as $\alpha < 1$. By substituting $L^* = [(1 - \alpha)/(1 + \alpha)]$ into the production function, we get $C^* = \{\ln[(1 - \alpha)/(1 + \alpha)]\}$. The illustration is as in Figure 8.4 with $L^* = [(1 - \alpha)/(1 + \alpha)]$ and $C^* = \{\ln[2/(1 + \alpha)]\}$.

An alternative solution method which does not use Lagrangians is to substitute the production function directly into U and then maximise with respect to the one variable L.

Thus, by substitution, $U(L) = \alpha \ln(1 - L) + \ln(1 + L)$ and FOC obtained by differentiation is $\alpha/(1 - L) - 1/(1 + L) = 0$ as before. It's easy to verify the SOC too.

Note that as α increases, leisure H becomes more important to Robinson and the planner would reduce L^* (and C^*) to reflect this.

Example 8.7: Robinson has the utility function $U(C, L) = C - \alpha L^{3/2}$ and production is given by $C = sL^{1/2}$. Find the Pareto efficient allocation. What happens as the technology parameter s gets bigger and as α gets bigger?

By substitution of production function into utility function, we get

$$U(L) = sL^{1/2} - \alpha L^{3/2}. \tag{8.8}$$

Hence, FOC is

$(1/2)sL^{-1/2} - (3/2)\alpha L^{1/2} = 0$ or $sL^{-1/2} = 3\alpha L^{1/2}$. Multiplying both sides by $L^{1/2}$ immediately yields $L^* = s/3\alpha$. Hence, $C^* = s\sqrt{[s/3\alpha]}$. It is straightforward to check SOC. As technology improves, reflected in increase in s, the payoff to work is greater so the planner increases L^* (and C^*). Since $U_L = -(3/2)\alpha L^{1/2}$ which is the marginal **disutility** of work, an increase in α increases Robinson's marginal disutility of work and hence the planner reduces L^*.

8.5 Production and Competition in the Robinson Crusoe Economy

Suppose now that the planner is replaced by a competitive market. What outcomes might be observed? At the outset, we need to specify how this market works. The market prices of corn and labour are given as P and W. Since there are only two goods, only one relative price is needed. This is the wage in units of corn or real wage $w = W/P$. The firm uses L^d units of labour to produce C^s units of corn in order to maximise profits. It makes profits of $\prod$ units of corn which are given to its sole shareholder who is Robinson. But Robinson is also a worker and if he works L^s labour units, he receives a wage income (in corn) of wL^s making his total income $wL^s + \prod$. Given this income, Robinson maximises utility to choose his optimal labour supply L^s and his optimum corn demand C^d. Start with any w. The firm will choose L^d (and consequently output supply C^s) so as to maximise profits given w. It then calculates the maximised value of profits $\prod$ which is passed on to its shareholder Robinson who treats it as non-labour income. He then maximises $U(C, L)$ subject to his budget constraint which is $C = wL + \prod$, where the real wage w is the same as the one faced by the firm. His optimal values are C^d and L^s. A competitive equilibrium wage is the wage at which these decisions of the firm and Robinson as worker-consumer are mutually consistent. The competitive equilibrium wage w^* must satisfy $C^d(w^*) = C^s(w^*)$, $L^d(w^*) = L^s(w^*)$ and $\prod(w^*) > 0$. We investigate the possibilities diagrammatically in Figure 8.5.

Consider first the firm facing a wage w and with production function as in Figure 8.5. Draw a straight line of slope w through an arbitrary point like Q. This is an iso-profit line — everywhere on the line, profit is constant. At Q, the firm would use L^q labour to produce C^q output. The slope of the iso-profit line through Q is $w = QA/AB$ which implies $QA = (w)(AB)$ or $QA = wL^q$ which is the wage bill. This is also equal to BC^q. But $0C^q$ is total output. Hence, $0B = [0C^q - BC^q]$ is therefore profit at Q. Could the firm do better? Yes. If the firm moves up the production function from Q towards T (as shown by the arrow), it will increase profit because the vertical intercept of the straight line of slope w through points higher than

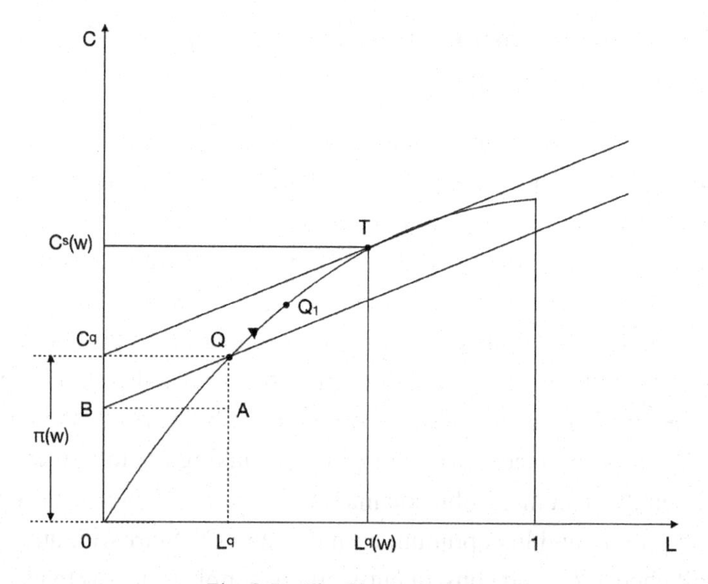

Fig. 8.5 The Firm's Optimum

Q (like Q_1) will increase. In other words, iso-profit lines with slope w have higher intercepts for a small movement from Q. This will continue till T where any further travel up the production function will lower profits. At T, the production function is tangent to an iso-profit line of slope w. This is the profit maximisation point where w = MPL. Hence, firms' optimum choices are $(L^d(w), C^s(w))$ which yield positive profit of $\prod(w)$.

Robinson receives this profit $\prod$ as his non-labour income. His budget constraint is therefore $C = wL + \prod$. In Figure 8.5, the line tangent at T has slope w and intercept $\prod$ and therefore has equation $C = wL + \prod$. Given Robinson's convex indifference curves between consumption and labour time, we can illustrate Robinson's problem in Figure 8.6.

Figure 8.6 shows Robinson's indifference curves and his budget constraint. The tangency optimum is at R where optimum labour supply is L^s and consumption demand is C^d. For convenience, the firm's optimum position for wage w, which is T (with labour demand L^d and corn output C^s), is also marked in Figure 8.6.

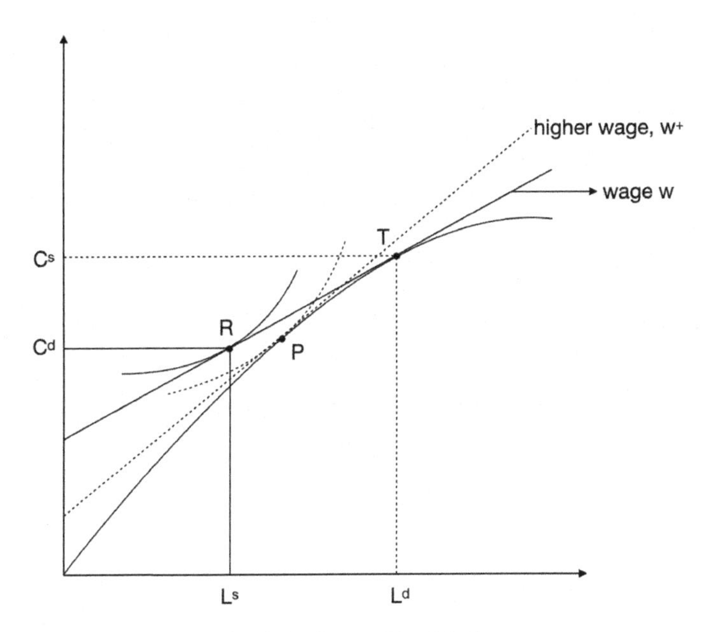

Fig. 8.6 Competitive Market

It is obvious that wage w is NOT an equilibrium since $L^s < L^d$. In terms of the diagrams, the productive optimum and the consumers' optimum do not coincide — T is different from R. We have a competitive disequilibrium. Since labour supply is too little, a higher wage is needed to induce greater labour supply and simultaneously choke off some labour demand. For some higher wage w^+, the steeper iso-profit line (the dashed line) is a tangent to both production function and indifference curve at the same point P. Then, w^+ is an equilibrium wage! In this situation, P locates the competitive equilibrium at the wage w^+, where the labour and the corn markets simultaneously clear. At P, MRS = w = MPL. But MRS = MPL is exactly the condition needed for Pareto efficiency as in Figure 8.4. Hence (under the assumed conditions), we have established the congruence between a competitive market and a Pareto efficient allocation. The following few examples illustrate these ideas in more detail.

Example 8.8: Robinson has the utility function $U = \alpha \ln(1 - L) + C$ and $\alpha < 1$. The production function is $C = \ln(1 + L)$. Find the competitive equilibrium allocation. Is it the same as the Pareto efficient allocation?

Starting with the firm, we write profits as

$$\prod(L) = \text{Ln}(1 + L) - wL. \tag{8.9}$$

Differentiating with respect to L, we get the FOC ($d\prod(L)/dw = 0$) as

$$1/(1 + L) = w, \tag{8.10}$$

which of course is the familiar MPL = w condition. It is easy to check SOCs are satisfied.

From (8.10), we get the firm's labour demand, output supply and maximised value of profits all as functions of the wage rate:

$$L^d = (1/w) - 1, \tag{8.11a}$$

$$C^s = -\ln w, \tag{8.11b}$$

$$\prod = -\ln w + w - 1. \tag{8.11c}$$

These solutions are only valid if $w < 1$ so that labour demand is strictly positive.

Robinson's optimum choice as consumer-worker is given by MRS $= w$ or $\alpha/(1 - L) = w$ which solves for labour supply as

$$L^s = 1 - E(\alpha/w). \tag{8.12}$$

Obviously, (8.12) only holds for $w > \alpha$ so that L^s is strictly positive. Coupled with $w < 1$ so that labour demand is also positive, we have $\alpha < w < 1$, which is consistent with $\alpha < 1$.

From (8.11) and (8.12), we can by setting $L^d = L^s$ solve for w^* and L^*: the equilibrium wage and employment.

$$w^* = (1 + \alpha)/2, \tag{8.13}$$

$$L^* = [(1 - \alpha)/(1 + \alpha)]. \tag{8.14}$$

We note from Example 8.6 that the Pareto efficient allocation is also given by $L^*= [(1 - \alpha)/(1 + \alpha)]$. Thus, a Paretian planner would choose exactly the competitive equilibrium allocation. To confirm that Eq. (8.14) does describe a competitive equilibrium, we need to show that profits are positive. From Eq. 8.11(c), note that $\prod (1) = 0$ and $\prod' (w) < 0$ for $w < 1$. Hence, $\prod(w) > 0$ for all $w < 1$. And from Eq. (8.13), w^* is indeed less than 1 because by assumption, $\alpha < 1$.

Example 8.9: Robinson has the utility function $U(C, L) = C - \alpha L^{3/2}$ and the firm's production function is given by $C = sL^{1/2}$, where both s and α are positive. Find the competitive equilibrium allocation. What happens as s gets bigger and as α gets bigger?

Following exactly the same steps as in Example 8.8, we get that

$$L^d = s^2/4w^2, \tag{8.15a}$$

$$C^s = -s^2/2w, \tag{8.15b}$$

$$\prod = s^2/4w, \tag{8.15c}$$

$$L^s = 4w^2/9\alpha^2. \tag{8.16}$$

Equating L^d and L^s gives $w^* = \sqrt{[(3/4)\alpha s]}$ and hence $L^* = s/3\alpha$ exactly the same answer as in Example 8.7. Once again, the competitive equilibrium is a Pareto efficient allocation.

Thus, we see that the congruence of Pareto efficient allocations chosen by a planner with a competitive allocation obtained through the price mechanism remains even with the introduction of production.

8.6 Efficiency and Competition with Increasing Returns

In the previous sections of this chapter, we have assumed that indifference curves and production sets are both convex. In other words, production functions are characterised by diminishing marginal productivity. In this section, we look at the complexity introduced by dropping the assumption of diminishing marginal product. Instead, we assume production is characterised by increasing marginal product which we loosely refer to as "increasing returns". Common examples of such production processes will include examples where a large fixed cost of production is allied to a small marginal cost, e.g., phone networks, electricity and gas production, etc. The presence of increasing returns will in general weaken the link between competitive equilibrium and Pareto efficiency as the following few examples show.

Example 8.10: Robinson has the utility function $U(C, L)$ given by $U = C(1 - L)$, where C is coconut consumption and L is labour supplied. The maximum value of L is 1. Suppose coconut production is given by (a) $C = L^{1/2}$ or (b) $C = L^2$, for $0 \leq L \leq 1$. Suppose economic life on Crusoe Island is managed by a benevolent Paretian dictator who informs Crusoe of his labour requirement L^* and his consumption basket C*. Find the values of (C*, L^*) in both cases. Also find the marginal product of labour at the **social optimum** (C*, L^*). Illustrate your answer with a diagram. Will a competitive market achieve the social optimum?

In this example, it's simpler to solve by direct substitution of production function into utility. Thus, for option (a), planner seeks to maximise $U = L^{½}(1 - L)$. From FOC, it follows that $L = 1/3$ and SOC for a maximum are satisfied as $U_{LL} < 0$. Hence, $L^* = 1/3$ maximises Robinson's utility subject to the production constraint.

If the planner was replaced by a competitive market, the firm would maximise profits by setting wage = MPL or $w = 1/(2\sqrt{L})$ (as in Examples 8.7 and 8.8) which gives labour demand $L^d = 1/4w^2$, output supply $C^s = 1/2w$ (by substitution into the production function) and maximised profits $\prod = C^s - wL^d = 1/4w$ as functions of the wage. To obtain labour supply, we first set MRS = w (as before). Thus, we get C/H = w or $C^d = w(1 - L^s)$. We then use Robinson's budget constraint which is $C^d = wL^s + \prod$ since firm's profits $\prod$ are Robinson's non-labour income. Setting the two expressions for C^d equal to each other and noting that $\prod = 1/(4w)$, we find $L^s = (1/2) - \prod/(2w) = (4w^2 - 1)/8w^2$. These values are summarised in the following:

$$L^d = 1/4w^2, \tag{8.17a}$$

$$C^s = 1/2w, \tag{8.17b}$$

$$\prod = 1/4w, \tag{8.17c}$$

$$L^s = -(4w^2 - 1)/8w^2. \tag{8.18}$$

Setting $L^d = L^s$, we solve for the competitive equilibrium wage $w^e = [(\sqrt{3})/2]$. Note that this is also the MPL at the social optimum $L^* = 1/3$. Since $w^e = (\sqrt{3})/2$, it follows that employment in the competitive equilibrium is $L^e = 1/3$. Hence, we have shown that the competitive equilibrium allocation equals the Pareto efficient allocation. Figure 8.6 illustrates this situation as indifference curves are convex and the production function has diminishing marginal product. At the Pareto efficient point P, the slope of the production equals that of the dashed separating line which has slope w^*. Hence, the separating line acts as both iso-profit line for the firm and budget line for the consumer-worker.

In case (b) when $C = L^2$, matters are quite different. Production is now characterised by increasing returns — the average output function is $C/L = L$ which increases continuously as L increases. The MPL function is given by $2L$ which also increases as L increases.

The social planner seeks to find the maximum of U which in this case by direct substitution of production function into utility function is given by $U = L^2(1 - L)$. From the FOC, there are two roots: $L = 0$ and $L = 2/3$. From the SOC, it follows that $L = (2/3)$ is the maximum point as $U_{LL} = 2 - 6L < 0$ when $L = (2/3)$. Thus, $L^* = (2/3)$. To check whether $L^* = (2/3)$ can also be the competitive equilibrium, we start by examining the firm's decision. The firm wishes to maximise $\prod(L) = C - wL = L^2 - wL$. Following the conventional approach, the FOC requires setting $\prod_L = 0$ (or wage = MPL) which implies $L = w/2$ but the SOC, viz. $\prod_{LL} < 0$, is NOT satisfied as $\prod_{LL} = 2$. Hence, $L = w/2$ is NOT a maximum for $\prod(L)$. Indeed, at $L = w/2$, profits are minimised and are negative for any w!

To find the maximum, we proceed from first principles. We know that the competitive wage w^e must be less than 1 since the maximum output of the economy (at $L = 1$) is 1. Since profits are minimised at the interior point $L = w/2$, moving away from $w/2$ must increase profits. If $L = (w/2 + k)$, where k can be positive or negative, then profits $\prod(w/2 + k) = \{[(w/2 + k)]^2 - [(w/2 + k)]w\} = \{k^2 + \prod(w/2)\}$. Thus, profits increase with larger k. The furthest we can move away is to go either to $L = 0$ or $L = 1$. For any $w < 1$, $\prod(1) = 1 - w > \prod(0) = 0$. Therefore, the firm will choose $L = 1$ for $w < 1$ and $L = 0$ for $w > 1$. At $w = 1$, the firm is indifferent. Hence, the only possible meaningful competitive equilibrium is at $L = 1$, NOT $L = 2/3$. The congruence between Pareto efficient allocation and competitive equilibrium is destroyed. At the Pareto efficient point $L^* = 2/3$, MPL $= 4/3$ which is bigger than unity and hence this cannot be an equilibrium wage as the firm will shut down at this wage! Figure 8.7 illustrates the problem of increasing returns.

In Figure 8.7, the feasible set bounded by the production function and $L = 1$ is shaded. It is clearly not convex since if any two points on the boundary OB are joined by a straight line, then all points on the line will

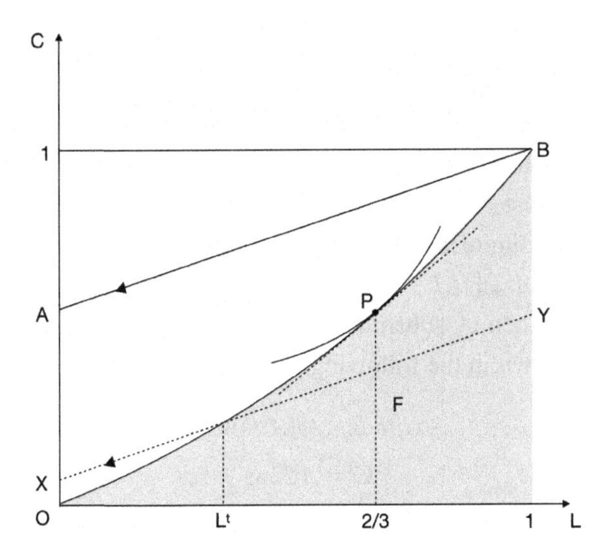

Fig. 8.7 The Problem of Increasing Returns

(except the two end points) lie outside the boundary. The Pareto allocation is at P where there is a common tangent (the dashed line) to both indifference curve and production function. BUT the common tangent is NOT a separating line. And it is this fact which implies that P cannot be sustained by a competitive equilibrium. The firm's profit maximising choice is at B since the iso-profit line through B has a slope less than 1 and thus yields positive maximum profit of OA. XY is another iso-profit with the same slope as AB. But the profit at $L = L^t$ is OX which is less than OA. Hence, the firm's optimum is $L = 1$. At $L = 1$, the average product of labour is a maximum. Hence, for any wage, $L = 1$ yields the maximum profit if the firm stays in production. But for high enough w, the profit at $L = 1$ is negative and the firm simply shuts down. The social planner's optimum position cannot be achieved by competition. The second theorem of welfare economics does not hold.

Example 8.11: Robinson has the utility function $U(\mathrm{C}, L)$ given by $U = \mathrm{C}(1 - L)$, where C is coconut consumption and L is labour supplied. The maximum value of L is 1. The production function in this economy is given by $y = 0$ if $L < L_{min}$, and $y = A(L - L_{min})^{1/2}$ if $L \geq L_{min}$. Find the labour demand and labour supply functions and hence find equilibrium employment, wage and coconut production in a competitive market. For what values of L_{min} will the second theorem of welfare economics NOT hold?

As usual, we start with the firm. For $L \geq L_{min}$, the production function is conventional (diminishing marginal productivity) and FOC is w = MPL or $w = dy/dL = (A/2)[1/(L - L_{min})^{1/2}]$ for $L > L_{min}$. From this, we immediately get L^d and then by substitution, we get C^s and $\prod$, all as functions of w. These are shown in the following.

$$L^d = L_{min} + (A^2/4w^2), \tag{8.19a}$$

$$C^s = A^2/2w, \tag{8.19b}$$

$$\prod = (A^2/4w) - wL_{min}, \tag{8.19c}$$

Note that $\prod > 0$ requires

$$w < A/(2\sqrt{L_{min}}). \tag{8.20}$$

Note also that profits fall as L_{min} gets larger.

As the utility function is the same as in Example 8.9, we get the following:

$$L^s = 1/2 - (\prod/2w), \tag{8.21a}$$

or using Equation (8.19c),

$$L^s = 1/2 - (A^2/8w^2) + (L_{min}/2). \tag{8.21b}$$

Setting $L^d = L^s$, we get wage w^* and employment L^* as

$$w^* = \sqrt{\{(3A^2/[4(1 - L_{min})]\}}, \tag{8.22}$$

$$L^* = (2/3)L_{min} + (1/3). \tag{8.23}$$

But from Eq. (8.20), we know $w < A/(2\sqrt{L_{min}})$ which together with Eq. (8.22) implies $L_{min} < 1/4$ for $\prod^* > 0$.

The planner would of course set MPL = MRS directly and hence planner's optimum is given by Eq. (8.23). To verify this, note that

$\text{MPL} = A/\{2[\sqrt{(L - L_{\min})}]\}$ and $\text{MRS} = C/(1 - L) = \{A[\sqrt{(L - L_{\min})}]/(1 - L)\}$. Equating and solving, we get exactly Eq. (8.23)!

For the planner, however, Eq. (8.23) is the solution whatever the value of $L_{\min}$. BUT under competitive markets, (8.23) is only a solution if $L_{\min} < (1/4)$ so that $\prod^* > 0$ in which case, (8.23) is the unique solution. Hence, the congruence does not hold and consequently, the second theorem of welfare economics does NOT hold if $L_{\min} > (1/4)$. The problem arises because the feasible production set is NOT convex. Figure 8.8 illustrates non-convex production and welfare.

In Figure 8.8, there are two production functions: one corresponding to a low value of $L_{\min}$ denoted as L^- and the other corresponding to a high value of $L_{\min}$ denoted as L^+. Both production sets are non-convex. If $L_{\min} = L^-$, then the planner's optimum is at P^- on IC^-. As can be seen, the separating (iso-profit) line cuts the vertical axis on the positive segment implying positive profits if the planner was replaced by a market. Hence, in this case, the second theorem holds. However, if $L_{\min} = L^+$, then the planner's optimum is at P^+ on IC^+. This optimum cannot be sustained by a competitive market because the separating (iso-profit) line cuts the vertical axis on the negative segment implying negative profits.

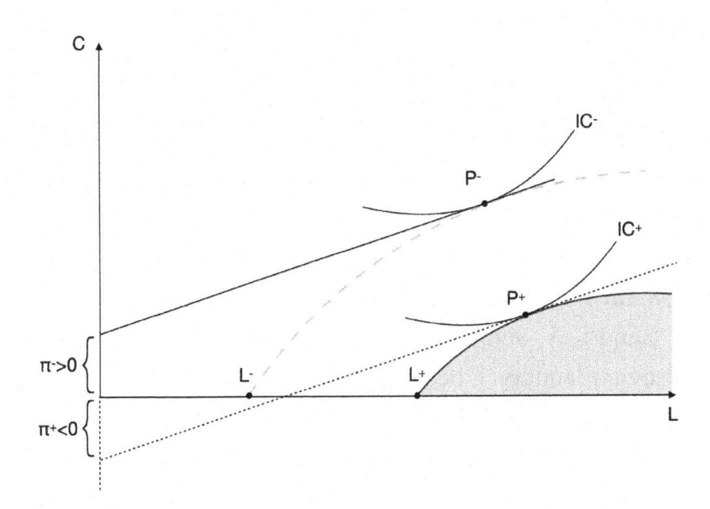

Fig. 8.8 Non-Convex Production and Welfare

Examples 8.9 and 8.10 illustrate several of the difficulties which stem from increasing returns. The planner will be able to find the socially optimum allocation. But there is no guarantee that this optimum can be achieved by a competitive market. Indeed, a competitive market equilibrium may not even exist.

8.7 Externalities and the Environment

Up until now, a fundamental assumption running through all the examples is that an individual's actions affect only their own welfare or profits. But there are many situations in which an individual carries out an action which has a direct beneficial or detrimental effect on someone else. An example of the former might be when an individual plants a lovely rose bush in her garden, neighbours get a direct benefit from the pleasure of viewing the roses. An example of the latter might be the impact of smoking by an individual on someone nearby or the impact of noisy parties on neighbours. Such effects are called **external effects**. They arise when individuals or firms are affected directly — negatively or positively — and without their consent by actions of other individuals or firms. Much of environmental economics is concerned with how to tackle the issues arising from pollution of various kinds, i.e., from negative externalities. From an economist's perspective, the fundamental question is whether such externalities damage the cosy relationship between competitive markets and Pareto efficient outcomes. The answer is an unqualified "Yes". We illustrate through examples which focus on the negative impacts of pollution on production.

Example 8.12: Two shirt laundries are located on the banks of a river. The upstream laundry, X, dumps waste in the river which negatively impacts the downstream laundry Y because Y has to devote labour to "clean" its water before use. The production functions of the two laundries are $x = 2\sqrt{(l_x)}$ and $y = 2\sqrt{(l_y - \alpha l_x)}$. The price of a laundered shirt is $p = 6$, and the wage is $w = 1$. Under perfect competition, find the profits of X and Y if $\alpha = 0.2$. What happens as α gets bigger?

Since profits are just revenue less labour costs, under perfect competition, each firm hires labour till the marginal product equals the real wage which implies for X and Y respectively that

$$w/p = 1/\sqrt{(l_x)}, \quad (8.24a)$$

$$w/p = 1/\sqrt{(l_y - \alpha l_x)}. \quad (8.24b)$$

These FOCs for profit maximisation are sufficient since both production functions have diminishing marginal product. They can be solved to yield the optimal labour demands, output and maximised profits of each firm using $p = 6$ and $w = 1$. From Eq. (8.24a), we immediately get

$$l_x^* = 36, \quad (8.25a)$$

$$x^* = 12, \quad (8.25b)$$

$$\Pi_x^* = 36. \quad (8.25c)$$

After substituting the value of $l_x^* = 36$ into the FOC for Y which is Eq. (8.24b), we also get

$$l_y^* = 36(1 + \alpha), \quad (8.26a)$$

$$y^* = 12, \quad (8.26b)$$

$$\Pi_y^* = 36(1 - \alpha). \quad (8.26c)$$

It can be seen from Eqs. (8.26) how increases in the external effect α impinge on y. As α rises, firm X imposes greater cleaning cost on firm Y and firm Y reacts by hiring more labour used for cleaning water supply which increases its costs but does not change its marketable output and consequently its profits fall. In the special case when $\alpha = 0.2$, firm Y's optima are

$$l_y^* = 43.2, \quad y^* = 12, \quad \Pi_y^* = 28.8. \quad (8.27)$$

Are these outcomes $\Pi_x^* = 36$ and $\Pi_y^* = 28.8$ Pareto efficient? Is there another arrangement which could increase one firm's profit without lowering that of the other? See the following example.

Example 8.13: Suppose the owners of the two firms in Example 8.12 Ari (who owns *X*) and Rani (who owns *Y*) agree to merge. What strategy should the **merged firm** follow? Will this strategy be Pareto efficient?

We can envisage the newly merged firm as treating *X* and *Y* as plants rather than firms. Recall that under separate existence of *X* and *Y* as firms, Ari received profit income of 36 and Rani of 28.8 so that the pooled profit income was 64.8. The merged firm will seek to maximise the pooled profit from its two plants which is given by $\prod$, where

$$\prod = 2p\sqrt{(l_x)} + 2p[\sqrt{(l_y - \alpha l_x)}] - w(l_x + l_y). \quad (8.28)$$

The merged firm will choose its two labour inputs l_x and l_y to maximise $\prod$. The two FOCs are $\prod_x = 0$ and $\prod_y = 0$ which when simplified yield

$$w/p = [1/\sqrt{(l_x)}] - \alpha/[\sqrt{(l_y - \alpha l_x)}], \quad (8.29a)$$

$$w/p = 1/[\sqrt{(l_y - \alpha l_x)}]. \quad (8.29b)$$

Equation (8.29b) is the familiar wage = marginal product condition for choice of l_y and is the same as in Eq. (8.24b). However, the FOC pertaining to choice of l_x (which is Eq. (8.29a)) is very different. Substituting Eq. (8.29b) into the right-hand side of Eq. (8.29a) eliminates l_y and yields

$$(w/p)\,(1 + \alpha) = [1/\sqrt{(l_x)}], \quad (8.30)$$

which can be interpreted as saying that the optimal condition for l_x requires MPL (the RHS of (8.30)) to equal wage *plus* an adjustment for the externality. If $\alpha = 0$ (no externality), then Eq. (8.30) reduces to the same as Eq. (8.24a) or wage = MPL.

Plugging in the values $p = 6$, $w = 1$ and $\alpha = 0.2$ into Eq. (8.30) yields $l_x{**} = 25$ and by substitution into Eq. (8.29b), we get $l_y{**} = 41$. Compared to the individual solutions of Example 8.11, employment is decreased in the polluting plant *and* in the non-polluting plant. Because the externality is now accounted for, plant *X* lowers its output and generates less waste thus allowing plant *Y* to also lower its employment as it no longer has to "clean" up so much.

Substituting these employment values (l_x** = 25 and l_y** = 41) into the production and profit functions, we immediately get optimal output and plant profits as x** = 10, $\prod_x$** = 35, and y** = 12, $\prod_y$** = 31. Combined or pooled profits $\prod$** = 66. Is the allocation (l_x** = 25 and l_y** = 41) Pareto efficient? Since it maximises total profit, any division of the profit income between Ari and Rani is Pareto efficient. It would be impossible to make one person better off without making the other person worse off. If we denote Ari's income by A and Rani's by R, then the set of Pareto efficient income distributions is given by A + R = 66. Note that under individual optimisation, A + R = 64.8 and is therefore Pareto inefficient. However, starting from individual optimisation, not all Pareto efficient distributions of income are Pareto dominant. Ari must receive at least 36 and Rani at least 28.8 or else they would not agree to joint maximisation of total profit. The "excess" profit made by joint maximisation is 66 – 64.8 = 1.2. Therefore, if we let A = 36 + G and R = 28.8 +(1.2 – G) = 30 – G, then so long as $0 \leq G \leq 1.2$, the allocation which maximises joint profit (l_x** = 25 and l_y** = 41) is both Pareto efficient and feasible.

We can get the same result as the joint ownership model described above through taxation. Suppose the government taxes firm X (Ari) by t per unit of labour employed. Then, firm X faces wage cost $w(1 + t)$ and will set MPL = $w(1 + t)$. If the government sets $t = 0.2$, then X will optimally choose l*** = 25 and consequently firm Y will optimally choose l*** = 41. Plugging these back into output and profit functions, we get $\prod_x$*** = 30, $\prod_y$*** = 31 AND government Tax Revenue, TR = 5. In order to achieve the same result, government will have to tax Rani (firm Y) a lump sum = 1 + G (where $0 \leq G \leq 1.2$). Government tax revenue is now 5 + 1 + G = 6 + G and government transfers all of that to Ari whose income is now 36 + G as before. Thus, a suitable tax policy can exactly replicate any Pareto efficient feasible outcome obtainable under joint maximisation. The following example is in the same spirit but more general.

Example 8.14: Two neighbouring firms X and Y have the same production function $x = \ln L_x$ and $y = \ln L_y$, where ln = natural logarithm. Firm X

has cost function $C(x) = 0.5(L_x)^2$ and firm Y has cost function $C(y) = 0.5(L_y)^2 + (1/2)d(L_x)^2$, where d measures the externality imposed by firm X on firm Y. The output price for both firms is p. Find the optimal production for each firm and show that it is Pareto inefficient. What tax policy can resolve this problem?

Note that in this example, the externality affects the total cost but not the marginal cost of Y. Under individual profit maximising, both firms will hire the same amount of labour by setting marginal revenue from one extra unit of labour equal to the marginal cost of one extra unit of labour. The profits for each firm are given by

$$\prod_x = p \ln L_x - 0.5L_x^2, \tag{8.31a}$$

$$\prod_y = p \ln L_y - 0.5L_y^2 - (1/2)d(L_x)^2. \tag{8.31b}$$

The FOC conditions for maximisation yield

$$L_x = L_y = L^* = \sqrt{p}. \tag{8.32}$$

Both firms hire the same amount of labour and produce the same output, $x^* = y^* = (\ln\sqrt{p})$. But because of the externality, the profits are very different with firm Y earning lower profits by the amount $(1/2)d(L_x)^2 = dp/2$.

To find the Pareto efficient labour allocations, we maximise the sum of profits ($\prod$) simultaneously as if the firms were merged. Thus, we maximise

$$\prod = p \ln L_x - 0.5L_x^2 + p \ln L_y - 0.5L_y^2 - (1/2)d(L_x)^2. \tag{8.33a}$$

Rewrite this as

$$\prod = \{p \ln L_x - [0.5L_x^2 + (1/2)d(L_x)^2]\} + p \ln L_y - 0.5L_y^2. \tag{8.33b}$$

The expression in square parentheses, i.e., $[0.5L_x^2 + (1/2)d(L_x)^2]$, can be interpreted as the **social cost** of firm X producing x units. The social cost is obtained by adding the external cost $(1/2)d(L_x)^2$ to the private cost $0.5L_x^2$. The Social Marginal Cost (SMC) is just the derivative with respect to L_x of total social cost $[0.5L_x^2 + (1/2)d(L_x)^2]$ and hence $\text{SMC} = (1 + d)L_x$.

The two FOCs for maximising joint profits which are $\prod_x = 0$ and $\prod_y = 0$ yield

$$L_x^{**} = \sqrt{[p/(1+d)]}, \tag{8.34a}$$

$$L_y^{**} = \sqrt{p}. \tag{8.34b}$$

Thus, optimal L_y does not change but optimal L_x falls because the externality d is now taken into account in the optimisation. For firm X, the optimal solution is to set value of marginal product (price times MPL $= p/L_x$) equal to social marginal cost $= (1 + d)L_x$ which solves to give Eq. (8.34a). Figure 8.9 illustrates private and social marginal costs.

In Figure 8.9, the downward sloping curve is the marginal revenue which in this case is value of marginal product or (price times MPL $= p/L_x$). The straight dashed line 0P is the private marginal cost. Under individual optimisation, the firm would choose L_x*, where MR = MC. The bold line 0S adds the external cost dL_x to the private MC to obtain SMC. Hence, the social planner would choose L_x**, where SMC cuts the value of MPL. The social optimum is less than the private optimum.

Exactly, the same result can be obtained through a tax of $(1/2)dL_x^2$ imposed on firm X. Individual optimisation by X will now result in a

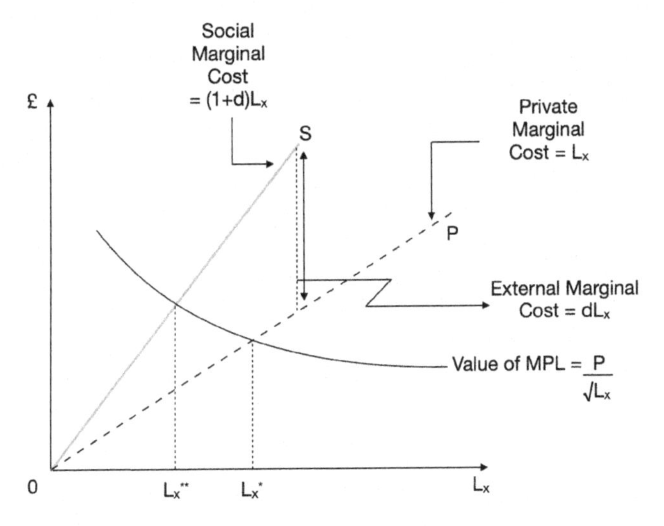

Fig. 8.9 Private and Social Marginal Costs

choice of Lx^{**} by firm X. However, X will now have lower profits due to the tax. Firm Y will be producing the same as before but making larger profits because the costs imposed on Y by X have fallen. A Pareto-dominating solution (relative to no taxation) would be that part of the tax revenue be returned as a lump sum to firm X to compensate for the lost profits.

These two examples illustrate the problem created by externalities. Under individual optimisation, the polluter (firm X) has no incentive to rein back production to the socially optimal level. The allocation is not Pareto efficient. Taxation can remedy this as can the merger of the polluting firm with the victim of the pollution. A feasible sustainable Pareto outcome can be obtained if suitable transfers are feasible and implemented.

8.8 Summary

- The fundamental philosophical judgement used by economists is that of the Pareto principle which states that an allocation is Pareto efficient (socially optimal) if and only if any movement away from the allocation cannot make one agent better off without making some other agent worse off.
- If a movement from one allocation A to another B results in at least one person being better off in B than in A and no one being worse off, then B is said to Pareto dominate A. The Pareto principle takes no account of distribution.
- In a pure exchange economy, the Edgeworth box represents the set of all feasible allocations.
- The contract curve is the set of all allocations which are Pareto efficient and characterised by back-to-back tangencies of convex indifference curves.
- The Pareto criterion provides only a partial ranking of allocations. No two points on the contract curve can be compared using Pareto.
- Every point off the contract curve is Pareto dominated by some point on the contract curve. But not every point off the contract curve is Pareto dominated by all points on the contract curve.

- Starting from any arbitrary initial allocation, a competitive market enables agents to trade to mutual advantage ending up at some point on the contract curve, i.e., at a Pareto efficient allocation. This is the first theorem of welfare economics.
- Starting from any arbitrary point on the contract curve as a target, a suitable redistribution of initial endowments will enable the market to achieve this target. This is the second theorem of welfare economics.
- With production, the congruence between competitive markets and Pareto efficiency is maintained whenever production sets are convex.
- With non-convex production sets (increasing returns), there is no assurance that a Pareto efficient allocation can be replicated by a competitive market equilibrium. Indeed, in this case, there is no assurance that a competitive market equilibrium can be found.
- If externalities are present, the competitive market allocation will not be Pareto efficient.
- Corrective taxes (or alternative ownership arrangements) will be required so that the externality is in effect "internalised" by the decision maker. This would enable a Pareto efficient allocation to be realised.
- In the case where joint ownership is considered as a means of bypassing the externality, the division of joint profits between the two parties requires both to be better off in order for the solution to be feasible.

Chapter 9

Macroeconomic Concepts and Measurement

Macroeconomics is concerned with the analysis of **aggregate variables** which affect human well-being. In particular, we will focus on the determinants of the level and growth of **national income**, the **price index** and **inflation**, **employment** and **unemployment**, and the balance of our economic relationships with other countries. The role of government in policymaking intended to improve macroeconomic outcomes is a central part of the analysis. In all economies, there are many economic agents taking decisions simultaneously. Consumers/workers are deciding what to buy, how much to save, how much to work, etc. Firms (including banks) are deciding what and how much to produce and sell, how much to invest, how many workers and machines to hire, etc. Government seeks to influence these decisions by changing the environment in which the private sector (consumers/workers and firms) operates.

9.1 National Income

The simplest National Income concept is **Gross Domestic Product** or GDP. It can be measured as the value of final goods and services in the economy or as the value of the sum of all incomes in the economy in a given time period, usually one year. Obviously, to find the value of total final goods and services, we need to use prices to aggregate. If the economy produces only two goods X and Y in quantities x and y respectively, there is no meaning which can be attached to $(x + y)$.

Example 9.1: Suppose an economy produces as *final* output 10 bikes and 5 cars in year 0 and their prices are £100 per bike and £4,000 per car. Compute the GDP in year 0.

$$\text{GDP} = \pounds[(10 \times 100) + (5 \times 4{,}000)] = \pounds 21{,}000.$$

Example 9.2: Suppose that in the economy described in Example 9.1, the bike-making firm employs 10 workers while the car firm employs 180 workers. Suppose further that the wage is £50 per annum. How much profit does the owner of the bike firm and the car firm make? What is the sum of all the incomes in this economy?

$$\text{Profits} = \text{Revenue} - \text{Costs} = \text{Revenue} - \text{Wage bill},$$

$$\text{Bike firm profits} = \pounds(1{,}000 - 500) = \pounds 500,$$

$$\text{Car firm profits} = \pounds(20{,}000 - 9{,}000) = \pounds 11{,}000,$$

$$\begin{aligned}\text{Sum of all incomes} &= \text{Wage bill in bike firm} \\ &\quad + \text{Wage bill in car firm} + \text{Profits in bike firm} \\ &\quad + \text{Profits in car firm} \\ &= 500 + 9{,}000 + 500 + 11{,}000 = \pounds 21{,}000.\end{aligned}$$

This shows that in computing GDP, an alternative to adding up the value of final production is simply to add up all incomes. Since the proceeds from production must go to the agents in the economy (workers and capital owners), the two ways of computing GDP must produce the same answer.

Example 9.3: Suppose that in the economy described in Example 9.2, the bike-making firm sells all its bikes to the car firm that uses them to give their workers free transport. How much profit does the owner of the bike firm and the car firm make? What is the sum of all the incomes in this economy?

The subtle distinction between Examples 9.2 and 9.3 is that in Example 9.3, bikes are an **intermediate** NOT a final good. The wage bill and profits of the bike firm are unchanged at £500 and £500, respectively. But now the car firm's costs are different. In addition to wage bill of £9,000, it has to pay for the bikes which cost £1,000. Hence, car firm profits now are £[(20,000 – 9,000) – 1,000] = £10,000. Hence, GDP = Total wages + Total profits = 500 + 9,000 + 500 + 10,000 = £20,000. What's going on here? The value of bike production (£1,000) is NOT included in GDP since it's not final output but only intermediate output as it is an input for the car firm. GDP is just the value of production in the car firm as it is the only final good in this economy.

9.2 Comparing National Incomes

In Section 9.1, current market prices were used to aggregate the various components of final production into a single number. This single number is called the **nominal** GDP to reflect the fact that **current** prices are being used. Suppose using the method of Section 9.1 that we find that nominal GDP increases from £20,000 in year 0 to £25,000 in year 1. This does not allow us to say how much production has actually increased because the rise in nominal GDP is driven by both production increases and price rises. Economists developed the concept of **real GDP** to measure GDP at **constant** prices to arrive at a national income concept purged of the distorting effects of price rises.

Example 9.4: Suppose an economy produces as *final* output 10 bikes and 5 cars in year 0 and their prices are £100 per bike and £4,000 per car. The same economy in year 1 produces 20 bikes and 10 cars whose prices are £200 and £8,000, respectively. Compute the real and nominal GDP in year 0 and year 1.

$$\begin{aligned}\text{Nominal GDP year 0} &= £[(10 \times 100) + (5 \times 4{,}000)] \\ &= £21{,}000 \text{ at year 0 prices,}\end{aligned}$$

$$\begin{aligned}\text{Nominal GDP year 1} &= £[(20 \times 200) + (10 \times 8{,}000)] \\ &= £84{,}000 \text{ at year 1 prices.}\end{aligned}$$

To calculate real GDP, we must first fix the base year whose prices are used for all calculations. Say we use year 0 as the base year. Then, we proceed as follows:

$$\text{Real GDP in year } 0 = £[(10 \times 100) + (5 \times 4{,}000)]$$
$$= £21{,}000 \text{ at year 0 prices,}$$
$$\text{Real GDP in year } 1 = £[(20 \times 100) + (10 \times 4{,}000)]$$
$$= £42{,}000 \text{ at year 0 prices.}$$

Thus, we say that real GDP in year 1 measured at year 0 prices is £42,000. Another way to describe this is to use what are called **index numbers**. We note that real GDP in year 1 is exactly twice that in year 0. Hence, if we set base year real GDP = 100, then we can say that real GDP in year 1 = 200. In using index numbers, only proportions matter, not the scale. We can proceed in this way for year 2, year 3, etc. to get a whole time series of real GDP expressed as index numbers or as absolute numbers at constant base year prices. In this simple example, we can see directly that both bike and car output double in year 1 (compared to year 0) so that production has obviously doubled. Our calculation confirms that.

Example 9.5: Suppose an economy produces as *final* output 10 bikes and 5 cars in year 0 and their prices are £100 per bike and £4,000 per car. The same economy in year 1 produces 20 bikes and 10 cars whose prices are £200 and £8,000, respectively. And in year 2, the data are bike output 24 bikes and 12 cars selling for £240 and £9,600, respectively. Compute the real and nominal GDP in year 0, year 1 and year 2.

The answers are shown in the following table:

	Year 0	Year 1	Year 2
Nominal GDP	£21,000	£84,000	£120,960
Real GDP (year 0 prices)	£21,000	£42,000	£50,400
Real GDP (index, year 0 = 100)	100	200	240

The discussion of real versus nominal GDP leads naturally to a discussion of the aggregate price index (or **GDP deflator**) which is defined as the ratio of nominal to real GDP in the same year. Using the table above, we can calculate the GDP deflator for years 0, 1, and 2. For the base year, this ratio is obviously 1. For year 1, it's 84,000/42,000 = 2, and for year 3, it's 120,960/50,400 = 2.4. Once again in index number form, one could write these as 100, 200 and 240, respectively. It is usual to think of a GDP deflator as an index number so its absolute value has little meaning.

9.3 Inflation

Denote the level of the aggregate price index at time t as $P(t)$. Then, the proportional rate of change of $P(t)$ is the inflation rate. Define the rate of inflation $\prod(t)$ as $\prod(t) = [P(t) - P(t-1)]/P(t-1) = \Delta P(t)/P(t-1)$. However, if we treat $P(t)$ as a continuous function, it is usual to replace "small change" $\Delta P(t)$ with the derivative $dP(t)/dt$ and $P(t-1)$ with $P(t)$. And using the chain rule of differentiation, we can see that $[d \ln P(t)/dt]$ is the same as $[dP(t)/dt]/P(t)$. Thus, we have three interchangeable measures of $\prod(t)$ which are $[P(t) - P(t-1)]/P(t-1)$ or $[dP(t)/dt]/P(t)$ or $d \ln P(t)/dt$.

It is important to distinguish between one burst of inflation and a steady inflation. Steady inflation is persistent whilst one burst implies no further inflation beyond the initial burst. These imply very different price paths over time.

Example 9.6: The price index has been constant at 120 for many years. There is a one-round bout of inflation of 10% at time T. Calculate the price level for year T, $T+1$,.... Compare and contrast this with continuous steady inflation of 10% from time T onwards. Illustrate your answers.

At time T, price level rises by 10% so $P(T) = 132$. But as it's only one bout of inflation, thereafter P does not change so that $P(t) = 132$ for $t = T$, $T + 1$, etc. On the other hand, when inflation is steady at 10%, then we

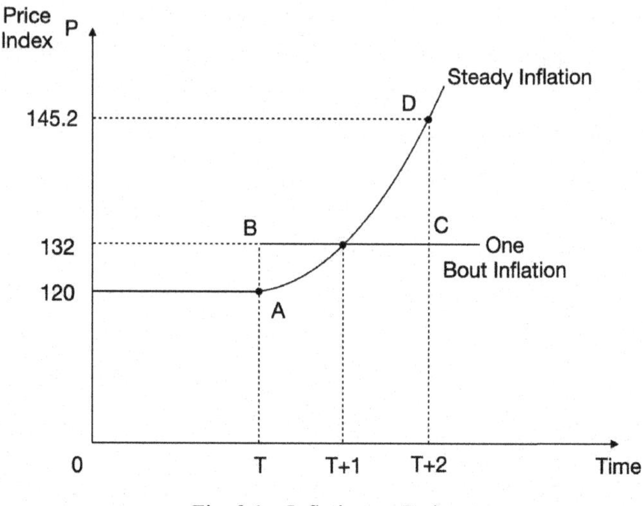

Fig. 9.1 Inflationary Paths

have compounding so that $P(T) = 132$, $P(T + 1) = 145.2$, $P(T + 2) = 159.7$, etc. This is a very different process. Figure 9.1 illustrates.

In Figure 9.1, the path of P for a single bout of inflation of 10% at T is shown by the step function which starts at $P = 120$ on the vertical axis continues to A, then jumps to B and continues along BC thereafter. Mathematically, we could describe this by writing $P(t) = 120$ for $t < T$ and $P(t) = 130$ for $t \geq T$. On the other hand, the path of steady inflation at 10% starting at time T is the exponential curve AD. Mathematically, we could describe this by writing $P(t) = 120 \exp[\pi(t - T)]$ for $t > T$ and $P = 120$ for $t \leq T$, where π is the steady inflation rate; in this example, $\pi = 10\%$.

9.4 Labour Market Measures

Most people derive their livelihood in the **labour market**. This fact alone makes it worthy of serious study. In macroeconomics, we take a highly aggregative approach and suppress the many variations of job and worker in the labour market. Typically, we assume one type of job which pays a weekly wage based on a standard working week of say 40 hours and requires standard workers of given skill. Each worker may be employed or maybe without work but looking for a job in which case they count as unemployed. Those who are not even looking for a job count as "**out of the labour force**" or "**non-participants**". Denoting each of these categories of worker by N for employment, U for unemployment and NP for non-participants, then the whole population is given by $N + U + NP$. Thus, these categories are mutually exclusive and exhaustive. Economists sometimes define the unemployment rate as $u = U/(U + N)$ and the employment rate as $n = N/(U + N)$ so that $u + n = 1$. Both **unemployment rate** and **employment rate** are defined as proportions of the active labour force LF which is $(U + N)$. And the ratio $\acute{p} = LF/(LF + NP)$ is defined as the participation rate. However, in official statistics, the employment rate is defined as $\acute{n} = N/[U + N + NP]$, i.e., employment as a proportion of total population. Obviously, $\acute{n}$ is always less than n.

Example 9.7: Find the relationship between $\acute{n}$ and $\acute{p}$ for constant u and n.

Since $\acute{n} = N/[U + N + NP]$, dividing numerator and denominator by $LF = N + U$, we have $\acute{n} = \{(N/LF)\}/\{(N + U + NP)/LF\} = n/[1 + (NP/LF)] = n/[1 + (1/\acute{p}) - 1] = n\acute{p}$. This shows how a rise in the official employment rate ń can be misleading. A rise in participation reflected in higher $\acute{p}$ can raise $\acute{n}$ the official employment rate even though n has not changed. Similarly, shifting one worker from the NP category to the U category lowers n but not $\acute{n}$.

9.5 Measuring Economic Growth

The study of **economic growth** has been at the forefront of macroeconomics for a long time. Its importance derives from the dynamic nature of the analysis. Studying the GDP level at a point in time is a snapshot but studying growth of GDP over time is a motion picture, a video.

Continuous rises in output over time are what we mean by economic growth. Thus, if $Y(t)$ stands for output at time t, and if $\Delta Y(t)$ is the change in output over a small interval of time $[t, (t + dt)]$, then the (proportional) rate of economic growth is defined as $\Delta Y(t)/dt$. And if dt is "small", we use derivatives to define growth rates as follows:

$$G_y = (dY/dt)/Y(t), \tag{9.1}$$

where (dY/dt) is the derivative of output with respect to time and measures the absolute change in output while G_y measures the proportional change in output (often expressed as a percentage).

Example 9.8: Suppose output Y evolves over time according to $Y(t) = a + bt^2$, find the rate of growth of output.

Since $(dY/dt) = 2bt$, then $G_y = 2bt/[a + bt^2]$. Note that in this example, G_y is not a constant but depends negatively on t since the numerator is of order t but the denominator is of order t^2. Economic growth will approach zero as t gets large.

In many cases, it is easier to calculate growth rates using log differentiation (similar to calculations of inflation). Thus, if $Y(t)$ is the time path of output, then we can write $G_y = (dY/dt)/Y(t) = d \ln Y(t)/dt$ where the equivalence is established by differentiating $d \ln Y(t)/dt$ using the chain rule.

Example 9.9: Suppose output Y evolves over time according to $Y(t) = A \exp(gt)$, find the rate of growth of output.

Using direct differentiation, $dY(t)/dt = [A \exp(gt)]g$ and hence, $G_y = (dY/dt)/Y(t) = [(A \exp(gt)g]/A \exp(gt) = g$.

Using log differentiation, we find $\ln Y(t) = \ln A + gt$ and hence, $G_y = d \ln Y(t)/dt = g$ as before.

Note that we did not specify exactly what "output" was. This is because the growth calculations above are entirely independent of the variable being measured. Whether Y is real or nominal GDP makes no difference. Indeed, Y could be any economic variable (Price level, Employment, etc.) and the methods used in this section still remain valid. Indeed, the method used here can be readily generalised to combinations of variables too.

Example 9.10: Suppose $X(t)$, $Y(t)$ and $Z(t)$ are three economic variables growing over time that are related according to $Z(t) = [X(t)^{\alpha}][Y(t)^{\beta}]$ where α and β are any constants. What is the relationship between the three growth rates G_x, G_y and G_z?

Taking (natural) logs of $Z(t) = [X(t)^{\alpha}][Y(t)^{\beta}]$, we have $\ln Z(t) = \alpha \ln X(t) + \beta \ln Y(t)$ and hence by log differentiation, we immediately get the following:

$$G_z = \alpha G_x + \beta G_y. \tag{9.2}$$

One special case of interest arises when $\alpha = 1$ and $\beta = 1$. Thus, consider the simple relationship Output (Z) = Employment (X) × Output per worker or productivity (Y). Putting $\alpha = 1$ and $\beta = 1$ into (9.2), it then follows that in growth rate terms, Growth of output = Growth of employment + Growth of productivity. If the level relationship is multiplicative, then the growth relationship is additive!

Another important special case is when say $\alpha = -1$ but $\beta = 1$ as in, for example, where Per capita income (Z) = Output (Y)/Population (X). In growth terms then, Growth of per capita GDP = Growth of output – Growth of population.

9.6 Summary

- National Income or GDP can be measured in nominal or real terms.
- Real GDP strips out the effects of price rises on nominal GDP and is often quoted as an index number.
- The aggregate price index measured as the GDP deflator links real and nominal GDP.
- Inflation can be either one burst (one shot) or a continuous process. It is measured as the rate of growth of the price index.
- Economists' definitions of labour market variables are not always the same as in official statistics.
- Growth calculations are most easily carried out using log differentiation.

Chapter 10

Equilibrium and Comparative Statics in Macro Models

When macroeconomists seek to analyse the economy, they construct a little miniature of the economy which embodies the key features of interest. Such an artificial construction is called a **model**. Typically, a model will consist of a set of equations that link the variables of interest. These equations are usually of two types. The first type is what is called an **equilibrium condition**. The concept of equilibrium is fundamental to a study of economics. An equilibrium is a situation in which there is no force for change — a situation which can be sustained. For example, in macroeconomics, a situation where planned expenditure equals national income is often described as an equilibrium. In later chapters, we will show how this can be justified. For now, we simply assume that planned expenditure equals national income represents a **macroeconomic equilibrium**. Denoting national income by Y, consumption by C and investment by I, then in a simple closed economy with no foreign trade, planned expenditure Z is simply the sum of consumption and investment. The equilibrium condition in this particularly simple economy is thus $Z = C + I = Y$ or

$$Y = C + I. \tag{10.1}$$

Example 10.1: If $Y = 10$, $C = 8$ and $I = 2$, do we have an equilibrium situation? What if $Y = 10$, $C = 8$ and $I = 3$?

If $Y = 10$, $C = 8$ and $I = 2$, then $Y = C + I$, and there is no force which can drive the economy away from it. However, if $Y = 10$, $C = 8$ and $I = 3$, we have a disequilibrium situation which is not sustainable. Something will have to change. But what? To investigate this question, we need to complete the model.

10.1 Behavioural Equations, Structure and Reduced Form

The other type of equation commonly found in macroeconomic models is one which represents behaviour. For instance, household's consumption plans may depend on national income. This implies a **behavioural equation** like

$$C = a + bY, \tag{10.2}$$

where $a > 0$ and $0 < b < 1$ are constants. In passing, note that the constant $b = (dC/dY)$ is called the **marginal propensity to consume**. It is the slope of the consumption function described by Eq. (10.2).

Suppose the value of investment is I. Then, these two linear Eqs. (10.1 and 10.2) can be 'solved' for the two 'unknowns' C and Y by substituting (10.2) into (10.1) to solve for Y and then substituting the answer for Y into (10.2) to get the solution for C. The answers are

$$C^* = (a + bI)/(1 - b), \tag{10.3a}$$

$$Y^* = (a + I)/(1 - b). \tag{10.3b}$$

These solutions — C^* and Y^* — are the equilibrium values of C and Y. Note that the answers are expressed in terms of I (and constants) which says that the model can only find the equilibrium values of C and Y, given the value of I. A variable like I whose value is pre-determined and set *outside* the model is called an **exogenous variable**. Variables like C and Y whose equilibrium values are determined within the model are called

endogenous variables. Equations (10.1) and (10.2) describe the structure of the economy and are called **structural equations.** Equations (10.3a) and (10.3b) which solve for the equilibrium values of the endogenous variables in terms of the pre-determined values of the exogenous variables together constitute the **reduced form** of the model. Thus, the interpretation of the reduced form equations (10.3) is as follows: "If the pre-determined value of the exogenous variable investment is I, then the equilibrium values of the endogenous variables consumption and income are given by Eqs. (10.3)". The distinction between the reduced form and structure is crucial to a proper understanding of macroeconomic models.

The reduced form is most helpful in answering the basic question 'How will the equilibrium change if one of the exogenous variables changes?' Straight from (10.3a) and (10.3b), it can be seen that a rise in I leads to a rise in both C^* and Y^*. We can actually compute the exact quantitative amount by which each endogenous variable will change for every unit change in the exogenous variable, all other things constant. These calculations are called **multipliers**. They measure the impact of a unit change in the value of an exogenous variable on the equilibrium values of each endogenous variable, all other things held constant.

Example 10.2: If $C = a + bY$ is the consumption function and $Y = C + I$ is the equilibrium condition, what will happen if the exogenous variable I increases?

Suppose that investment is higher by an amount ΔI so that the new level of exogenous investment is $(I + \Delta I)$. Let the corresponding equilibrium values of consumption and income be C^{**} and Y^{**} so that the induced changes in equilibrium consumption and income are ΔC^* and ΔY^* respectively where, by definition, $\Delta C^* \equiv [C^{**} - C^*]$ and $\Delta Y^* \equiv [Y^{**} - Y^*]$. Then, the two multipliers we seek are given by $(\Delta C^*/\Delta I)$ and $(\Delta Y^*/\Delta I)$, respectively.

To calculate these multipliers, note that C^{**} and Y^{**} are the equilibrium values of C and Y when investment is $(I + \Delta I)$. Therefore, they must satisfy

$$C^{**} = (a + b(I + \Delta I))/(1 - b), \tag{10.4a}$$

$$Y^{**} = (a + I + \Delta I)/(1 - b). \tag{10.4b}$$

Subtracting (10.3a) from (10.4a) and (10.3b) from (10.4b) gives us the answers immediately as

$$\Delta C^* = [b/(1 - b)]\Delta I, \tag{10.5a}$$

$$\Delta Y^* = [1/(1 - b)]\Delta I. \tag{10.5b}$$

Equation (10.5) relates the total change in the equilibrium values of the endogenous variables to the total change in the exogenous variable. These changes are sometimes called **differentials**. From the relationship between differentials, we can calculate the impact multipliers.

In this case, from (10.5b), the investment multiplier on income, i.e., $(\Delta Y^*/\Delta I)$, is $[1/(1 - b)]$ while from (10.5a), the investment multiplier on consumption, i.e., $(\Delta C^*/\Delta I)$, is $[b/(1 - b)]$. In this simple linear model, the multipliers are simply the coefficients of the reduced form equations (10.3). The multiplier $[1/(1 - b)]$ tells us that if for whatever reason, investment is higher by one unit, then equilibrium income is higher by $[1/(1 - b)]$ units. The multiplier for consumption, i.e., $[b/(1 - b)]$, has a similar interpretation.

We could have arrived at this conclusion by means of a diagrammatic analysis. Figure 10.1 illustrates comparing equilibria.

The consumption function $C = a + bY$ has slope b which is less than unity. The bold thick line represents the sum of the consumption function and exogenous investment. It is parallel to the consumption function. The 45-degree line represents the equilibrium condition where expenditure equals income. This intersects the thick bold line at E^* which is the initial equilibrium position yielding an equilibrium income of Y^*. If investment increases by ΔI, the thick bold line shifts upwards parallel to itself by ΔI to the dashed line. The vertical distance AE^{**} thus represents ΔI. The new equilibrium is at E^{**} yielding a new equilibrium income of Y^{**}. The horizontal distance E^*B represents ΔY^*.

From the right-angled isosceles triangle E^*BE^{**}, it follows that $E^{**}B = E^*B = \Delta Y^*$. But $E^{**}B = E^{**}A + AB$. Thus, $\Delta Y^* = \Delta I + AB$. But $AB/\Delta Y^* = b$, the slope of the bold line. Hence, $AB = b\Delta Y^*$. Substitute this

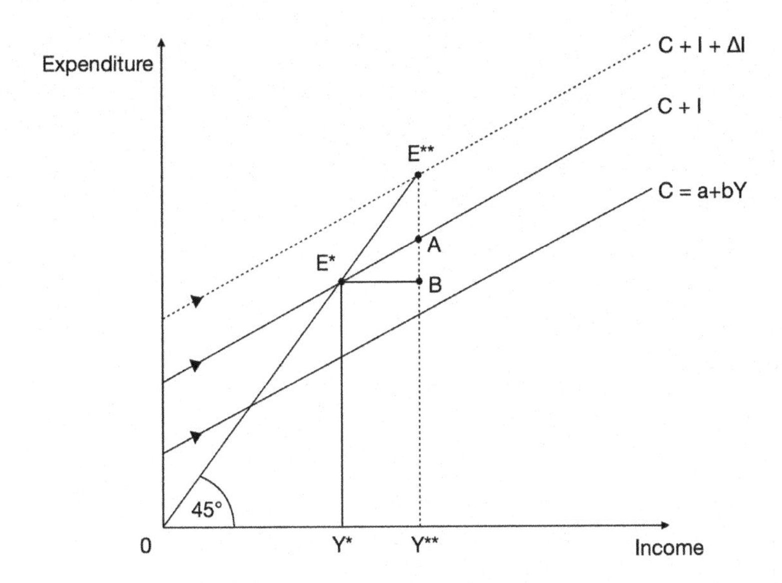

Fig. 10.1 Comparing Equilibria

into $\Delta Y^* = \Delta I + AB$ to get $\Delta Y^* = \Delta I + b\Delta Y^*$ or $\Delta Y^*/\Delta I = [1/(1-b)]$ which is the multiplier for income as before. The mathematical and diagrammatic treatments must give the same answer and they do. They are alternative but complementary methods. In more complex examples, the diagrams can get rather complicated and so it is important to be fluent in both modes of analysis.

In any model, the choice of which variables are exogenous and which are endogenous is not unique. It is imposed from out with the model.

Example 10.3: In Example 10.2, suppose that Y is exogenous. Solve and interpret the model.

Now C and I are endogenous and Y is exogenous. The very same structural equations (10.1) and (10.2) now lead to a very different reduced form (10.6a) and (10.6b) and the multipliers are different.

$$C^* = a + bY, \tag{10.6a}$$

$$I^* = -a + (1-b)Y. \tag{10.6b}$$

The reduced forms (10.6) answer a different question from the structural equations (10.3). In (10.6), we ask 'By how much do the equilibrium values of C and I change when the exogenous variable Y changes by one unit?' The multipliers of the exogenous variable income on consumption and investment are thus b and $(1 - b)$. Figure 10.1 now needs different interpretation. Suppose the consumption function is as before and Y is exogenously given at Y^*. Endogenous consumption C^* is now read off from the intersection of consumption function with $Y = Y^*$. And E^* is determined by making E^*Y^* equal to OY^*. And the difference between E^*Y^* and C^* is I^*. Investment has to change endogenously till the $C + I$ line passes through E^*.

10.2 The Method of Comparative Statics

The method we have described above is known as the **comparative static** method. It is a thought experiment in which we are comparing two equilibrium situations. Each equilibrium is a snapshot of an economy at a point in time. The two equilibrium situations could be one economy in two different time periods or equally, they could be two different economies at the same point in time. All that is being done is investigating how an equilibrium value of an endogenous variable changes in response to a hypothetical change in the value of some exogenous variable. The conclusions are always of the "if-then" variety. This comparison between two "static" equilibria has nothing much to say about how an economy might move from one equilibrium to another. Such movements may take a long time and there be many snags on the path. There are many interesting and important questions about how the economy might move from one equilibrium situation to another. For now, we ignore such dynamic issues and focus on comparative statics only.

In essence, the 'what if' variety thought experiment of comparative statics consists of a set of ordered steps which are as follows:

1. State the macroeconomic issue.
2. Specify the variables whose behaviour we are concerned with.

3. Specify the structural equations — both equilibrium conditions and behavioural relationships.
4. Specify the variables to be treated as exogenous and endogenous.
5. Obtain the reduced forms for the endogenous variables.
6. Derive the impact of a change in exogenous variables on endogenous variables both qualitatively and quantitatively (multipliers).
7. Interpret.

Let us recast our simple example 10.2 in terms of these seven steps:

1. We are concerned with the impact of investment on consumption and income.
2. Our variables are therefore C, I and Y.
3. The structural equations are (10.1) and (10.2).
4. Since we are concerned with the impact of investment, it is natural to treat I as exogenous and C and Y as endogenous.
5. The reduced forms are obtained as (10.3a) and (10.3b).
6. The impact multipliers of I on C and Y are obtained as $[b/(1 - b)]$ and $[1/(1 - b)]$, respectively.
7. We interpret as follows: "If there are two identical economies (the same 'a' and 'b' values), and in one I is higher by one unit, then the economy with the higher I has a higher equilibrium consumption level by $[b/(1 - b)]$ units and a higher equilibrium income level by $[1/(1 - b)]$ units". Note that we are NOT saying anything about dynamics, that is to say, the transition path the economy might follow in moving from the "lower" to the "higher" equilibrium. Indeed, the two economies being compared might well be two different countries rather than the same country at two different points in time in which case there is of course no transition path to discuss.

The importance of pre-designating the endogenous and exogenous variables cannot be overstated. Consider again a disequilibrium situation with $Y = 10$, $C = 8$ and $I = 3$, which is not sustainable. If as in (10.3), investment is exogenous, then C and/or Y must change till the difference between them is 3 in order to correct the disequilibrium. If on the other hand, income is exogenous as in (10.6), investment and/or consumption must change in order for their sum to equal 10 to correct the disequilibrium. There is no way for the mathematical model by *itself* to tell us which of these adjustments will happen.

10.3 More Complex Models

While the examples above do illustrate the nature of the comparative static method, they are limited in scope for direct applicability for two separate reasons. First, the structural Eqs. (10.1) and (10.2) contain only one exogenous variable because a two-equation system requires two endogenous variables and there are only three variables in total, viz. C, Y and I. Second, both structural equations are linear. In practice, neither of these conditions will hold in macro models of any complexity. We start our analysis of more complex and realistic model structures by introducing more exogenous variables into the two-equation linear system. A natural way to expand the simplistic model of Section 10.2 is by adding a government sector.

Suppose we introduce a government sector which spends and **taxes**. Let G denote real government spending on goods. These could be defence, public jurisdiction, education, health, etc. On the taxation side, we will assume a particularly simple form of tax levy. Specifically, we assume that government levies a tax T which is independent of income. It is called a **lump sum tax**. Examples of this are Mrs Thatcher's notorious poll tax and taxes on property levied by local government. The tax impacts consumption by reducing **disposable income** which is now $(Y - T)$. The simple macro model of income determination can now be written as

$$Y = C + I + G, \tag{10.7}$$

$$C = a + b(Y - T). \tag{10.8}$$

Example 10.4: If a macroeconomy is described by (10.7) and (10.8), and I is exogenous along with G and T, find the impact multipliers and interpret.

We treat I as exogenous along with G and T. The models (10.7) and (10.8) now consist of two independent equations, two endogenous variables (C and I) and three exogenous variables (I, G and T). Each of the two reduced form equations will thus have three exogenous variables on the right-hand side. To solve the model, substitute (10.8) into (10.7) to solve for Y^* and then substitute the answer for Y^* into (10.8) to solve for C^*. The answers are as follows:

$$C^* = [(a)/(1-b)] + [b/(1-b)]I + [b/(1-b)]G + [-(b)/(1-b)]T, \quad (10.9a)$$

$$Y^* = [(a)/(1-b)] + [1/(1-b)]I + [1/(1-b)]G + [-(b)/(1-b)]T. \quad (10.9b)$$

The expressions in square parentheses are the impact multipliers of which there are now six — one for each endogenous/exogenous pair. Each multiplier shows the impact of an exogenous unit change in a given exogenous variable on a given endogenous variable, all other things constant. The "all other things constant" clause is important because it implies that the multipliers are, in effect, "one change at a time" multipliers. Thus, if the exogenous variable G was to change by one unit, but I and T were held constant, the impact on Y^* (from Eq. (10.9b)) is a change of $[1/(1-b)]$ units. Using the notation of differentials, we could write this as follows:

$$\Delta Y^*/\Delta G \text{ (if } I \text{ and } T \text{ are constant)} = [1/(1-b)]. \quad (10.10)$$

The clause "I and T are constant" on the left-hand side of Eq. (10.10) serves as a reminder of the "one change at a time" nature of the impact multiplier.

But what if two or more of the exogenous variables change simultaneously? Then, we are looking for the total *effect* on the endogenous variable, not just the "one at a time" impact. Let the simultaneous exogenous changes be ΔI, ΔG and ΔT. Let the total effect of these three changes on Y^* be ΔY^* which is what we seek to evaluate. From Eq. (10.9b), we know that the new equilibrium value, i.e., $(Y^* + \Delta Y^*)$, must satisfy

$$\begin{aligned} Y^* + \Delta Y^* = {} & [(a)/(1-b)] + [1/(1-b)]\,(I + \Delta I) \\ & + [1/(1-b)](\underline{G} + \Delta G) + [-(b)/(1-b)](T + \Delta T). \end{aligned} \quad (10.11)$$

As before, we subtract the old equilibrium from the new to obtain the answer which is

$$\Delta Y^* = [1/(1-b)]\,\Delta I + [1/(1-b)]\Delta G + [-(b)/(1-b)]\Delta T. \quad (10.12)$$

Note that in this case of simultaneous change in exogenous variables, the total effect on the endogenous variable depends not only on the one at a time impact multipliers but on the size of the exogenous changes themselves. Note also that this method of obtaining the total effect can yield the impact multipliers too. From (10.12), we can see that if $\Delta G = \Delta T = 0$ and $\Delta I = 1$, then the change in Y^* is induced solely by the unit level exogenous change in I and the magnitude of this change is just $[1/(1-b)]$ — the one at a time impact multiplier of I on Y.

A major use of the reduced form is to evaluate **government policy**. In the reduced form equation (10.12), the effect of policy is captured by the effect of its instruments, viz. G and T. Quite often, the government's choice of its instruments may be constrained. Thus, for reasons to do with containing its deficit or because of the national constitution, the government may be required to balance its budget. This effectively means that the government must always set $T = G$ and consequently in (10.12), $\Delta T = \Delta G$. Hence, the impact effect on Y^* is of the whole fiscal package. If $\Delta I = 0$, then setting $\Delta T = \Delta G$ in Eq. (10.12) gives the total effect of the fiscal package as

$$\Delta Y^* = \Delta G. \quad (10.13)$$

Put another way, we could restate (10.13) as

$$\Delta Y^*/\Delta G \text{ (if } \Delta G = \Delta T) = 1. \quad (10.13a)$$

This remarkable result states that for fixed investment, a fiscal package consisting of a balanced budget expansion ($\Delta G = \Delta T$) still has an expansionary effect on income with a multiplier of unity. The multiplier of unity for the package is simply the sum of the one at a time impact multipliers of G and of T.

As a final reflection on comparative statics, we note that all our examples have been linear. In reality, most economic relationships are not linear. If, for example, the consumption function is not linear, how might one proceed? The answer is by approximation. In effect, we replace the nonlinear function with a linear segment at the equilibrium. We omit the details of such procedures.

10.4 Summary

- Key concepts of model, equilibrium condition, structural equations, reduced form, exogenous variable, endogenous variable, multipliers and total differentials are the essential tools.
- Every model which has k endogenous variables must have k independent structural equations.
- The choice of endogenous and exogenous variables lies outside the model building exercise.

Chapter 11

The Classical Labour Market

This model of the labour market has enjoyed popularity for a considerable length of time. It is based on the idea of perfect competition which implies that all agents in the market are price takers. The price-taking assumption means that agents take the price as given and simply choose optimising quantities in the belief that any action they take cannot influence the price. At its simplest, the agents are of two opposite types. First, there are firms which use labour (together with other inputs) to produce output which is sold in the search for profits. This is the source of the demand for labour. On the other side are workers. They supply labour in return for remuneration which finances their consumption. Given relevant prices, firms only have to choose how much labour to hire while workers have to decide whether to work or not.

11.1 Labour Demand

Each firm is assumed to have a production function which shows the relationship between labour employed and output. At a basic level, we do not deal explicitly with how individual firms' decisions are aggregated up to derive the "macro" picture. Rather we rely on the notion of the "representative" firm. What is true for the representative firm will be true for the whole economy. We start by examining the "representative" firms' behaviour as a profit maximiser. How much labour will it seek to hire given the environment? The representative firm is assumed to have a production function which shows the relationship between labour employed and output on the basis of which it derives its labour demand function.

Example 11.1: The representative firm has production function given by $Y = s\sqrt{L}$, where L is the labour employed and Y is the output of the single good: corn or convenience. L is measured in workers and corn in bushels. The term "s" captures all other positive influences on output: technology, hours of work, capital, etc. Find the firm's labour demand function, sketch and interpret. What happens as s increases?

The firm's profit (in £) is given by

$$\prod = PY - WL. \tag{11.1}$$

Substitute $Y = s\sqrt{L}$ into the above and differentiate with respect to L to obtain

$$\frac{d\prod}{dL} = Ps/2\sqrt{L} - W. \tag{11.2}$$

Note that the expression $s/2\sqrt{L}$ is the marginal product of labour (MPL). The first-order condition for profit maximisation is $\frac{d\prod}{dL} = 0$. The SOC is satisfied because MPL is decreasing as L increases.

On solving the first-order condition for profit maximisation (setting $\frac{d\prod}{dL} = 0$) and solving for L yields

$$L = [Ps/2W]^2. \tag{11.3}$$

Note that the expression $[Ps/2W]^2$ on the right-hand side (RHS) of Eq. (11.3) contains P and W only in ratio. Doubling or halving both has no impact on L. Thus, (11.3) can be rewritten as

$$L = [s/2w]^2, \tag{11.4}$$

where the lower-case w is the **real wage**, that is to say, the wage measured in corn. This could also be written in the familiar form of real wage = MPL or $w = s/2\sqrt{L}$.

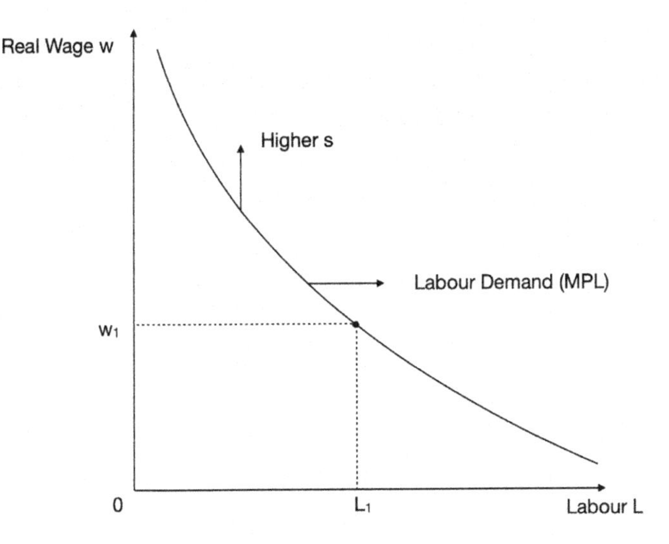

Fig. 11.1 The Labour Demand Curve

Because Eq. (11.4) shows the firm's labour choice given $w = (W/P)$, we refer to it as the **labour demand function** $L^d = [s/2w]^2$. Note that labour demand is a decreasing function of the real wage. Figure 11.1 illustrates the labour demand curve.

In Figure 11.1, we plot w, the real wage on the vertical axis (following economic conventions) and labour L on the horizontal axis. The downward-sloping curve is the MPL $s/2\sqrt{L}$. For any wage, labour demand is read off from this curve. Thus, if wage is w_1, then labour demand is L_1. Clearly, labour demand increases as wage decreases. As s increases due to say technological improvement, then labour demand increases for every w. The labour demand curve shifts upwards as shown by the vertical arrow.

Example 11.2: The representative firm has production function given by $Y = s \ln L$ with notation as in Example 11.1. Find the firm's labour demand function, sketch and interpret. What happens as s increases?

Once again, the firm's solution will require real wage = MPL or $w = s/L$ and therefore labour demand is given by $L^d = [s/w]$. All the properties of L^d remain as in Example 11.1 so that Figure11.1 is still relevant.

To derive the **aggregate labour demand** curve from individual ones, one simply laterally sums the individual demand curves. Thus, think of K as being the number of factories, each with an identical labour demand curve $L^d(w)$. Then, the aggregate demand for labour $\Lambda(w) = KL^d(w)$. From now on, we do not distinguish between the representative firm and the aggregate economy in effect by setting $K = 1$.

Example 11.3: For the production function, $Y = sL^a$, $0 < a < 1$, find the firms' labour demand as a function of the real wage (and the parameter s). What happens as s increases? Interpret. Show mathematically and diagrammatically the relationship between real wage, labour demand and output supply (Y^s). Discuss what happens if the nominal wage W changes? What if P changes? What if both W and P change?

The MPL function is given by MPL $= as/L^{1-a}$ which is clearly decreasing in L which ensures the SOC is satisfied. From real wage = MPL, which is the FOC for profit maximisation, we get that $w = as/L^{1-a}$ which simplifies to $L = [sa/w]^{1/(1-a)}$. And substituting in the production function, we get $Y = \{s \ln[sa/w]^{1/(1-a)}\}$. Thus, the required answers are $L^d = [sa/w]^{1/(1-a)}$ and $Y^s = \{s \ln[sa/w]^{1/(1-a)}\}$. Output supply is also decreasing in the real wage. Figure 11.2 illustrates real wage, labour demand and output supply.

Figure 11.2 is an extension of Figure 11.1. The lower panel shows the production function. If real wage is say $w = w_1$, then the corresponding values of labour demand and output supply are L_1 and Y_1, respectively. A decrease in real wage w leads to an increase in both labour demand and output supply. Changes in W or P or both only impact through the impact on the real wage. Thus, for example, if W and P both rise but W rises more, then the real wage rises and from Figure 11.2 and our earlier calculations both labour demand and output supply fall. In general, we can write labour demand as $L^d = H(w)$ with $H'(w) < 0$.

11.2 Labour Supply

How many workers will wish to work at the going daily real wage w? For simplicity, we assume workers can either work a full day or not at all.

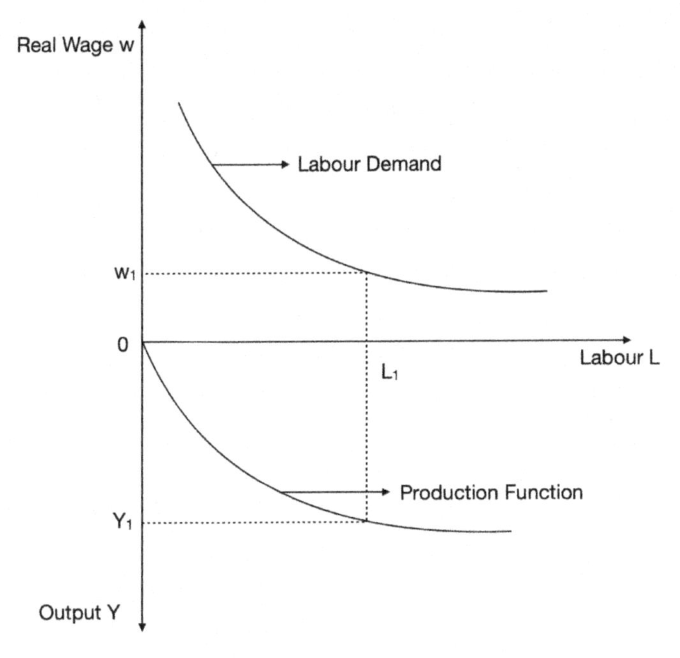

Fig. 11.2 Real Wage, Labour Demand and Output Supply

Part-time work is not considered. All potential workers dislike work. Workers also have daily non-labour income. Together, these two — dislike of work and non-labour income — determine their "work resistance" which is summarised in the workers' "reservation wage" — the minimum real wage required to induce him to work. Other things equal, the higher the non-labour income, the greater the work resistance or equivalently, the higher the reservation wage. Note that workers are assumed to be free of "money illusion". They only care about the real wage, not the money wage.

Example 11.4: A worker has utility function given by $U = \ln C - \ln(1 + H)^2$, where C is consumption and H is time worked measured as a fraction of a day, so $0 < H < 1$. A job offers a real wage w per full day. Hours of work are fixed at T, where $0 < T < 1$ so that his labour income if he works is wT per day. In addition, the worker has non-labour real income K per day. For what wage will he work?

Utility from working for the fraction T of a day = $\ln(K + wT) - \ln(1 + T)^2$ whereas utility from not working is $\ln K$. Hence, he works if $[\ln(K + wT) - \ln(1 + T)^2] > \ln K$ which simplifies to $w/K > 2 + T$. Thus, the higher the wage relative to his non-labour income, the more likely he is to work. There is a critical wage $\bar{w}$ at which he is just indifferent between work and non-work where $\bar{w}$ is given by $\bar{w} = (2 + T)K$. For all wages higher than $\bar{w}$, he will choose to work. This critical wage $\bar{w}$ is his reservation wage. Note that the reservation wage increases with non-labour income K. This makes intuitive sense. If a worker is richer (higher K), the more likely he is to reject any wage offer that is not high enough.

Example 11.5: Suppose all workers are different in that they each have a different reservation wage. The reservation wage is uniformly distributed between w^- and w^+. Find the labour supply curve at the aggregate macro level.

At a very low wage, no one will offer to work. As the wage offered rises to go above the minimum reservation wage, those with low reservation wages will supply labour. Further rises in the wage induce yet more workers to enter the market. Thus, at the macro level, the supply of labour increases as the real wage rises. Eventually, for a sufficiently high wage (in excess of the highest reservation wage), everyone enters the labour market and participation is 100%. For any wage w, the proportion of the labour force which wants to work is given by the fraction $[w - w^-]/[w^+ - w^-]$. If the total labour force is given by $\bar{L}$, then **labour supply** L^s is $L^s = [w - w^-]/[w^+ - w^-]\bar{L}$, for $w^- \leq w \leq w^+$. Figure 11.3 illustrates labour supply.

In Figure 11.3, w^- is the lowest wage which just induces some worker to overcome his/her work resistance. As the wage rises higher than this minimum, more and workers are persuaded to overcome their work resistance and enter the market. Eventually, at a high wage w^+, the entire population enters the labour market and further rises in the wage have no effect — the labour supply curve is vertical. We could write this

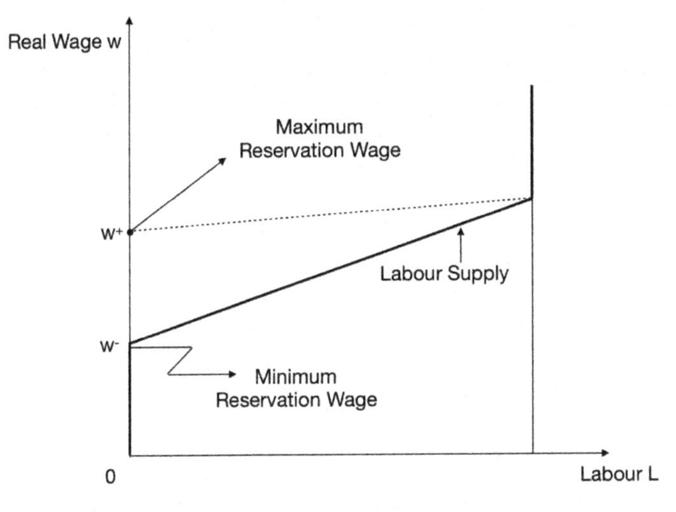

Fig. 11.3 Labour Supply

relationship formally as $L = G(w)$ with $G' \geq 0$, where $g(w)$ is the labour supply curve and $g' \geq 0$ to reflect the upward slope.

11.3 Market Equilibrium

Equilibrium refers to a state or a configuration where there is no force tending to move the configuration away from its current position, and hence, it is a sustainable situation. Consider the real wage w^* in Figure 11.4.

At this wage, firms want to hire L^* workers (as read off the labour demand curve) — and as exactly L^* workers want to work; the firm is able to satisfy its (profit maximising) labour demand and is content. Likewise at w^*, the L^* workers who want to work (as read off the labour supply curve) all find jobs and are thus content. Hence, there is no force for change and therefore there is no tendency to move away from (w^*, L^*). We refer to w^* as the equilibrium real wage and L^* as the equilibrium employment. In fact, (w^*, L^*) represents a **market-clearing** equilibrium where demand and supply are equal. Not all equilibria are of this nature. It should be noted that there is no other wage which has this property.

The equilibrium is unique. Formally, the equilibrium requires demand for labour equal to supply of labour, or $H(w) = G(w)$ to first obtain w^* and hence L^*. Employment and output are simultaneously determined. Note that the equilibrium is characterised by "full employment". All workers who want work at the equilibrium wage w^* are employed. The level of output corresponding to this equilibrium is the full employment level of output, $Y^* = F(L^*)$. Full employment does not mean that the entire labour force $\bar{L}$ is necessarily employed. At the real wage w^*, there are $(\bar{L} - L^*)$ workers who are not working because their reservation wages are higher than w^*. It is a moot point whether these $(\bar{L} - L^*)$ workers are described as "unemployed" or "not in the labour force".

What if for some reason the market real wage is NOT w^*? Then, either workers or firms cannot fulfil their plans. Hence, there is at least a latent force for change. This is an example of a "disequilibrium" situation. As shown in Figure 11.4, if the wage is "too high" at w_H, there is excess supply of labour measured by AB.

The classical model assumes that forces are set in motion that will quickly cause the wage to adjust downwards till equilibrium is re-established at w^*. But there is no convincing description of what these

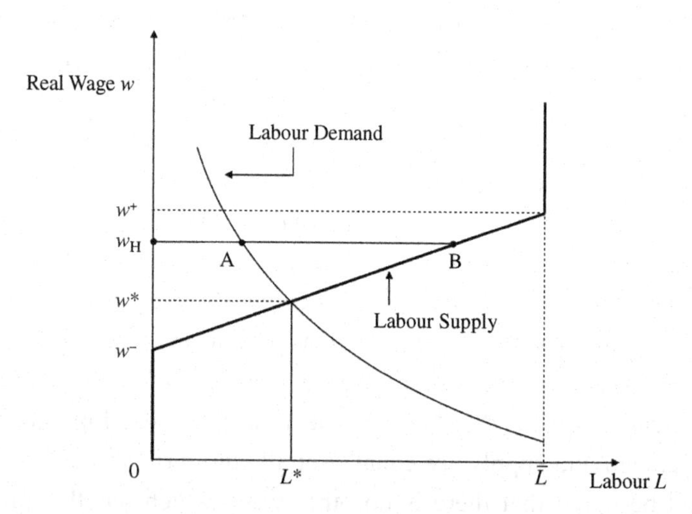

Fig. 11.4 Labour Market Equilibrium

equilibrating forces might be. How exactly does the excess supply of labour at w_H get eliminated? (A similar argument would apply if we considered a real wage w_L which is lower than w^*.)

Example 11.6: Suppose that production function is $Y = s\ \ln(1 + L)$ and $\bar{L} = 120$ and $w^- = 100$ and $w^+ = 160$. It is known that the equilibrium real wage is 160. Find the corresponding equilibrium employment. What happens as s increases?

Since wage $= w^+ = 160$, it follows that all workers enter the labour force and employment is maximal at 120. From wage = MPL, we know that $s/(1 + L) = w$. But once maximum employment is reached, increases in s only increase the real wage continuously. And as shown by $s/(1 + L) = w$, it follows that w is proportional to s. The driver of real wage growth is technological progress which increases s. The rate of growth of real wages must equal the rate of growth of the technological progress parameter s.

Example 11.7: The aggregate production function of an economy is given by $Y = sL^{1/2}$, where L is the labour and Y is the corn output measured in tons. The economy has 1,000 workers each with the same reservation wage of $\hat{w}$ tons of corn. The real wage w is fully flexible and the market is competitive.

(a) State the equation(s) which represent labour supply and sketch the labour supply curve for this economy based on the equations.
(b) Find the competitive equilibrium real wage.
(c) Is there any possibility of unemployment in equilibrium?
(d) What happens as technology improves continuously?

L^s is discontinuous in the real wage w. For $w < \hat{w}$, $L^s = 0$ and for $w \geq \hat{w}$, $L^s = 1{,}000$. To find the equilibrium, we calculate L^d from real wage = MPL as $L^d = s^2/4w^2$. The equilibrium wage rate must exceed or equal $\hat{w}$. There are two possibilities. If labour demand evaluated at $\hat{w}$ is less than 1,000, then equilibrium wage w^* is $\hat{w}$ and equilibrium employment

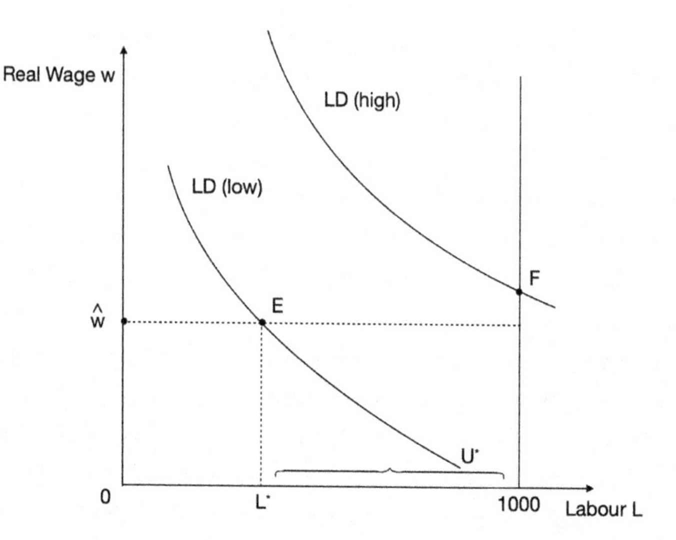

Fig. 11.5 Unemployment and Technical Progress

$L^* = [s^2/4\hat{w}^2]$. And unemployment $U^* = 1{,}000 - [s^2/4\hat{w}^2]$. If however, $[s^2/4\hat{w}^2] \geq 1{,}000$, then equilibrium employment $L^* = 1{,}000$ and $U^* = 0$ and $w^* = s/200$. As s increases, w increases proportionally with no change in L^*. The gains from technology growth fall entirely on real wages. Figure 11.5 illustrates unemployment and technical progress.

Figure 11.5 shows two labour demand curves — LD (low) and LD (high) — with the latter corresponding to a higher value of the technology parameter s. LD (low) intersects $w = \hat{w}$ at E so that equilibrium employment is L^* and unemployment is $1{,}000 - L^*$. If s is larger so that labour demand is given by LD (high), then there is maximum employment and equilibrium wage is w^{**} where LD (high) intersects $L = 1{,}000$. This is shown at point F. As s gets bigger and LD (high) shifts out in northeast direction, employment remains fixed at 1,000 but real wage increases continuously.

11.4 Unemployment

One might describe the situation at w_H (in Figure 11.4 where there is excess supply of labour) as one characterised by "unemployment".

This unemployment is due to too high a real wage and is sometimes called **structural unemployment**. However, given real wage flexibility, this cannot persist and eventually, unemployment will get eliminated as the real wage returns to w^*. If this adjustment process takes a long time, then the market will exhibit structural unemployment for a long time. Indeed, it is sometimes argued that the classical model is an accurate description of the labour market only in the long run when all unemployment has been eliminated. But a basic fact is that even in the longest of long runs, we do observe unemployment. The model needs some change to incorporate this.

The labour market is always in a state of flux which the static classical model cannot describe. Existing jobs are always getting destroyed and new jobs getting created. Workers who are made unemployed by job destruction will take time to search for and find new jobs. During this search period, they remain unemployed. This is what we call **frictional unemployment**. Suppose the job separation rate is σ, then the number of workers entering unemployment — the inflow — is σL, where L is employment. On the other hand, suppose that the job-finding rate is ϕ so that if the stock of unemployed is U, then ϕU find jobs and leave the unemployment pool. Thus, the outflow from unemployment is ϕU. The total amount of unemployment at any time is thus given by last periods' unemployment plus inflow less outflow or

$$U_t = U_{t-1} + \sigma L_{t-1} - \phi U_{t-1}, \tag{11.5}$$

where the t subscript denotes time.

In a long-run steady state, by definition, both unemployment and employment stocks are constant so that setting $U_t = U_{t-1} = U$ and $L_{t-1} = L$ in Eq. (11.5), we have

$$\sigma L = \phi U, \tag{11.6}$$

which simply asserts that in steady state, inflows must equal outflows. Noting that the active labour force is by definition $\bar{L}$, it follows that

$$L + U = \bar{L}. \tag{11.7}$$

Defining $u = U/\overline{L}$ and $l = L/\overline{L}$ as the unemployment/employment rates respectively, it follows that $l + u = 1$. Hence, from Eqs. (11.6) and (11.7), it follows that u^*, the steady state unemployment rate — called the "natural rate of unemployment" — is given by

$$u^* = [\sigma/(\phi + \sigma)]. \tag{11.8}$$

And the corresponding steady-state employment rate is

$$l^* = [\phi/(\phi + \sigma)]. \tag{11.9}$$

Note from Eq. (11.8) that u^* can be rewritten as $u^* = 1/[(\phi/\sigma) + 1]$ and hence that the fundamental determinant of u^* and l^* is the ratio σ/ϕ which may be thought of as an index of labour market friction. The *higher* this ratio, the higher the u^*. So long as ϕ and σ are exogenous, these steady-state *rates* do not depend on the real wage. If $\sigma = 0$, then $u^* = 0$ and $l^* = 1$, and we are then back in the world of the static model.

Example 11.8: An economy with 1,000 workers has $\sigma = 0.1$ per period and $\phi = 0.4$ per period, what is the natural rate of unemployment and how many workers are unemployed in the steady state? Suppose the government makes sacking workers illegal so that $\sigma = 0$, what happens to unemployment in the short run and in the long run?

Initially, the unemployment rate $u^* = \sigma/(\sigma + \phi) = 0.1/(0.1 + 0.4) = 0.2$ or 20%. Since labour force = 1,000, the stock of unemployed is 20% of 1,000 = 200 workers. Cutting σ to 0 implies that in the long run, the unemployment rate u^* goes from 20% to zero.

In the short run, U falls steadily by ϕU every period. Initially, U falls 4% of 200 = 8 so that the new value of $U = 200 - 8 = 192$. Then, in the next period, by 0.4 of 192 = 7.68, etc. Dynamically, we represent the path of the unemployment stock U as given by $U_t = (1 - \phi)U_{t-1}$ which is a declining geometric series which solves as $U_t = (1 - \phi)^t U_0$. In this case, $U_0 = 200$ and $(1 - \phi) = 0.96$ so that $U_t = (0.96)^t 200$ for $t = 1, 2, \ldots$. Obviously, as t gets large (tends to infinity), U will shrink towards zero. A common measure of the speed of decline is the "half-life" of the process, i.e., how

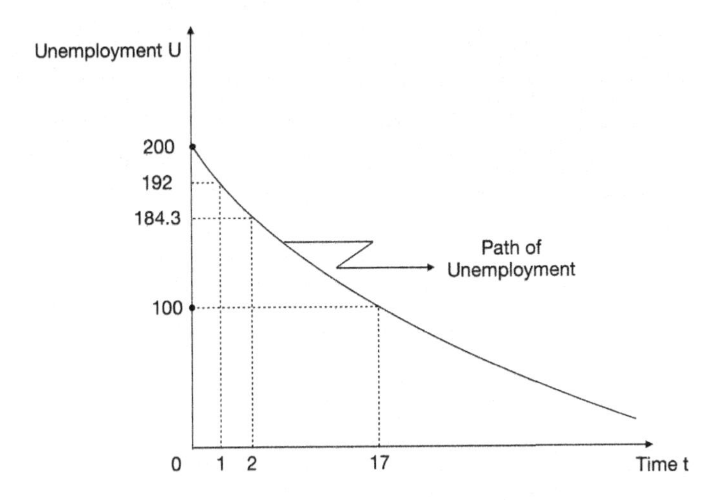

Fig. 11.6 Unemployment Dynamics

long before U reaches halfway to its target of zero. In other words, how long before U is (approximately) 100. The answer is obtained by solving for t in $U_t = (1 - \phi)^t U_0$ when $U_t = 100$, $U_0 = 200$ and $\phi = 0.04$. Taking natural logs on both sides of $U_t = (1 - \phi)^t U_0$, we get $\ln(U_t/U_0) = t \ln(1 - \phi) = -t\phi$ or $\ln(1/2) = -0.04t$ which gives $t = 17$ (approximately). Figure 11.6 illustrates unemployment dynamics.

In Figure 11.6, we show the path of unemployment as the exponentially declining curve starting at $U = 200$ and declining towards zero. The points marked 1 and 2 on horizontal axis show the situation in periods 1 and 2 while the point 17 on the horizontal axis shows the half life shows the "half-life".

Example 11.9: There are three types of workers in a labour market. Those with permanent contracted jobs P, those with zero-hour contracts C and those who are unemployed U. Those with permanent jobs retire and become unemployed at rate r. Those on zero-hour contracts get permanent jobs at rate π but also get fired at rate f. Those who are unemployed can only move to zero-hour contracted jobs at rate σ. Find the natural rate of unemployment. What happens if the government bans firing those on zero-hour contracts?

In steady state, the net inflow into P, C and U must be zero. Equivalently, for each of P, C and U, inflow must equal outflow. For convenience, we measure labour so that total labour force = 1 (million). This has the advantage that for all types of workers, P, C and U, the stock levels and rates are the same so that, for example, U is both the stock and the rate of unemployment.

Writing down inflow = outflow for each of P, C and U, we get

$$\pi C = rP, \tag{11.10a}$$

$$\sigma U = \pi C + fC, \tag{11.10b}$$

$$fC + rP = \sigma U. \tag{11.10c}$$

From Eq. (11.10a), we get that

$$C = (r/\pi)P. \tag{11.11}$$

Substituting from Eq. (11.11) into Eq. (11.10c), we get P in terms of U as

$$P = \sigma U/r[(f/\pi) + 1], \tag{11.12}$$

which on substituting back into Eq. (11.11a) yields C in terms of U as

$$C = \sigma U/[\pi + f]. \tag{11.13}$$

Since $P + C + U = 1$, we use Eqs. (11.12) and (11.13) to get

$$\sigma U/[(fr/\pi) + r] + \sigma U/[\pi + f] + U = 1. \tag{11.14}$$

And hence, we solve for U^* as

$$U^* = 1/[D], \tag{11.15}$$

where $D = [\sigma/r\{(f/\pi) + 1\}] + \sigma/(f + \pi) + 1$. If government bans firing of C-type workers, then $f = 0$ and D rises and U^* falls. The intuition is that $f = 0$ means the only source for augmenting U is from retirements of the permanent workers P.

These frictions which sustain long-run unemployment also have an impact on the real wage. Due to frictions, those willing to work at any wage are a bigger number than those willing and able to work at that wage. And it is those willing and able to work which constitutes the effective labour supply. At any wage w, the effective supply of labour is not $G(w)$ any longer but rather $l^*g(w)$, where the fraction l^* is the natural rate of employment. Thus, the labour market equilibrium condition $G(w) = H(w)$ must be modified. The equilibrium real wage is now determined by

$$l^*G(w) = H(w), \tag{11.16}$$

In effect, there are fewer workers available to work at every wage because some workers who are active in the labour force are searching rather than working. Figure 11.7 (which is an augmented version of Figure 11.4) illustrates classical labour market with frictions.

In Figure 11.7, we measure labour on the horizontal axis and real wage on the vertical. The demand curve for labour is the downward-sloping curve. The bold upward-sloping curve is the conventional static labour supply curve whereas the dotted version is the effective labour

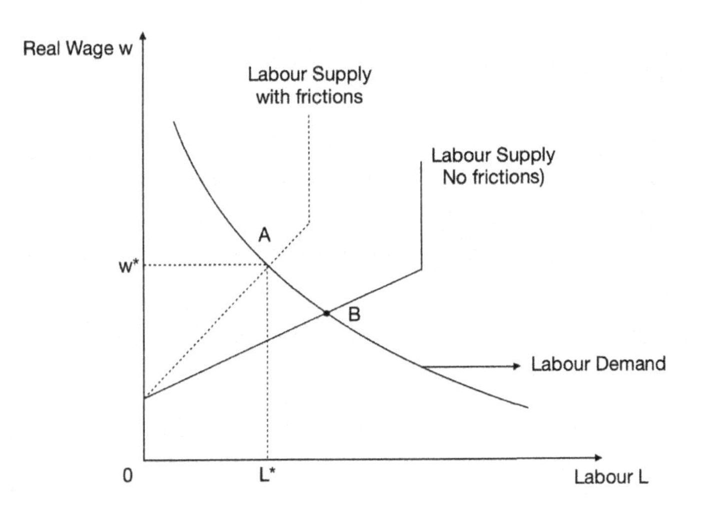

Fig. 11.7 Classical Labour Market with Frictions

supply. The difference between these curves is a constant proportion equal to l^*.

The equilibrium at A is (w^*, L^*) where demand equals effective labour supply. L^* is no longer full employment but rather the "natural level of employment". The corresponding "natural level" of output Y^* is read off from the production function. The natural level of unemployment U^* is measured by the horizontal distance between the two labour supply curves at w^*. These natural levels will change as factors determining the labour demand and static labour supply change. However, the natural rates of unemployment and employment are independent of such changes depending only on σ and ϕ as set out in Eqs. (11.8) and (11.9), respectively. This equilibrium can be contrasted with the frictionless equilibrium at B.

As a result of the frictions, the real wage is higher and employment is lower than in the absence of frictions. The higher the σ relative to ϕ, the lower the l^*. And the lower the l^*, the greater the impact of frictions on the real wage. If the separation rate is zero, then there is no unemployment, the equilibrium employment rate is unity and we are back in the static classical model.

11.5 Summary

- On the assumption of (i) perfect competition in the labour market so that all agents are price takers and (ii) a production function with diminishing returns to labour, the demand curve for labour summarising firm's optimal plans is downward sloping in the *real* wage.
- On the assumption that each worker has a different reservation wage, the supply curve of labour is upward sloping in the real wage and becomes vertical for high enough real wages.
- The (static) labour market equilibrium is unique. This equilibrium is established by assuming real wage flexibility which eliminates either excess demand or supply of labour. In the static classical model, structural unemployment due to too high a real wage can exist as a temporary phenomenon only.

- The presence of frictions as embodied in a job separation rate σ and a job finding rate ϕ creates long-term permanent unemployment which may be called frictional unemployment.
- In the presence of frictions, the classical model does not predict full employment but rather a natural level of employment and output.
- The natural rate of unemployment is determined uniquely by these rates as $u^* = [\sigma/(\phi + \sigma)]$.
- The presence of frictions as measured by σ/ϕ raises the real wage and lowers employment in equilibrium.
- The higher these frictions, the greater the impact on real wages and the natural level of employment.
- From the level of employment, the output level is uniquely determined through the production function.

Chapter 12

The Classical Model of Money, Interest and the Price Level

In the previous chapter, we showed how real wage flexibility determines both the level of employment and output. In this chapter, we extend the analysis to the other main macroeconomic variables, namely interest rates and the price level. The role of the money supply is emphasised particularly in the determination of the price level. We assume a **closed economy** in which there is no foreign trade. And in the spirit of the classical theory, we assume all relevant prices are fully flexible.

12.1 The Goods Market

In this section, we analyse how the output determined in the labour market is split between different uses. In a closed economy, the purchasers of goods are private consumers, firms and the government. Private consumers buy goods for *consumption*, firms buy goods for *investment* in order to add to future production capacity and government buys goods for a variety of purposes — defence, schools, hospitals, etc. Denoting consumption plans by C, investment plans by I and **government spending** by G, total spending (or expenditure) plans Z are given by

$$Z = C + I + G. \tag{12.1}$$

Since one domestic individual's expenditure is another domestic individual's income, the goods market is said to be in equilibrium when spending plans exactly match production or output Y so that $Y = Z$. In other words, the condition for goods market equilibrium is given by

$$Y = C + I + G. \tag{12.2}$$

This equilibrium condition is often confused with the national income identity which states that realised output must equal the sum of realised spending. The distinction between plans and realisations is important. If planned spending and output are not equal, disequilibrium prevails, and some plans will have to be adjusted. In the classical model, this adjustment process essentially involves price changes. Once equilibrium is reached, plans and realisations become equal so that the national income identity does in fact hold.

The equilibrium condition (Eq. (12.2)) can be written in an alternative more helpful form. Let government taxes paid by consumers be T and let private saving be S_{pvt}. Then, it follows that total income Y must be $C + S_{pvt} + T$. Substitute $C + S_{pvt} + T$ for Y in Eq. (12.2) to yield

$$S_{pvt} + (T - G) = I. \tag{12.2a}$$

In the left-hand side (LHS) of the equilibrium condition (Eq. (12.2a)), the term $(T - G)$ is government revenue less government spending and hence may be properly thought of as government saving. Hence, the LHS of Eq. (12.2a) is the sum of private and government saving which we call **national saving** S; that is, $S = S_{pvt} + (T - G)$. The goods market equilibrium thus boils down to saying national savings equals private investment or

$$S = I. \tag{12.2b}$$

To understand the implications of this, the determinants of S and I need to be investigated. Since private savings are part of national savings, we start by studying the determinants of private savings.

Since $S_{pvt} = Y - C - T$ and the most common explanation of C is given by

$$C = a + b\,(Y - T), \qquad (12.3)$$

where $(Y - T)$ is disposable *income*, b is the marginal propensity to consume out of disposable income (which is less than unity) and a is a positive constant representing autonomous consumption. This description is the most basic version of the consumption function which describes the determinants of consumption. Provisionally, we assume that taxes T are a lump sum, not dependent on income. It follows from Eq. (12.3) that

$$S_{pvt} = -a + (1 - b)\,[Y - T]. \qquad (12.3a)$$

To obtain S, note that $S = [Y - C - T] + [T - G] = Y - C - G$ so that from (12.3), we get

$$S = -a + (1 - b)Y + bT - G. \qquad (12.4)$$

Some properties of national saving that follow from Eq. (12.4) are worth emphasising. If Y increases, so does S but by less than the increase in Y; the same is true for T. But a rise in G causes an equal fall in S.

Example 12.1: The consumption function is given by $C = 100 + 0.8(Y - T)$. Find the national savings function if taxes T are given by (i) a lump sum $T = T_0$ and (ii) a proportional income tax so that $T = tY$, where t is the tax rate. What happens if government which is committed to balancing the budget increases G?

$S_{pvt} = Y - C - T = 0.2Y - 100 - 0.2T_0$ by direct substitution. Therefore, national saving is $S = S_{pvt} + T - G$ is given by

$$S = 0.2Y - 100 + 0.8T_0 - \text{G}. \qquad (12.5a)$$

This is exactly as in Eq. (12.4). If $T = tY$, then the expression for S_{pvt} changes to $S_{pvt} = Y - C - T = Y - [100 + 0.8(Y - tY)] - tY = 0.2(1 - t)$ $Y - 100$ and hence national savings is given by

$$S = 0.2Y + 0.8tY - G - 100. \qquad (12.5b)$$

If the government balances its budget, we need to substitute $T_0 = G$ in Eq. (12.5a) and $t = G/Y$ in Eq. (12.5b) to yield

$$S = 0.2Y - 100 - 0.2G, \tag{12.6a}$$

$$S = 0.2Y - 100 - 0.2G. \tag{12.6b}$$

Note that the expressions for S are the same which leads to the result that if government spending is financed by taxation, whether lump sum or proportional income tax, then national savings will fall as G is raised. Equal rises in G and T are not neutral because increases in tax produce a smaller impact on S than an equal increase in G.

Turning to private investment, it is commonly assumed that the determinant of investment is its opportunity cost which is the **real rate of interest** which we denote by r. The real interest rate is measured in units of the good, NOT money. Thus, if $r = .05$ or 5%, per annum, this means that a lender who lends 100 units of the good will receive 5 units of the good in interest making the total payable to him at the end of one year equal to 105 units of the good. We write this investment function as

$$I = I(r), \tag{12.7}$$

where $I'(r) < 0$ to signify that as r rises, I falls.

Recall from Eq. (12.2b) that goods market equilibrium condition is $S = I$ or

$$I(r) = S = -a + (1 - b)Y + bT - G. \tag{12.8}$$

Up to this point, we have not introduced any classical assumptions into the model. Indeed, the equilibrium condition (Eq. (12.8)) is quite general. Classical economics is based on the presumption of rapid price adjustment. One consequence of this is that Y is determined in the labour market by real wage flexibility at its full employment or "natural level" Y^* as discussed in Chapter 11. This "full employment" level is determined in the labour market. To be clear, the direction of causality is that the labour market determines the level of full employment L^* and then by substitution in the aggregate production function, one arrives at Y^*, the exogenous value of the "natural level of output" for the classical model of the goods market.

Thus, in Eq. (12.8), Y is treated as predetermined or exogenous as are T and G — which makes the whole RHS of Eq. (12.8) exogenously given. Hence, the goods market equilibrium will determine the equilibrium value of the real interest rate at r^*, given the values of Y^*, G and T. It may be slightly confusing that output which is endogenous in the labour market has now become exogenous in the goods market. This peculiarity stems from the "hierarchical" nature of the classical model which will be explained in full later. Figure 12.1 illustrates determination of the real rate of interest.

In Figure 12.1, real interest rate is measured on the vertical axis and both savings and investment on the horizontal axis. The vertical line S is national savings which are independent of r. The downward-sloping curve $I(r)$ is the investment function (as in Eq. (12.8)) which is declining as r increases. Where these two curves intersect is the equilibrium.

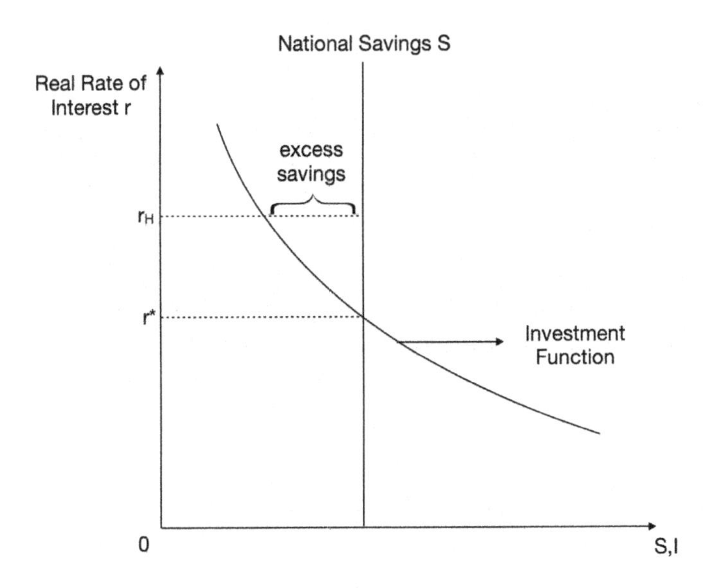

Fig. 12.1 Determination of the Real Rate of Interest

The goods market is in equilibrium at interest rate r^* and Investment level I^*. It is only at these values that planned spending equals output.

What if the interest rate is higher at r_H? Then, there are excess savings so that planned spending is less than output. The goods market is in disequilibrium. The classical model assumes rapid price adjustment so the real interest rate will be "bid down" till the market clears. This is analogous to the real wage adjusting to clear the labour market. Since the endogenous variable is the real interest rate which adjusts to equate investment and national savings, the goods market equilibrium is sometimes referred to as equilibrium in the market for **loanable funds**.

Example 12.2: Suppose $I(r) = I_0 - \theta r$ and the consumption function is $C = C_0 - b(Y - T)$, where T is lump sum, i.e., $T = T_0$. Find the equilibrium value of r when Y is pre-determined as Y^*. How does it change if G increases by ΔG? How does it change if $\Delta G = \Delta T_0$? What are the consequences for private investment I? Illustrate diagrammatically.

From (12.8), we get

$$I_0 - \theta r = -C_0 + (1 - b)Y^* + bT_0 - G, \qquad (12.9)$$

which solves for r^* as

$$r^* = [1/\theta][I_0 + C_0 - (1 - b)Y^* - bT_0 + G]. \qquad (12.10)$$

It is clear from Eq. (12.10) that as Y^* or T rises, r^* falls whereas a rise in G raises r^*. However, if G and T both rise by the same amount, then r^* rises. In Eq. (12.10), the absolute value of the impact multiplier of G on r^* is $[1/\theta]$ which is larger than the absolute value of the impact multiplier of T on r^* which is $b[1/\theta]$ because $0 < b < 1$. Note that the overall impact is bigger when θ (the slope of the investment function) is smaller. Figure 12.2 illustrates changes in real rate of interest.

The investment function is the downward-sloping straight line (similar to the curved investment function in Figure 12.1). The initial equilibrium is at A where equilibrium interest rate is r^*. If Y^* or T_0 rises, this shifts S to the right (dashed line) lowering r^* to r^{*-} as shown at B. If G rises or even if G and T_0 rise by equal amounts ($\Delta G = \Delta T_0$), then S shifts

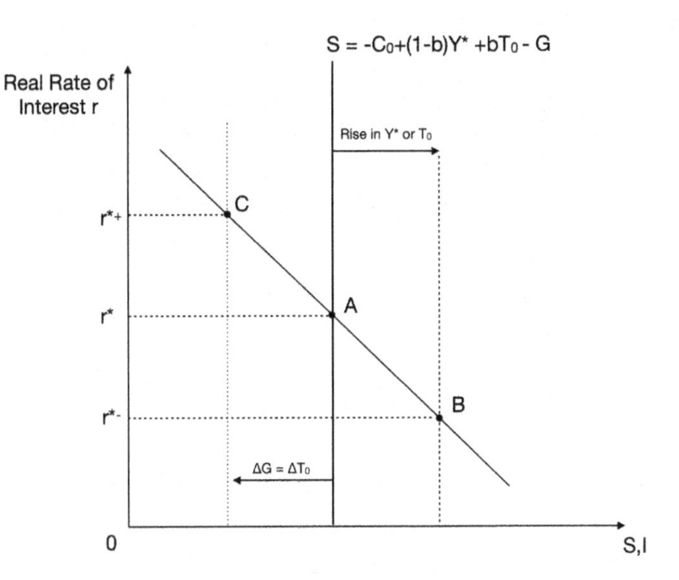

Fig. 12.2 Changes in Real Rate of Interest

to the left (dotted line) and r^* will rise to r^{*+} as shown at C. The rise in r^* necessarily lowers investment. Note also from Eq. (12.10) that since $\Delta I^* = -\theta\Delta r^* = -\theta\,[1/\theta]\Delta G = -\Delta G$ that investment falls one for one with an increase in G. This is known as **"full crowding out"**. Since Y is fixed, the only impact of increasing G is to reshuffle the components of Y. Since T is unchanged, then so must C be constant. Hence, $I + G$ is constant, ergo there is full crowding out of private investment if G rises as $\Delta I^* = -\Delta G$. If, however $\Delta G = \Delta T_0$, then from Eq. (12.10), $\Delta r^* = [1/\theta]\,[b\Delta G - \Delta G] = -[1/\theta](1 - b)\Delta G$ and hence $\Delta I^* = -(1 - b)\Delta G$ which is less than ΔG. Crowding out of investment is less than 100% because the rise in T means that S shifts by less than before. Part of the crowding out burden is borne by consumption.

12.2 Real and Nominal Rates of Interest

In the previous section, we saw the role of the real interest rate in bringing about equilibrium in the loanable funds market. Later, we will see how the nominal interest rate plays a role in the money market. But first, we need to establish the relationship between nominal and real interest rates. Recall the definition of real interest rate as being the rate of return obtained by lending out one unit of a physical good, say corn. Thus, by lending one unit of corn at real rate r, a lender will receive $(1 + r)$ units of corn in one year. For the nominal interest rate, we simply replace units of corn with units of money. Thus, if i is the nominal rate of interest, it means that by lending £1 now, one will receive £$(1 + i)$ in one year's time. What is the relationship between r and i?

Example 12.3: Two investment options exist. Option A is to invest £1 at an annual rate of return i (the nominal rate of return). Option B is to invest £1 via the real loan market in corn where the annual real rate of return is r. If the expected inflation rate over the period of the investment is expected to be π^e, find the payoff in £ from each option at the end of one year. Comment on your answers.

The return on investing £1 in option A is £I so yields £$(1 + i)$ at the end of the period. Investing £1 in option B, the investor must first buy the corn. With £1, she buys $1/p_0$ units of corn, where p_0 is the current price of one unit of corn. Investing this produces $(1/p_0)(1 + r)$ units of corn at the end of the period which is worth £$(1/p_0)(1 + r)p_1$ if the current price of corn is p_1. So, at end of the year, option A produces £$(1 + i)$ while option B produces £$(1/p_0)(1 + r)p_1$. If there is free entry into both loan markets, these end of year values must be the same. Rewriting option B end value as £$(1 + r)(p_1/p_0) =$ £$(1 + r)(1 + \pi^e)$, we must have $(1 + i) = (1 + r)(1 + \pi^e)$. For small r and π^e (and hence ignoring the term $r\pi^e$), we have $i = r + \pi^e$. This relationship is known as the **Fisher equation** and provides the link between real and nominal sides of the economy. It is an equilibrium condition based on free entry **arbitrage**. In the classical model, it is r which determines i. If r increases by one percentage point, so will i increase by the same amount, for constant expected inflation rate π^e.

12.3 Money and the Price Level

In this section, we analyse the nominal or monetary side of the economy. The model assumes that there are two financial assets: money (M) and

bonds (B). Consumers divide their wealth between the two. Bonds are an interest-bearing asset yielding an interest rate i per annum. Money in the form of cash earns no interest while bonds earn interest i. So, why would anyone hold money when it earns nothing? The answer is convenience yield. Money can be exchanged for goods or labour (or bonds) but bonds are not usable as a medium of exchange for goods or labour. Bonds are issued by the government **Treasury** at what is called "face value". If one held all one's wealth in bonds, one would have to sell some each day to finance daily purchases. This is both costly and inconvenient. Thus, some money is held to deal with transactions. This is called the **transactions demand for money**. The higher the interest rate on bonds, the greater the incentive to hold bonds. Thus, as i goes up, bond demand rises and money demand falls. Individuals keep some cash in order to take advantage of changes in the interest rate on bonds. This is the **speculative demand for money**. The total demand for money is the sum of these two separate demands for holding money. The supply of money is determined by the **Central Bank**. In order to understand how the money market works, we first need to understand how the market for bonds (which is the alternative to money) works.

A bond is an instrument which pays the holder a fixed sum of money called an **annuity** each year. Bonds are typically issued by the Treasury on behalf of the government at face value. In this simple model, we assume bonds last forever unless the Treasury buys them back. Till then, the only way to sell or buy bonds is on the secondary bond market. On the day of issue, if the issue price is say £100 — called the face value — and the annuity rate is A%, then in effect, the bond will pay £A every year into perpetuity. A is sometimes called the **coupon rate**. The present discounted value of the bond is given by the infinite stream discounted at the rate i. This will be the price at which the bond will trade on the secondary market.

Example 12.4: A bond offers a coupon rate of 5%. Its face value is £100. The current interest rate is 2%. What is the present discounted value of the bond?

Denote the present as year 0. In year 1, the bond pays £5 (the coupon value). Today, that £5 is worth 5/(1 + 0.02) = £4.90 because by lending

£4.90 for one year at 2%, now an investor can get exactly £5 in year 1. The process of dividing by $(1 + i)$ is called "discounting". Similarly, £5 payable in year 2 is worth $5/(1 + 0.02)^2 = £4.81$ today because by lending £4.81 for two years at 2%, now an investor can get £5 in year 2. Thus, the entire income stream of £5 each period for ever has present discounted value (PDV) given by

$$\text{PDV} = 5/(1 + 0.02) + 5/(1 + 0.02)^2 + 5/(1 + 0.02)^3. \qquad (12.11)$$

The expression on the right-hand side of Equation (12.11) is a geometric series with first term $5/(1 + 0.02)$ and common ratio $1/(1 + 0.02)$. How do we find the sum of a geometric series? This is a slight digression to which we turn now.

A geometric series is one where each term is obtained from the previous term by multiplying by a constant called the *common ratio* R. Thus, the series takes the form A, AR, AR^2, etc. The nth term of the series is AR^{n-1} and hence S^n, the sum to n terms, is given by

$$S^n = A + AR + AR^2 + \cdots + AR^{n-1}. \qquad (12.11a)$$

Multiply Eq. (12.11a) throughout by R to get

$$RS^n = AR + AR^2 + AR^3 + \cdots + AR^{n-1} + AR^n. \qquad (12.11b)$$

Now, subtract Eq. (12.12b) from (12.12a) to get

$$S^n(1 - R) = A - AR^n. \qquad (12.11c)$$

And hence, we get the sum of n terms of the geometric series as

$$S^n = A/(1 - R) - AR^n/(1 - R). \qquad (12.11d)$$

As n gets large (tends to infinity), the second term on the RHS of Eq. (12.12) goes towards zero and hence we get the sum of an infinite number of terms of a geometric series with first term A and common ratio R as

$$S = A/(1 - R). \qquad (12.11e)$$

Applying this result to Eq. (12.11), and noting that first term is 5/(1 + 0.02) and common ratio $R = 1/1.02$, we get

$$\text{PDV} = [5/(1.02)]/[1 - 1/(1.02)] = 250. \tag{12.12}$$

Thus, the value of the bond today is £250. If there is free entry into the market, then the price of the bond will be £250. If the price exceeded £250, all bondholders would try to sell the bond till its price fell to £250. Conversely, if the price of the bond was below £250, everyone would demand the bond pushing up its price.

Example 12.5: A bond offers a coupon rate of £A every year into perpetuity. Its face value is £100. The current interest rate is i. What is the current price of the bond?

By the previous example, the price of the bond P_B is given by

$$P_B = A/(1 + i)/+ A/(1 + i)^2 + \cdots, \tag{12.13}$$

or

$$P_B = A/(1 + i)\,[1 + 1/(1 + i) + 1/(1 + i)^2 + \cdots]. \tag{12.13a}$$

The geometric series in square parentheses on the RHS of Eq. (12.13a) has first term 1 and common ratio $1/(1 + i)$. Summing, we get

$$P_B = A/(1 + i)[1/\{1 - 1/(1 + i)\}] = A/i. \tag{12.14}$$

This establishes the simple relationship between bond price and nominal interest rate, namely $P_B = [A/i]$. The intuition behind this result is given by the fact that an individual by spending £P_B now gets an annual income of £A forever and this amounts to a rate of return equal to A/P_B and therefore the interest rate i must equal A/P_B.

If the interest rate i falls, that means the price of bonds rises and demand for bonds falls. But the demand for bonds plus the demand for money equals total wealth. Hence, the (speculative) demand for money rises as interest rate falls. A rise in interest rate causes consumers to adjust their bond/money portfolios without total wealth changing.

The transactions demand for money is based on the need to finance consumption which depends on income, and therefore transactions demand for money depends positively on income. Combining these ideas, we can write the demand for money in real terms as

$$L = L(Y, i), \tag{12.15}$$

with $L_Y > 0$ (transactions demand for money increases as income increases) and $L_i < 0$ (speculative demand for money falls as interest rate rises). The supply of money M^s is determined by the Central Bank. For now, it is treated as exogenous. For equilibrium in the money market, we must have

$$L(Y, i) = M^s/P, \tag{12.16}$$

where P is the aggregate price level so that M^s/P measures the real supply of money. In analysing Eq. (12.16), note that Y is pre-determined in the labour market and hence is exogenous in Eq. (12.16). Similarly, i is pre-determined by the real interest rate r and expected inflation π^e. Thus, the whole of the LHS of Eq. (12.16) which is the demand for money is exogenous. So is M^s. Hence, the equilibrating variable in the money market is P. And from Eq. (12.16), it follows that P is proportional to M^s since $L(Y, i)$ is a constant.

Another way to consider the money market is in terms of the **velocity of money** V which is the number of times a pound note changes hands in a given period. The total nominal value of transactions in the economy is PY if each unit of output represents one transaction. But these transactions are financed by money. If the stock of money is M^s and velocity is V, this means total monetary expenditure $= M^sV$. Since total expenditure equals total nominal value of output, we must have $PY = M^sV$. This is the famous quantity theory of money. From Eq. (12.16), $M^s = PL(Y, i)$, it follows that $V = Y/L(Y, i)$. This is intuitive since $L(Y,i)$ represents real money stock kept at home, and its inverse represents money that is turning over or velocity. It also shows that the strict version of the quantity theory which requires constant velocity is only true if the nominal interest rate is constant.

Example 12.6: The real demand for money is given by $L = Y^{\alpha}i^{-\beta}$. The real interest rate is r and expected inflation is exogenous at π^e. The rate of growth of the money supply is m. Find the rate of inflation. What happens if π^e is endogenous?

Since $L = Y^{\alpha}i^{-\beta} = M^s/P$, it follows by taking logs and then first differences and then utilizing Fisher equation that

$$\alpha \, \Delta\ln Y - \beta\Delta\ln (r + \pi^e) = \Delta\ln M^s - \Delta\ln P. \tag{12.17}$$

Noting that for any variable X, that $\Delta\ln X = g_X$ or growth rate of X (approximately), and noting that Y is constant, Eq. (12.17) can be rewritten as

$$-\beta \, \Delta\ln(r + \pi^e) = m - \pi, \tag{12.18}$$

where π is the rate of inflation. If π^e is exogenous and constant, then the LHS of Eq. (12.18) is zero and $\pi = m$. This is the strict version of the quantity theory. But if π^e is endogenous, then the relationship is more complex. Suppose we start from a situation in which $\pi^e = \pi$. Imagine then the Central Bank announcing an increase in m in the future to m^+. Expected inflation should immediately jump to m^+ even though actual money supply growth has not changed. But this rise in π^e will lower demand for money and so there will be an immediate jump in the price level. Once m is actually increased, we will return to a long run equilibrium in which $\pi^e = \pi = m^+$.

12.4 Overview and Classical Dichotomy

We have shown how the classical model of the macroeconomy is developed. There are two notable features of the model which require comment. The first is that of **unidirectional causation**. We start in the labour market and determine employment (and unemployment), output and real wages by relying on rapidly flexible real wages. From there, we go to the goods market and determine the real interest rate. Then, we use Fisher to obtain the nominal interest rate and finally use the predetermined nominal

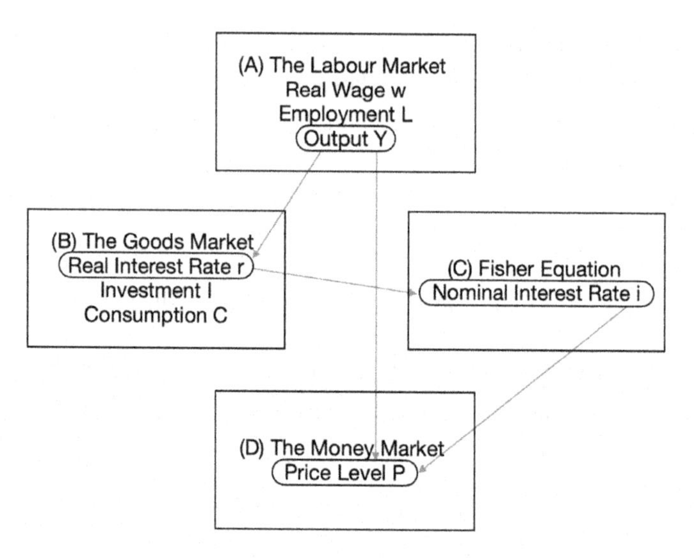

Fig. 12.3 The Structure of the Classical Model

interest rate and output to obtain the aggregate price level. This is a top-down model. There is no feedback from lower echelons to higher echelons. Figure 12.3 illustrates the structure of the classical model.

As Figure 12.3 shows, we solve the model starting in the top block and working our way down. Variables solved for in a higher block are used as inputs in the lower blocks. Thus, output solved for in block A feeds into determination of real interest rate r in block B and price level P in block D. Similarly, real interest rate r is determined in block B but then feeds into determination of nominal interest rate in block C. Output from block A and nominal interest rate from block C both feed into determination of price level P in block D. Any change to one of the parameters in the upper-most block has repercussions for the variables determined in the lower blocks BUT not conversely! Thus, for example, a change in labour productivity (the parameter s) will affect real wages, employment and output in block A and consequently feed through into all the other variables. However, a change in money supply (which only enters into block D) just affects the price level in block D but no other variable.

Example 12.7: Consider a simplified version of the full classical model. The production function is $Y = s\sqrt{L}$. The labour market is characterised by no friction and all workers are willing to work at any wage. There are $\bar{L}$ workers in the economy. The investment and consumption functions are as in Example 12.1. That is, $I(r) = I_0 - \theta r$ and the consumption function is $C = C_0 - b(Y - T)$, where T is the lump sum, i.e., $T = T_0$. The money demand function is $Y^{\alpha} i^{-\beta}$. Solve for the equilibrium values of L, Y, r, i and P. What happens as the exogenous parameters s, G, T and M^s change?

From the full employment assumption, we have

$$L^* = \bar{L}. \tag{12.19a}$$

And hence from the production function,

$$Y^* = s\sqrt{\bar{L}}. \tag{12.19b}$$

And since w^* = MPL at full employment, we have

$$w^* = s/(2\sqrt{\bar{L}}). \tag{12.19c}$$

From the goods market condition and using the result for Y^*, we get the real interest rate as

$$r^* = [1/\theta][I_0 + C_0 - (1 - b)s\sqrt{\bar{L}} - bT_0 + G]. \tag{12.19d}$$

From Fisher, we now get the nominal interest rate as

$$i^* = [1/\theta][I_0 + C_0 - (1 - b)s\sqrt{\bar{L}} - bT_0 + G] + \pi^e. \tag{12.19e}$$

And finally, from the money market equation, we get

$$P^* = \ln M^s - \alpha \ln (s\sqrt{\bar{L}}) - \beta \ln\{[1/\theta][I_0 + C_0 - (1 - b)s\sqrt{\bar{L}} - bT_0 + G] + \pi^e\}. \tag{12.19f}$$

Equations (12.19a)–(12.19f) are the solutions for each of the endogenous variables in terms of exogenous variables (the reduced forms). Finally, as an aside, note that the money wage W^* is obtained as w^* times P. It is convenient to summarise the qualitative impacts of the main exogenous variables in the form of a table as follows.

Exogenous Variables' Impacts on Endogenous Variables

	s	$\bar{L}$	G	T	C_0	I_0	π^e	M^s
w	+	−	0	0	0	0	0	0
L	+	+	0	0	0	0	0	0
Y	+	+	0	0	0	0	0	0
r	−	−	+	−	+	+	0	0
i	−	−	+	−	+	+	+	0
P	−	−	+	−	+	+	+	+

In the table, endogenous variables are in the rows and exogenous variables are in the columns. The table summarises the qualitative information contained in Eqs. (12.19a)–(12.19f). A zero indicates no impact, a plus sign indicates positive impact and a minus sign indicates a negative impact. The structure of the zeros (above the diagonal) is a reflection of the "block" structure of the model. A consequence of this is that all real variables (w, L, Y, I, r) are solved independently of the nominal variables. This is what is called the **classical dichotomy**. Real variables have to be solved first. The irrelevance of money for real variables is known as "money neutrality". With slight modifications to the classical assumptions, this property of the model does not hold. See the following example.

Example 12.8: Suppose consumption depends on real money balances (as they are part of wealth), does the classical dichotomy still hold? What is the impact of expected inflation?

Let us abstract from all aspects not central to this question. Write the model as $C = bY + d(M^s/P)$, where $d > 0$ is the real balance effect. Let $I = I_0 - \theta r$ as before. Let $G = T = 0$. Let money demand be $L = kY - \lambda i$. The money market equilibrium requires $kY - \lambda i = (M^s/P)$. Substituting this into the consumption function and noting that $i = r + \pi^e$, we get that

$$C = bY + d[kY - \lambda(r + \pi^e)]. \tag{12.20}$$

Hence, the goods market equilibrium, $Y = C + I$, now requires

$$Y^* = bY^* + d[kY^* - \lambda(r + \pi^e)] + I_0 - \theta r, \tag{12.21}$$

which solves for Δr^* as a function of $\Delta \pi^e$

$$\Delta r^*(\lambda d + \theta) = (-\lambda d)\Delta \pi^e. \tag{12.22}$$

And hence, $\Delta r^* = -[(\lambda d)/(\lambda d + \theta)]\Delta \pi^e$ which says that a one-percentage point increase in π^e leads to a less than one-percentage point fall in r^*. And if $d = 0$ (no real balance effect), then of course there is no impact on r^*. But for nominal interest rate i, we have that $\Delta i^* = \Delta r^* + \Delta \pi^e$ which can be written as $\Delta i^*/\Delta \pi^e = (\Delta r^*/\Delta \pi^e) + 1$. Hence, we see that $\Delta i^*/\Delta \pi^e < 1$ because $(\Delta r^*/\Delta \pi^e) < 0$ but numerically less than one. In the usual case, a one-percentage point rise in π^e is fully passed on to nominal interest rate, but here, the real interest falls (by less than one-percentage point) and hence the rise in nominal interest rate is less than one-percentage point and the classical dichotomy is broken.

12.5 Summary

- The classical model has a top-down hierarchical structure, starting in the labour market, then goods or loanable funds market, followed by money market.
- The equilibrium values of all real variables are determined through rapid price flexibility.
- The real rate of interest which is the rate obtained by lending one unit of a good is determined in the goods market through the interaction of national savings with private investment.
- Full flexibility of the real interest rate implies that any increase in government spending "crowds out" private investment. A government spending increase matched by equal tax rise also fully crowds out private expenditure with the induced fall in private expenditure being split between private investment and consumption.

- Arbitrage summarised by the Fisher equation determines the nominal rate of interest which moves one for one with expected inflation.
- The price level is determined in the money market by the quantity theory of money (or its modified version). From the basic version, we have that inflation rate equals the rate of monetary growth if output is constant.
- The usual version exhibits classical dichotomy — real variables are determined without any reference to nominal variables.

Chapter 13

Sticky Prices and Keynesian Macroeconomics

In the previous two chapters, we analysed the macroeconomy from the classical perspective which is based on the presumption of fully flexible real prices. In particular, we showed how real wage flexibility determines both the level of employment and output in the labour market. In this chapter, we explore another view — one associated with John Maynard Keynes and referred to as Keynesian macroeconomics. The essence of this view is that real and nominal prices are sticky, even rigid and do not adjust at least in the short run. Hence, output is not predetermined by the prior determination of employment in the labour market. On the contrary, it is output that determines employment.

13.1 The Simple Keynesian Model

The essence of this view is that real prices do not adjust to equilibrate the economy. The fundamental equilibrium condition does not change. It is still given by Eqs. (12.1) and (12.2) reproduced as follows:

$$Z = C + I + G, \tag{12.1}$$

$$Y = C + I + G. \tag{12.2}$$

The difference lies in the choice of what is endogenous. In the classical view, Y is not endogenous as it is pre-determined by the workings of the labour market. In the Keynesian view, Y is endogenous in Eq. (12.2). It is determined by total expenditure Z, part of which is exogenous. See Example 13.1.

Example 13.1: Suppose the consumption function is $C = C_0 + b(Y - T)$, where T is the lump sum, i.e., $T = T_0$, and b the marginal propensity to consume lies in (0, 1). Find the equilibrium value of Y when investment I is pre-determined (exogenous) as $\bar{I}$. Illustrate diagrammatically. How does equilibrium value of Y change if G increases by ΔG? How does it change if T_0 changes by ΔT_0? How does it change if $\Delta G = \Delta T_0$?

Substituting $C = C_0 + b(Y - T_0)$ and $I = \bar{I}$ into Z (expenditure), we get

$$Z = C_0 + \bar{I} + G - bT_0 + bY. \tag{13.1}$$

Since the equilibrium condition remains unchanged as output equals spending or expenditure, we have (repeating Eq. (12.2) as above) that

$$Y = Z = C + I + G. \tag{13.2}$$

Hence, solving for Y, we get

$$Y^* = [1/(1 - b)][C_0 + \bar{I} + G - bT_0]. \tag{13.3}$$

Equation (13.3) is the reduced form of the model — it shows the value of the endogenous variable (Y^*) in terms of all the exogenous variables (the terms in square parentheses on RHS). Note that private investment $\bar{I}$ is treated as exogenous unlike in the classical model.

Denote the term in square parentheses by A (for *autonomous spending*), then A is given by $A = [C_0 + \bar{I} + G - bT_0]$ and Eq. (13.3) can be written as

$$Y^* = [1/(1 - b)]A. \tag{13.4}$$

From Eq. (13.4), it follows immediately that $(\Delta Y^*/\Delta A) = [1/(1 - b)]$ for any change ΔA. If only G is increased, then from $A = [C_0 + \bar{I} + G - bT_0]$, it follows that $\Delta A = \Delta G$ and hence the impact multiplier of G is $\Delta Y^*/\Delta G = [1/(1-b)]$. If tax is increased by ΔT_0, then from $A = [C_0 + \bar{I} + G - bT_0]$, it follows that $\Delta A = -b\Delta T_0$ and hence $\Delta Y^*/\Delta A = [1/(1-b)] = \Delta Y^*/(-b\Delta T_0)$ so that $(\Delta Y^*/\Delta T_0) = -[b/(1-b)]$. These are called the government spending multiplier and the (lump sum) tax multiplier, respectively. If the policy experiment is to do a balanced budget expansion so that $\Delta G = \Delta T_0$, then from $A = [C_0 + \bar{I} + G - bT_0]$, we have $\Delta A = \Delta G - b\Delta T_0 = (1-b)\Delta G$ and substituting this into $(\Delta Y^*/\Delta A) = [1/(1-b)]$, we have $[(\Delta Y^*/(1-\mathrm{b})\Delta G] = [1/(1-b)]$ so that $\Delta Y^*/\Delta G = 1$ if $\Delta G = \Delta T_0$.

The **balanced budget multiplier** is not neutral, it's expansionary! This is an important result. Another way to think of this is that the balanced budget multiplier must be the sum of the government spending and tax multipliers which is unity. The tax multiplier is (numerically) smaller than the government spending multiplier because when T is increased by 1, consumption and therefore total expenditure fall by only b. Part of the tax increase is borne by savings. But if G is raised by 1, then total expenditure rises by 1. Hence, a unit rise in G and T raises expenditure by $1 - b$. This is the source of the expansion. In every case, what needs to be done is to first calculate $\Delta Y^*/\Delta A$ (which equals $[1/(1-b)]$) and then calculate ΔA when G or T or any combination of them changes. Figure 13.1 illustrates the Keynesian cross diagram.

In Figure 13.1, income or output is measured on the horizontal axis and expenditure on the vertical axis. All equilibria must lie on the 45-degree line through the origin so that expenditure equals income. The parallel lines marked Z_1 and Z_2 represent expenditure. Both have a slope of b — the marginal propensity to consume which is less than unity. The difference between the two lines is that Z_2 represents a higher level of autonomous expenditure by the amount ΔA which is the vertical distance between Z_1 and Z_2. The two equilibria corresponding to Z_1 and Z_2 are Y_1^* and Y_2^*, respectively. Starting from Z_1, let A increase by ΔA so that the new expenditure line is Z_2. The consequent increase in income is $\Delta Y^* = Y_2^* - Y_1^*$. Consider the isosceles triangle E_1E_2G in which $E_1G = E_2G = \Delta Y^*$. Therefore, we can write $\Delta Y^* = E_2H + HG = \Delta A + HG$. But note that from the triangle E_1HG, $HG = b\Delta Y^*$. Hence, $\Delta Y^* = \Delta A + HG$ can be

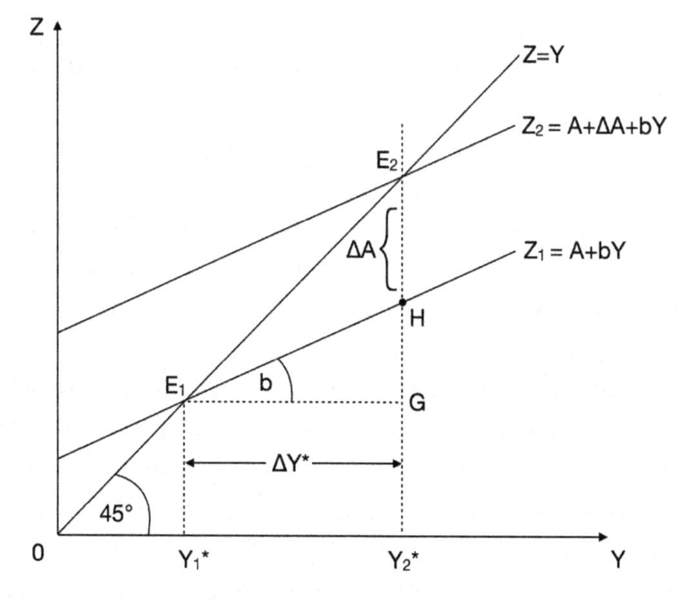

Fig. 13.1 The Keynesian Cross

written as $\Delta Y^* = \Delta A + b(\Delta Y^*)$. Therefore, we get the impact multiplier as $[\Delta Y^*/\Delta A] =[1/(1-b)]$. This multiplier is greater than unity as $0 < b < 1$. And from the definition of A, it follows that (i) $\Delta A = \Delta G$ if G increases by ΔG; (ii) $\Delta A = -b\Delta T_0$ if T increases by ΔT_0; and (iii) $\Delta A = (1-b)\Delta G$ if both G and T increase such that $\Delta G = \Delta T_0$ in the three cases. From these and the result $\Delta Y^*/\Delta A = [1/1 - b]$, the impact multipliers are immediate. Throughout this example, we have proceeded in three steps. First, find the impact of A on Y, which is given by $\Delta Y/\Delta A$. Then, find the impact of any change (G, T, or both) on A. Then, finally combine the two.

Example 13.2: If tax is proportional to income so that $T = tY$, is the balanced budget multiplier still positive?

$Z = C_0 + \bar{I} + G + b(Y - tY)$ and hence $Z = C_0 + \bar{I} + G + b(1-t)Y = C_0 + \bar{I} + G + bY - btY$. Balanced budget implies $tY = G$ which we substitute in Z above which implies $Z = C_0 + \bar{I} + G + bY - bG$ or that A is now given by $A = C_0 + \bar{I} + (1-b)G$. Hence, Y can be written as $Y = A + bY$ as before. Hence, $\Delta Y^*/\Delta A = [1/(1-b)]$ and $\Delta A/\Delta G = (1-b)$ as before. Hence, the impact multiplier given by $[\Delta Y^*/\Delta G] = [\Delta Y^*/\Delta A]\ [\Delta A/\Delta G]$ is still unity. So, the value of the balanced budget multiplier is unity regardless of the shape of the tax function! This is an important result.

Comparing Examples 13.1 and 13.2 with Example 12.1 shows the contrast between the Keynesian and classical models. There is no crowding out of private investment or consumption in the Keynesian model. In the simple Keynesian model of Examples 13.1 and 13.2, investment is assumed to be exogenously fixed so that a one unit rise in G leads (with T constant) to a unit rise in A and hence through the multiplier output will rise by $1/(1 - b)$. Assuming T is constant, the induced rise in consumption is $(b/1 - b)$ which added to the rise in G of 1 equals the total change in equilibrium output of $1/(1 - b)$. Also, note that in the Keynesian model, an exogenous rise in saving (a fall in C_0) does not increase investment unlike in the classical model where it does. In the simple Keynesian model, a fall in C_0 is accommodated by fall in income and hence consumption, leaving savings unchanged. This is the so-called **paradox of thrift** — attempts to save more lowers income and doesn't add to savings! It is investment that drives saving not the other way round as in the classical model.

13.2 Investment Functions and Goods Market Equilibrium

The assumption of exogenously given investment is at best a first approximation. It is difficult to pin down the drivers of investment as it is notoriously unstable compared to other components of national income. We have already seen in Chapter 12 one investment model in which investment depends negatively on the real interest rate. We will explore that investment model in the context of a modified Keynesian model later. But first, we turn to another view of investment which we call the political investment model.

It is sometimes argued that private investment could be driven by a reaction to government spending. Suppose the government spending plans increase so that private firms perceive that the government budget deficit

$G - T$ increases. The political investment model hypothesises that investment is given by

$$I = I_0 + \tau(G - T). \tag{13.5}$$

If private firms pessimistically believe that a rise in $G - T$ implies government is grabbing more resources (so that less is left for the private sector), they may cut investment. This implies that in Eq. (13.5), the coefficient τ is negative. On the other hand, to the extent some private investment is geared to receiving government contracts (in armaments industries, healthcare, etc.), then the reverse could be true, i.e., the coefficient τ is positive and private sector is optimistic when budget deficit expands.

Example 13.3: Suppose the consumption function is $C = C_0 + b(Y - \text{T})$, where T is the lump sum, i.e., $T = T_0$, and b the marginal propensity to consume lies in (0, 1). Find the equilibrium value of Y when I is given by Eq. (13.5). How does equilibrium value of Y change if G increases by ΔG? How does it change if $\Delta G = \Delta T_0$?

Substitute the C and I functions into the goods market equilibrium condition, $Y = C + I + G$, to get

$$(1 - b)Y = C_0 + I_0 - (\tau + b)T_0 + (1 + \tau)G. \tag{13.6}$$

Denote the RHS of Eq. (13.6) as D so that $D = C_0 + I_0 + (\tau - b)T + (1 - \tau)G$ is the autonomous expenditure component. The impact multiplier of G alone is given by $(\Delta Y/\Delta G) = (1 + \tau)/(1 - b)$. If private investors are pessimistic so that τ is negative, then the government spending multiplier is reduced. Partial crowding out of private investment is happening. Indeed, if τ exceeds one numerically, then the government spending multiplier becomes negative. The direct effect of G in increasing Y is reversed by the indirect effect of a big fall in I due to private sector pessimism. On the other hand, if τ is positive so that private sector is optimistic, then the government spending multiplier gets larger than $[1/(1 - b)]$. Crowding "in" rather than crowding out is occurring.

Now, let $\Delta T_0 = \Delta G$ so that the budget deficit $(G - T)$ is unchanged. Then, investment is unchanged and the impact multiplier of G is the same as in the standard case, i.e., $(\Delta Y/\Delta G) = 1$.

In the following example, we revert to the same investment function as was used in Chapter 12, viz. that investment was a declining function of the real interest rate r. Without significant loss of generality, we shall assume a straight-line investment function.

Example 13.4: Suppose the consumption function is $C = C_0 + b(Y - T)$, where T is the lump sum, i.e., $T = T_0$, and b the marginal propensity to consume lies in (0, 1). Find the equilibrium value of Y when $I(r) = I_0 - \theta r$. How does the equilibrium depend on the value of r? What happens as G increases? Illustrate graphically.

Substitute for C and I in the equilibrium condition $Y = C + I + G$ to get

$$Y = [1/(1 - b)][C_0 + I_0 - bT_0 + G - \theta r], \tag{13.7}$$

which can be rewritten conveniently as

$$Y = [1/(1 - b)][K] - [\theta/(1 - b)]r, \tag{13.8}$$

where the exogenous components are lumped together into K which is given by $K = [C_0 + I_0 - bT_0 + G]$. Clearly, an exogenous rise in r will lower Y via lowering investment.

We can rewrite Eq. (13.8) with r as the subject,

$$r = K/\theta - [(1 - b)/\theta]Y. \tag{13.9}$$

From Eq. (13.9), it is clear that the relationship between r and Y is negative. As r increases, I falls, and hence output falls. This relationship is called the **IS curve** in (r, Y) space. It represents all combinations of r and Y such that there is equilibrium in the goods market. It is downward sloping in (r, Y) space where r is normally measured on the vertical axis. The shift parameters of IS are the exogenous components in K. Any change in these components will cause IS to shift for every level of r.

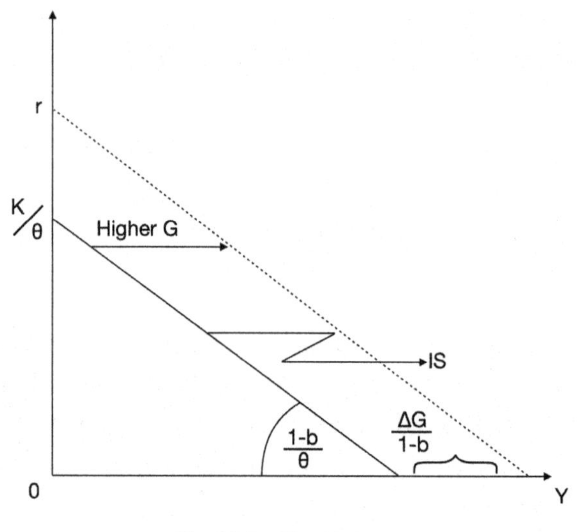

Fig. 13.2 The IS Curve

For example, given r, if G increases, then K is bigger and so Y increases through the multiplier. This implies a rightward shift of IS. Figure 13.2 illustrates the IS curve.

In Figure 13.2, we measure r on vertical axis and Y on the horizontal axis. The IS curve slopes downward. The intercept on the vertical axis is (K/θ). The slope is (negative) $(1 - b)/\theta$. An increase in G leads to a rise in K and hence to a parallel rightward shift of the IS curve as shown by the arrow. The horizontal amount of the shift is $\Delta G/(1 - b)$ — which is the same as the increase in Y when investment was fixed. The effect of a rise in $(C_0 + I_0)$ or a fall in T_0 is the same. An equal increase in G and T_0 increases K by ΔG and hence shifts IS outwards by ΔG which is of course less than $\Delta G/(1 - b)$.

Before turning to the role of money in the Keynesian macro model, we note that using Fisher's equation, we can rewrite the IS relationship in terms of nominal rather than real interest rate. Since nominal interest rate $i = r + \pi^e$, then we can rewrite the IS equation $r = K/\theta - [(1 - b)/\theta]Y$ as $i = K/\theta - [(1 - b)/\theta]Y + \pi^e$ where expected inflation is exogenous. What this means is that the IS curve in (i, Y) has an additional shift factor, namely the expected rate of inflation π^e. Any increase in π^e will shift the IS curve in (i, Y) space to the right with no change in slope. Note that the larger the θ — the impact of interest rate on investment — the smaller the slope of IS (numerically). If in Figure 13.2 we replace r with i on the vertical axis, then any increase in π^e will have the same effect on IS as a rise in G. All other properties of IS are unchanged. It represents all combinations of (i, Y) that keep the goods market in equilibrium given autonomous consumption and investment, government spending and taxes, and expected rate of inflation.

13.3 The Money Market

The analysis of the money market is similar to that in Chapter 12. The equilibrium is characterised by real demand for money equal to real supply of money, encapsulated in Eq. (12.16) reproduced as follows:

$$L(Y, i) = M^s/P. \tag{12.16}$$

The major difference is that in the sticky price model, we treat P as exogenously given so that Eq. (12.16) now represents an equilibrium relationship in (i, Y) space. The following example illustrates the properties of this relationship.

Example 13.5: The real demand for money is given by $L = Y^\alpha i^{-\beta}$. Find the equilibrium relationship in the money market in (i, Y) space. What causes shifts in the relationship?

Since $L = Y^\alpha i^{-\beta} = M^s/P$, by taking natural logs of both sides and simplifying, we get

$$\ln i = (\alpha/\beta) \ln Y - (1/\beta) [\ln M^s - \ln P]. \tag{13.10}$$

This relationship which is linear in logarithms can be written as

$$i = Y^{(\alpha/\beta)}/[M^s/P]^{(1/\beta)} \tag{13.11}$$

This relationship depicting money market equilibrium is called the **LM curve**. Clearly, the slope of the LM curve in (i, Y) space is positive. Given M^s and P and starting from any point on the LM curve, a rise in Y increases transactions demand for money and therefore speculative demand for money must fall since real money supply (M^s/P) is constant. Thus, an increase in Y is associated with an increase in nominal interest rate i. Shifts in the LM curve will occur if exogenously given money supply M^s or exogenously given price level P changes. If money supply increases (or price level decreases), then for any Y, there is downward pressure on nominal interest rate and hence i falls which means that LM shifts downwards. Figure 13.3 illustrates the LM curve.

In Figure 13.3, we measure Y on the horizontal axis and i on the vertical axis. The bold upward-sloping curve is the LM curve for given (M^s/P) — the real money supply. Its intercept is given by $(M^s/P)^{-1/\beta}$. If percentage rise in M^s exceeds percentage rise in P, then M^s/P gets bigger which lowers $(M^s/P)^{-1/\beta}$, i.e., the intercept of LM falls and the new LM curve is the dashed curve. It is often convenient to simplify the LM curve as a linear relationship (see Example 13.7).

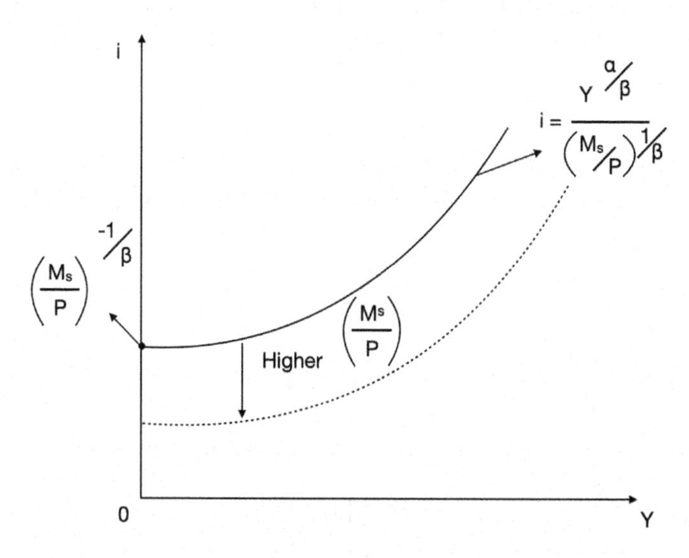

Fig. 13.3 The LM Curve

13.4 Output and Employment in the Generalised Keynesian Model

The IS curve in (i, Y) is an extension of the simple Keynesian model when investment is no longer exogenous but determined by the real interest rate. The LM curve shows how nominal interest and output are linked in the money market. Together, they jointly determine the equilibrium values of output and nominal interest rate. This is the generalised Keynesian model.

Example 13.6: Suppose the consumption and investment functions are as in Example 13.5 and that the demand for money is given by $L = \alpha Y - \beta i$. Find the equilibrium output level. If the production function is $Y = sL^a$, what is the equilibrium level of employment and unemployment? What role if any do prices play? Illustrate diagrammatically.

We start by deriving the IS and LM curves. The IS curve in (i, Y) is given by Eq. (13.9) augmented by the term in expected inflation, π^e. Thus,

$$i = K/\theta - [(1 - \mathrm{b})/\theta]Y + \pi^e \tag{13.12}$$

where K is as before the sum of all autonomous components, i.e., $K = [C_0 + I_0 - bT_0 + G]$.

The LM curve is obtained by setting $\alpha Y - \beta i = (M^s/P)$ and solving for i. The result is shown in Eq. (13.13) as follows:

$$i = (\alpha/\beta)Y - (1/\beta)[M^r] \tag{13.13}$$

where to simplify notation, we have written the real money supply (M^s/P) as M^r. To further simplify notation, we write $\sigma = [\theta/\beta]$.

These two equations (13.12 and 13.13) form a simultaneous linear system of two equations in two unknowns which is easily solved to get Y^* and i^*.

The solution for Y^* is shown in Eq. (13.14) as follows:

$$Y^*(1 - b + \alpha\sigma) = K + \sigma M^r + \theta\,\pi^e \tag{13.14}$$

Note that in Eq. (13.14), we have the equilibrium value Y^* (and some fixed parameters) on the LHS and only exogenous variables — K, M^r and

π^e — on the RHS so that it is a genuine reduced form for Y^*. To determine the employment level, we insert the value of Y^* into the production function $Y = sL^a$ and solve for L^* as

$$L^* = (Y^*/s)^{1/a}. \tag{13.15}$$

This is an increasing relationship. A rise in the exogenous value of the price level P will lower $M^r = M^s/P$ and hence lower Y^* and L^*. Note that implicitly we have taken the nominal wage W as exogenously fixed too. Hence, the real wage W/P is exogenous. For Eqs. (13.14) and (13.15) to represent equilibria, it is necessary that the exogenous value of W/P is high enough to induce a labour supply L^s which is at least as great as L^*. Only then is L^* feasible. The difference $L^s - L^*$ is U^*, the level of equilibrium unemployment. Figure 13.4 illustrates goods, money and labour markets.

Figure 13.4 depicts overall macroeconomic equilibrium in the sticky price economy. In the upper and lower panels, output Y is on the horizontal axis. In the upper panel, nominal interest rate i is on the vertical axis

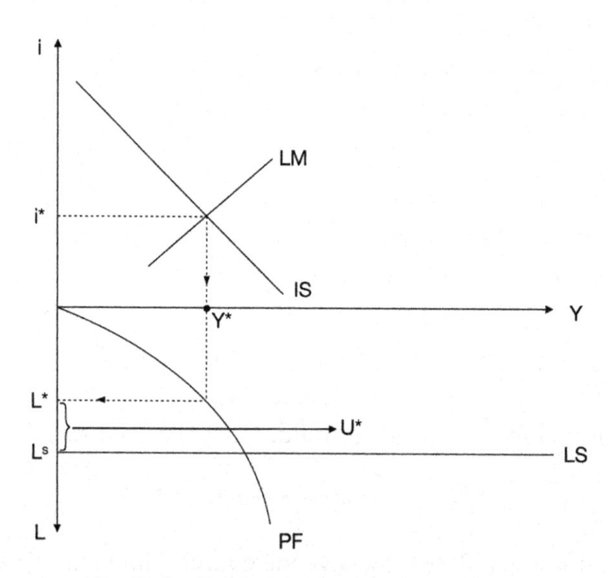

Fig. 13.4 Goods, Money and Labour Markets

with i increasing in northerly direction. In the lower panel, labour Y is on the vertical axis with increasing L in southward direction. The intersection of IS and LM curves in the upper panel yields Y^* (and i^*) and reflects Eq. (13.14). Given this determination of Y^*, the lower panel determines L^* from the production function PF. As shown by the horizontal line LS in the lower panel, labour supply L^s is greater than L^* and hence L^* is feasible and is the equilibrium employment level and $U^* = L^s - L^*$ is the equilibrium level of unemployment. Given the assumption of fixed W and P, it is perhaps best to think of these equilibria as short-run equilibria. Note the difference with the classical macro model of Chapter 12. Output and interest rate are simultaneously determined given the consumption, investment and money demand functions whereas in the classical model, causation is unidirectional running from employment to output to interest rate. In the classical model, unemployment is zero as real wage adjusts to clear the labour market. By contrast, in the Keynesian model, unemployment will typically be positive and will be zero only in a special case.

13.5 Fiscal Policy

In this section, we examine the role that **fiscal policy** can have on output (and therefore) employment. The policy instruments which government has are assumed to be government spending G, taxation T and money supply M^s. In the model, these are exogenous variables. From Eq. (13.14), it is clear that equilibrium output Y^* is influenced by all three. In this section, we explore fiscal policy, or the consequences of changing the fiscal variables G and T, leaving monetary policy for later. We study the details in the following examples.

Example 13.7: Suppose the consumption and investment functions are as in Example 13.5, i.e., $C = C_0 + b(Y - T)$ and $I(r) = I_0 - \theta r$. T is the lump sum, i.e., $T = T_0$, and b the marginal propensity to consume lies in (0,1). Find the government spending multiplier when r is fixed. What is the multiplier when increased G is matched by increased T? Illustrate by showing how much IS shifts.

Since $Y = C + I$, we get Eq. (13.7) which is

$$Y = [1/(1 - b)][C_0 + I_0 - bT_0 + G - \theta r]. \quad (13.7)$$

Hence, $\Delta Y/\Delta G = 1/(1 - b)$ if T is constant. However, if $\Delta G = \Delta T_0$, then from Eq. (13.7), $\Delta Y = 1/(1 - b)[\Delta G - b\Delta T_0] = 1$ as $\Delta G = \Delta T_0$. So, we can write the two answers as

$$\Delta Y/\Delta G \text{ (when } T \text{ constant)} = [1/(1 - b)], \quad (13.16a)$$

$$\Delta Y/\Delta G \text{ (when } \Delta G = \Delta T) = 1. \quad (13.16b)$$

Clearly, the government spending multiplier is lower when increased G is matched by increased T. Figure 13.5 shows the impact on the IS curve in the two cases.

Figure 13.5 is an extended version of Figure 13.2. IS_0 is the original IS curve (Eq. (13.9)). If the fixed interest rate is r_0, then output would be Y_0. Suppose G increases by ΔG but T is held constant. The multiplier is thus $1/(1 - b)$. Output then would be Y_1 and the new IS curve, IS_1, would

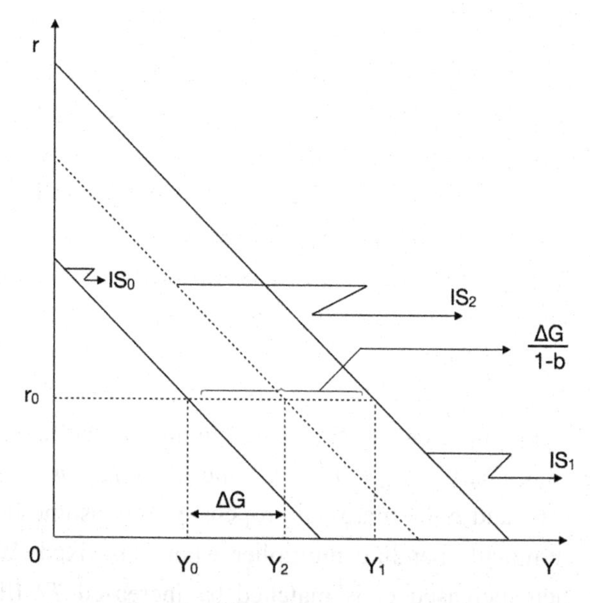

Fig. 13.5 IS Curve and Fiscal Policy

pass through (r_0, Y_1). If, however, G increases by ΔG but simultaneously T is increased by the same amount, then for fixed r (or fixed I), the multiplier is 1 so that $\Delta Y = \Delta G$. In this case, the shift in IS is smaller. The IS curve, IS_2, passing through (r_0, Y_2) reflects this case.

The previous example is based on the idea of a constant interest rate, but in reality, the interest rate will change if the government holds the money supply M^s constant. We must take into account the impact of the upward-sloping LM curve. A rightward shift of IS due to positive fiscal policy will lead to a rise in interest rate and hence a decline in investment. This decline in investment is referred to as the "crowding out" effect which we encountered in Chapter 12. The following examples are based on this idea.

Example 13.8: Suppose the consumption and investment functions are as before, i.e., $C = C_0 + b(Y - T)$ and $I(r) = I_0 - \theta r$, where T is the lump sum. The demand for money is given by $L = \alpha Y - \beta i$. Find the government spending multiplier if the increase in G is financed by a sale of new bonds to the public who pay cash for these bonds. Illustrate by IS/LM diagram showing clearly the extent of "crowding out" and the final outcome.

Since the government finances its spending by selling new bonds to the public, there is no change in money supply. The basic functions in this example are exactly as in Examples 13.5 and 13.7 so that the reduced form solution for Y is given by Eq. (13.14) reproduced as follows:

$$Y^*(1 - b + \alpha\sigma) = K + \sigma M^r + \theta\pi^e. \tag{13.14}$$

Recall that K is a combination of autonomous (exogenous) components given by $K = [C_0 + I_0 - bT_0 + G]$, M^r is real money supply and $\sigma = \theta/\beta$. Hence, we obtain

$$\Delta Y^*/\Delta G = \{1/[(1 - b) + \alpha\sigma]\}. \tag{13.17}$$

This is smaller than the government spending multiplier with fixed interest rate which is just $1/(1 - b)$. The extra term in the denominator of the RHS of Eq. (13.17) is $\alpha\sigma$, which reflects (partial) crowding out of private investment. The difference in the two multipliers is the output lost due to crowding out of private investment by the interest rate rise. Its value is given by $\{1/(1-b)\} - \{1/[(1-b)+\alpha\sigma]\} = \alpha\sigma/[(1-b)+\alpha\sigma] = 1/[\{(1-b)/\alpha\sigma\}+1]$. Clearly, as σ gets bigger, the denominator $[\{(1-b)/\alpha\sigma\}+1]$ gets smaller and the crowding out effect is larger. This can also be inferred directly from Eq. (13.17). The larger the $\sigma = [\theta/\beta]$, the larger the denominator in Eq. (13.17), and hence the larger the crowding out and consequently, the smaller the multiplier. If $\sigma = 0$ ($\theta = 0$ or $\beta \rightarrow \infty$), then the multiplier value converges on $1/(1-b)$ which is the same as if interest rate was fixed or investment didn't depend on the interest rate. Intuitively speaking, a large θ implies a large cut in investment if real interest rate increases. Figure 13.6 illustrates bond-financed increase in G.

In Figure 13.6, IS_0 is the original IS curve and IS_1 is the IS curve after G increases by ΔG. The LM curve labelled LM_0 does not shift because no new money is being created by the Central Bank. The initial equilibrium is at E with output Y_0 and interest rate i_0. Increasing G by ΔG shifts the IS curve parallel to itself to IS_1. If interest rate was constant at i_0, then the

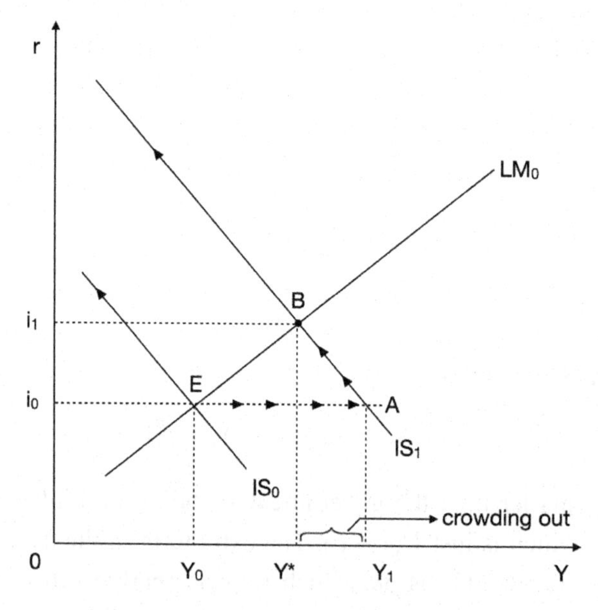

Fig. 13.6 Bond-Financed Increase in G

new equilibrium would be at A with output level Y_1. The economy would travel from E to A as shown by the arrows. The output increase of $(Y_I - Y_0)$ is given by $\Delta G/(1 - \mathrm{b})$. But due to new bonds being issued, the price of bonds must fall as the supply of bonds rises, and hence the interest rate rises to i_1. The final equilibrium is at B and the economy travels from A to B as shown by the arrows with output at Y^*. The difference $Y^* - Y_0$ is obviously smaller than $(Y_1 - Y_0)$ and is given by $(Y^* - Y_0) = \{\Delta G/[(1 - b) + \alpha\sigma]\}$. The distance $(Y_1 - Y^*)$ represents output lost due to crowding out.

Example 13.9: Suppose the consumption and investment functions are as before, i.e., $C = C_0 + b(Y - T)$ and $I(r) = I_0 - \theta r$, where T is the lump sum. The demand for money is given by $L = \alpha Y - \beta i$. Derive the multiplier when government spending is financed by the Central Bank buying new bonds from the government which then spends the cash. Illustrate by IS/LM diagram.

In this case, the mechanism for increasing G is very different. Government issues new bonds and sells them to the Central Bank for cash and uses the cash to increase G. New cash is being injected into the economy and hence real money supply increases with $\Delta M^r = \Delta G$. Both IS and LM shift. Recall the equilibrium value of Y^* is given by Eq. (13.14) reproduced as follows:

$$Y^*(1 - b + \alpha\sigma) = K + \sigma M^r + \theta\,\pi^e. \tag{13.14}$$

Ignoring all other terms in K except G, it follows that when both G and M^r increase that $\Delta Y^*(1 - b + \alpha\sigma) = \Delta G + \sigma\Delta M^r$ and since $\Delta M^r = \Delta G$, it follows that

$$(\Delta Y^*/\Delta G) = \{[1 + \sigma]/[(1 - b) + \alpha\sigma]\} \tag{13.18}$$

We may call the expression on the RHS of Eq. (13.18) "the money financed government spending multiplier". It is clearly larger than the bond-financed money multiplier described by Eq. (13.17). This is because the crowding out effect is mitigated by an increase in the real money supply which shifts out the LM curve too. Figure 13.7 illustrates money-financed increase in G.

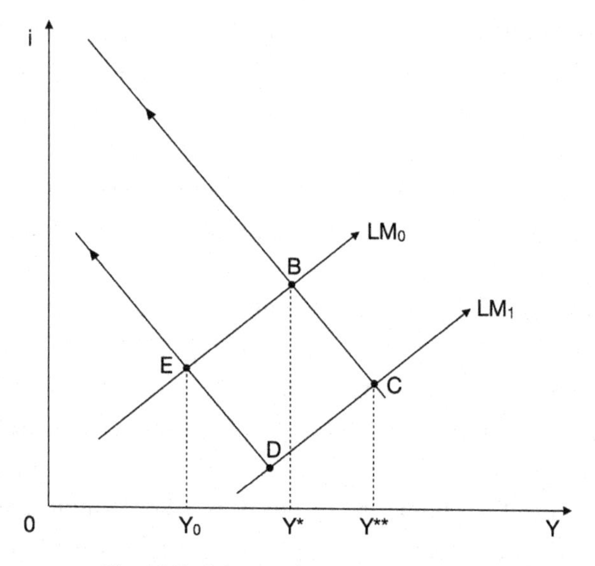

Fig. 13.7 Money-Financed Increase in G

Figure 13.7 is simply Figure 13.6 augmented by a shifted LM curve labelled LM_1. The equilibrium is at C with $Y = Y^{**}$ as compared to the bond-financed case with equilibrium at B and output = Y^*. Crowding out is diminished in this case. The rise in interest rate is muted compared to bond finance and hence the impact on output is greater. The "extra" output per unit of government spending gained by this method is obtained by subtracting the RHS of Eq. (13.17) from the RHS of Eq. (13.18) and is given by $[\sigma/[(1-b)+\alpha\sigma]] = 1/[\{(1-b)/\sigma\} + \alpha]$. In Figure 13.7, it is the distance $(Y^{**} - Y^*)$. Once again, we see that the bigger the σ, and hence the smaller the $(1-b)/\sigma$, the bigger the gain from money financing of G.

13.6 Summary

- Output is determined by real expenditure when prices are rigid.
- Employment is determined from output. The role of prices (output price and money wage) is mainly restricted to ensuring the feasibility of output.

- Government spending has a positive impact on output. The extent of this impact per real unit of government spending is called the government spending multiplier.
- If increased taxation matches increased government spending, the net impact on output remains positive but is smaller than when just government spending increases. The balanced budget multiplier is positive.
- The multiplier is not a fixed number but changes with the model specification, in particular with the determinants of investment and money demand.
- When investment depends on the real interest rate and real money demand on nominal interest rate and real output, the analysis of goods and money markets must be carried out simultaneously using IS/LM analysis. The one-way hierarchical structure of the classical model is broken in this generalised Keynesian approach.
- The size of the government spending multiplier is larger with money financing than bond financing.

Chapter 14

Monetary Economics

In the previous chapter, we analysed the role of Fiscal Policy — government spending and tax — on the macroeconomy from the Keynesian perspective which is based on the presumption of fixed price level in the short run. We saw that changes in government spending and taxation or both can influence output and hence employment. The size of the impact — the multipliers — was dependent on how government spending was financed. In this chapter, we extend the ideas of the previous chapter to focus on **monetary policy**. Initially, we take monetary policy to mean a change in money supply M^s brought about by the Central Bank (CB). The CB does this by buying government bonds from or selling government bonds to the public. CB sale of bonds reduces money supply while CB purchase of bonds increases money supply. If the price level P is fixed, then every change in nominal money supply M^s produces a similar change in the real money supply M^r because $M^r = M^s/P$.

14.1 Changing the Money Supply

In this section, we study examples in which the CB operates by changing the money supply. We hold all other policy variables like government spending (G) and tax (T) constant. We also hold P constant.

Example 14.1: Suppose the consumption function is $C = C_0 + b(Y - T)$, where T is the lump sum, i.e., $T = T_0$, and b the marginal propensity to consume lies in (0, 1). Suppose further that the investment function is $I(r) = I_0 - \theta r$ and the money demand function is $L = \alpha Y - \beta i$. What happens as M^s increases? What is the importance of $\sigma = (\theta/\beta)$. Illustrate graphically.

The functions are exactly as in Example 13.7 and the IS and LM curves exactly as in Eqs. (13.12) and (13.13), respectively. The reduced form (the solution) for equilibrium output Y^* is given by Eq. (13.14) reproduced as follows:

$$Y^*(1 - b + \alpha\sigma) = K + \sigma M^r + \theta\,\pi^e, \qquad (13.14)$$

where $\sigma = \theta/\beta$. As all fiscal variables are constant, only real money supply M^r changes and the impact multiplier of M^r on equilibrium output is thus given by

$$\Delta Y^*/\Delta M^r = \sigma/(1 - b + \alpha\sigma). \qquad (14.1)$$

Equation (14.1) can be rewritten as

$$\Delta Y^*/\Delta M^r = 1/[\{(1 - b)/\sigma\} + \alpha]. \qquad (14.1a)$$

This makes it easy to see the impact of σ on the impact multiplier of M^r. A rise in σ lowers $\{(1 - b)/\sigma\}$ which is in the denominator of the money multiplier. Hence, the money multiplier increases. In the limit if $\sigma \to 0$, then $\Delta Y^*/\Delta M^r = 0$ while if $\sigma \to \infty$, then $(\Delta Y^*/\Delta M^r) \to (1/\alpha)$ which is its maximum value. To understand what the role of σ is, suppose M^r increases by 1 unit. From the demand for money function, nominal interest rate i will fall by $(1/\beta)$, given constant Y. The real interest rate also falls by $(1/\beta)$. This then feeds into investment. A unit fall in r raises investment by θ. Hence, a $(1/\beta)$ fall in r raises investment by $(1/\beta)\theta = \sigma$. Thus, σ measures the impact on investment of a unit rise in real money supply and hence determines how large the money multiplier is.

The diagrammatic analysis is shown in Figure 13.7. If BC is the IS curve, then the increase in M^r shifts the LM curve from LM_0 to LM_1.

Output rises from Y^* to Y^{**}. The flatter the IS curve (the higher θ as shown by Eq. (13.9) and the bigger the absolute value of the intercept of the LM curve (the higher $(1/\beta)$)), the larger Y^{**}.

14.2 Changing the Interest Rate

In the previous section, it was assumed that CB controlled money supply and this then determined nominal interest rate. However, monetary policy is often conducted by CB setting the nominal interest rate and allowing the demand for money to determine what the money supply should be. Furthermore, given exogenous inflation expectations, the CB is effectively setting the real interest rate by choosing a particular value of the nominal interest rate. Denote the CB's desired real rate of interest as R. Then, the way monetary policy works is that CB chooses R and then sets $i = R + \pi^e$. Effectively, the LM curve is redundant in the determination of output. Rather it simply tells us what the required money supply is.

Example 14.2: Suppose the consumption function is $C = C_0 + b(Y - T)$, where T is the lump sum, i.e., $T = T_0$, and b the marginal propensity to consume lies in (0, 1). Suppose further that the investment function is $I(r) = I_0 - \theta r$ and the money demand function is $L = \alpha Y - \beta i$. Government spending is fixed at G. The CB desired real interest rate is R. Find the equilibrium value of output Y^* and the equilibrium value of the real money supply. What happens as R increases? Illustrate graphically how monetary policy might respond in order to increase output.

Since $r = R$ is fixed, the solution is exactly as in Eq. (13.8) and is as given as follows:

$$Y^* = [1/(1 - b)]\ [K] - [\theta/(1 - b)]R. \tag{14.2}$$

Clearly, a rise in R lowers equilibrium output via the negative impact on investment. And since $i^* = R + \pi^e$, then the money market determines the real money supply $(M^r)^*$ as $(M^r)^* = \alpha Y^* - \beta i^*$. Figure 14.1 illustrates interest rate setting.

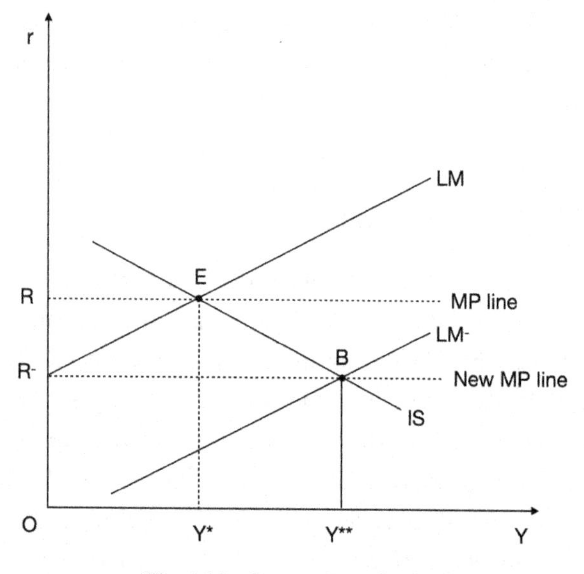

Fig. 14.1 Interest Rate Setting

In Figure 14.1, the IS and LM curves are shown in (r, Y) space. Given the target R, the equilibrium output Y^* is given by the intersection of the horizontal target line at R with the IS curve at E. This horizontal line is the **Monetary Policy (MP) line**. The position of the LM curve is determined by allowing the money supply to adjust till the LM curve passes through E. If higher output, say Y^{**}, is required, the CB will have to lower its target interest rate to R^-. The new equilibrium is at B and equilibrium output is Y^{**}. The CB will have to increase money supply till the new LM curve is LM^- which passes through B.

Example 14.3: Suppose the consumption function is $C = C_0 + b(Y - T)$, where T is the lump sum, i.e., $T = T_0$, and b the marginal propensity to consume lies in (0, 1). Suppose further that the investment function is $I(r) = I_0 - \theta r$ and the money demand function is $L = \alpha Y - \beta i$. The level of full employment output is Y^f. Government spending is at its long-run value G_N. Inflation expectations are exogenous at π^e. What monetary policy can achieve full employment? What happens if there is a lower bound to the real interest rate so that $r \geq r_{\min}$? Illustrate graphically.

If $Y = Y^f$, then from Eq. (14.2), we get r^f, the full employment interest rate, as

$$r^f = [K/\theta] - [(1 - b)/\theta]Y^f. \quad (14.3)$$

So, CB can either set $R = r^f$ (in effect, set $i = i^f = r^f + \pi^e$) or it can choose the money supply such that the real money supply is given by

$$(M^r)^f = \alpha Y^f - \beta i^f. \quad (14.4)$$

Equations (14.3) and (14.4) describe alternative but equivalent monetary policies for achieving full employment when G is fixed. Figure 14.2 illustrates full employment monetary policy.

In Figure 14.2, we measure real interest rate on the vertical axis and output on the horizontal axis. Full employment output is shown as Y^f on the horizontal axis. A vertical line through Y^f cuts IS at E. The horizontal line through E shows the value of r^f which is required to sustain full employment.

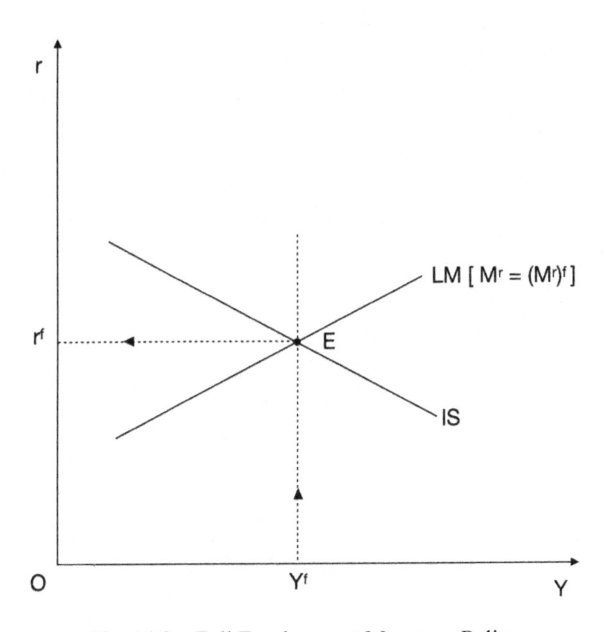

Fig. 14.2 Full Employment Monetary Policy

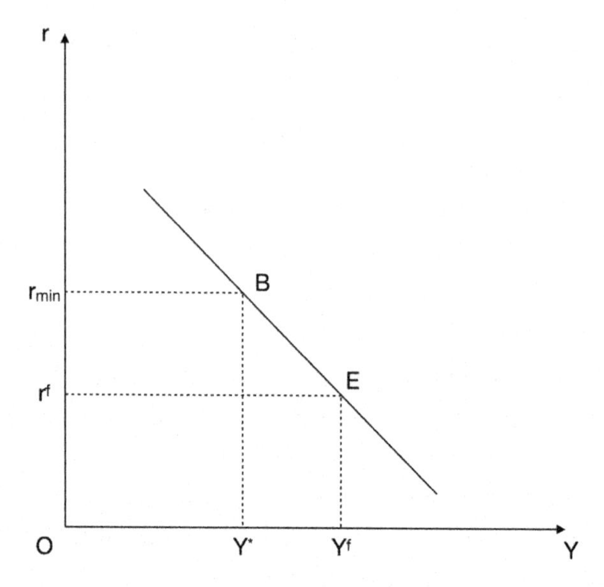

Fig. 14.3 The Impact of Lower Bound on r

But what if $r_{\min}$ — the effective lower bound to the real interest rate — exceeds r^f? Then, full employment cannot be achieved by monetary policy alone. Output will be determined by the intersection of the horizontal line at $r_{\min}$ with the IS curve and output will be below Y^f as illustrated in Figure 14.3.

In Figure 14.3, the equilibrium is at B where output is at Y^* and $r = r_{\min}$ which is the lowest feasible interest rate. Y^* is less than the full employment output Y^f which cannot be achieved unless the IS curve itself can be shifted rightwards by fiscal policy or some unconventional monetary policy. One reason why there might well be an effective lower bound on r is because nominal rate i must be greater than zero and hence r must exceed $(-\pi^e)$.

Unconventional monetary policies can take the form of quantitative easing or forward guidance. Quantitative easing refers to a policy where CB targets long-term bonds and seeks to drive up their price by buying.

This lowers long-term interest rates which then acts as a force driving up investment. Forward guidance refers to the CB trying to "talk up" the economy by assurances that the present low-interest rates will remain going forward in an attempt to induce higher levels of private investment. Neither has been particularly successful. The following example illustrates the potential role of forward guidance.

Example 14.4: Suppose the consumption function is $C = C_0 + bY$, where b the marginal propensity to consume lies in (0,1). Suppose further that the investment function is $I(r) = I_0 - \theta(r + r^e)$, where r^e is the expected future interest rate. Inflation expectations are exogenous at π^e. When can conventional monetary policy achieve full employment? If there is a lower bound to the real interest rate so that $r \geq r_{\min}$, what role is there for forward guidance?

Let Y^f denote the full employment level of output. From $Y = C + I + G$ and setting $G = 0$, and substituting for C and I, we get $I^d = (1 - b)Y^f - C_0$, where I^d is the desired investment required to maintain full employment. For any given r^e, there is a unique value of r denoted r^d which is required to generate I^d. Given the investment function, r^d solves $I^d = I_0 - \theta(r^d + r^e)$ and hence r^d is given by

$$r^d = (1/\theta)\,[I_0 + C_0 - (1 - b)\,Y^f] - r^e. \tag{14.5}$$

Should this be greater than $r_{\min}$, full employment can be achieved by conventional monetary policy. If not, an unconventional solution is required.

If r is constrained to equal $r_{\min}$ which exceeds r^d, then r^e will have to take up the slack. Forward guidance in the form of strong announcements can lead investors to perceive a lower r^e when r^d is too low ($<r_{\min}$) to be operational. This will lead to enough investment to sustain full employment.

A major question is how the CB sets its target R (or M^s). Often, Central Banks are mandated by the government or indeed by constitution to control inflation. If the CB has an inflation target π^T, then it is assumed to respond to deviations in actual inflation from the target. For instance, a simple MP rule for setting R might be

$$R = r^f + m_\pi (\pi - \pi^T),\ m_\pi > 0. \tag{14.6}$$

This says that CB raises R whenever actual inflation exceeds target inflation in order to reduce spending which fuels inflation. The feedback coefficient m_π measures the change in R when inflation exceeds target by one percentage point. Such a rule does not change the analysis much as the MP line still remains horizontal as in Figures 14.1, 14.2 and 14.3. However, the CB may well take responsibility for stabilising output too. In this case, an appropriate MP rule might be

$$R = r^f + m_\pi (\pi - \pi^T) + m_Y(Y - Y^f). \tag{14.7}$$

This generalised rule (sometimes called the **Taylor rule** after its "proposer" John Taylor) implies that MP line is upward sloping in (r, Y) space with a slope equal to m_Y which is the feedback coefficient on output deviations from the full employment target. In effect, the feedback rule for R as in Eq. (14.7) replaces the LM curve.

14.3 Aggregate Supply, Aggregate Demand and Inflation

Up to now, little has been said about inflation. Earlier in Chapter 12, we saw that in the long run, inflation equals expected inflation equals rate of monetary growth. But we had no apparatus for dealing with inflation dynamics. For this, we need to examine the **aggregate supply curve** and the **aggregate demand curve**. In some textbooks, both aggregate supply curve and the aggregate demand curve are written as relationships in price level and output space. However, given our focus on inflation dynamics, we set up both the aggregate supply curve and the aggregate demand curve as a relationship between inflation and output. There are several ways in which one can approach the aggregate supply curve and we focus on the simplest one which has reasonable plausibility.

Example 14.5: Derive the aggregate supply curve in (π, Y) space if some firms can adjust prices instantaneously when new information arrives but some are constrained and must set prices in advance.

Consider first the firms which must set prices in advance. For these sticky price firms which are a proportion s of all firms, their price $p^s = P^e$, where P^e is the expectation of the average (or aggregate) price level. All prices are measured in logarithms. Flex price firms which can set their prices instantaneously can do better by taking account of the actual average price P and also the pressure on factor prices (wages in particular) as measured by deviation of actual output Y from full employment output Y^f. For these firms, which are a proportion $1 - s$ of all firms, $p^f = P + a(Y - Y^f)$, where $a > 0$ reflects how much prices rise as costs rise. The average price level then must satisfy

$$P = sp^s + (1 - s)p^f. \tag{14.8}$$

Now, substituting $p^s = P^e$ and $p^f = P + a(Y - Y^f)$ in Eq. (14.8), we get

$$P = sP^e + (1 - s)[P + a(Y - Y^f)]. \tag{14.8a}$$

which then simplifies to

$$P = P^e + [a(1 - s)/s]\,[Y - Y^f]. \tag{14.8b}$$

This is the short-run aggregate supply curve in (P, Y) space. Subtracting last periods price P_{-1} from both sides converts to inflation space as prices are measured in logarithms so that $P - P_{-1} = \pi$ and $P^e - P_{-1} = \pi^e$ (provided inflation rates are low). Hence, Eq. (14.8b) can be converted to the aggregate supply (AS) curve in (π, Y) space as

$$\pi = \pi^e + v[Y - Y^f], \tag{14.9}$$

where $v = [a(1 - s)/s]$ is the slope of the AS curve. The AS curve states that actual inflation exceeds expected inflation whenever output exceeds full employment output.

An alternative way to write this is by making Y the subject so that

$$Y = Y^f + (1/v)[\pi - \pi^e], \tag{14.9a}$$

which states that actual output exceeds full employment output only when inflation exceeds expected inflation.

Note that if all firms are flex price so $s \to 0$, then $(1/v) \to 0$ and we are back to the classical model with $Y = Y^f$. On the other extreme, if all firms are sticky price firms so $s \to 1$, then $v \to 0$ and from Eq. (14.9), actual inflation is whatever it's expected to be! Furthermore, in the long run, $\pi = \pi^e$ so that from Equation (14.9a), it follows that $Y = Y^f$ — the classical result holds. The long-run AS curve (LRAS) is vertical at Y^f.

The aggregate demand curve (AD) is much simpler to derive. Intuitively, as inflation increases, CB will respond by raising the interest rate which lowers investment and hence output. Thus, the AD curve is downward sloping in (π, Y) space. If the CB is passive and holds money supply constant, then a rise in P due to inflation will lower real money supply and hence put upward pressure on the interest rate and thus lower investment and output. Either way, the AD curve is downward sloping in (π, Y) space.

Example 14.6: Derive the aggregate demand curve when monetary policy is set by CB setting interest rate according to the Taylor rule.

From Eq. (14.2), we know the relationship between CB set R and the output level Y that clears the goods market as

$$Y = [1/(1 - b)][K] - [\theta/(1 - b)]R. \qquad (14.2a)$$

Equation (14.2a) has a slight change in notation from Eq. (14.2) in that output is now Y not Y^* to reflect the fact that in the full equilibrium Y^* will depend on both AD and AS.

The full employment relationship is given by inverting Eq. (14.3) as

$$Y^f = [1/(1 - b)][K] - [\theta/(1 - b)]r^f. \qquad (14.3a)$$

Subtracting Eq. (14.3a) from Eq. (14.2a) gives the output deviation as

$$Y - Y^f = [\theta/(1 - b)](r^f - R). \qquad (14.10)$$

The Taylor rule is shown by Eq. (14.7) reproduced as follows:

$$R = r^f + m_\pi (\pi - \pi^T) + m_Y(Y - Y^f). \tag{14.7}$$

Substituting for $R - r^f$ from this into Eq. (14.10) gives the AD curve as downward sloping in (π, Y) space as

$$\pi = \pi^T - \{[(m_Y \theta) + (1 - b)]/(m_\pi \theta)\} (Y - Y^f). \tag{14.11}$$

The AS curve (Eq. (14.9)) and the AD curve (Eq. (14.11)) can be used to discuss inflation dynamics where changing expectations of inflation play a major role.

Example 14.7: An economy is in long run equilibrium with inflation at 2%. What is the impact of the CB raising the inflation target to 4%? Use graphical analysis.

In the new long-run equilibrium, we must have $\pi = \pi^e = \pi^T = 4\%$ and $Y = Y^f$ as before. How does the economy transition from initial equilibrium to the final one after π^T is raised? Figure 14.4 illustrates inflation dynamics.

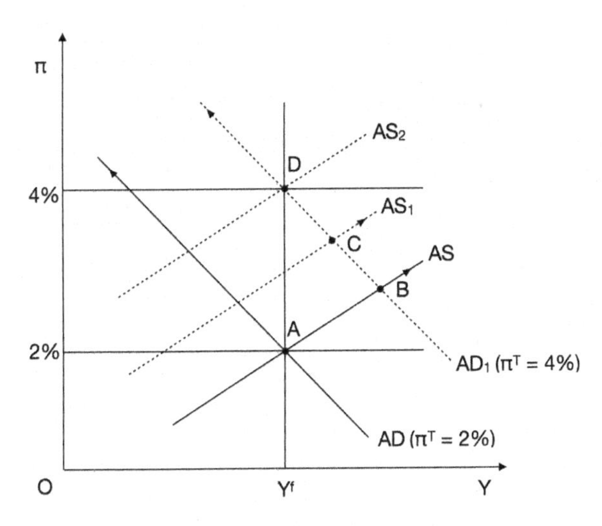

Fig. 14.4 Inflation Dynamics

We measure inflation on the vertical axis and output on the horizontal axis. The initial SRAS is AS and it intersects AD at A. Output is at full employment level Y^f and $\pi = \pi^e = \pi^T = 2\%$. This is the initial equilibrium. When π^T jumps to 4%, AD shifts upwards parallel to itself by two percentage points to AD_1. The new equilibrium is now at B where inflation is higher than 2%. This rise will drag up expected inflation π^e which in turn means that AS will now shift upwards as well to say AS_1. Hence, the new equilibrium is at C. This process of AS moving upwards continues till AS_2 is reached and the economy is in a full equilibrium again at D with $\pi = \pi^e = \pi^T = 4\%$ and $Y = Y^f$. The points B and C are temporary equilibria. At these, inflation expectations are below actual inflation and hence it is assumed that expected inflation is dragged upwards by actual inflation which in turn is dragged upwards by expected inflation till they both converge on 4% which is the only stable point. The following example is instructive in that it uses the conceptual material developed in the earlier examples.

Example 14.8: Spending in an economy is given by $Z = a + bY - \theta r + \varepsilon$, where ε is a random shock with zero mean. The CB sets the interest rate according to $r = r^f + m(\pi - \pi^T)$. The short-run AS curve is given by $\pi = \pi^e + v(Y - Y^f)$. Furthermore, the CB has a good track record of keeping inflation at target in long run. Explain the impact of the shock on output and inflation in the short run and long run.

As the CB has a good track record, economic agents will expect inflation to be at target so that $\pi^e = \pi^T$. Hence, the structural equations for this economy can be written as

$$Z = a + bY - \theta + \varepsilon, \qquad (14.11a)$$

$$r = r^f + m(\pi - \pi^T), \qquad (14.11b)$$

$$\pi = \pi^T + v(Y - Y^f). \qquad (14.11c)$$

In the full (long-run) equilibrium with no shocks, $Z = Y = Y^f$, $r = r^f$, $\pi = \pi^T$ and $\varepsilon = 0$. Substituting these in Eq. (14.11a), we get $Y^f = a + bY^f - \theta r^f$ which solves for r^f as $r^f = [a - (1 - b)Y^f]/\theta$.

To find the impact of the shock, allow ε to be non-zero. Substitute Eq. (14.11c) into Eq. (14.11b) to eliminate $(\pi - \pi^T)$ and then substitute the result obtained for r into Eq. (14.11a) to get

$$a + bY - \theta\,(r^f + mv(Y - Y^f) + \varepsilon = Y. \qquad (14.12)$$

Now, substitute for r^f in above by using $r^f = [a - (1 - b)Y^f]/\theta$. This allows us to solve for $(Y - Y^f)$ as

$$Y - Y^f = \varepsilon/[1 - b + \theta mv]. \qquad (14.12a)$$

Equation (14.12a) shows that the shocks cause output to deviate from its full employment level.

Substitution of Eq. (14.12a) into the AS curve (Eq. (14.11c)) solves for the deviations of inflation from the long-run value as

$$(\pi - \pi^T) = v\varepsilon/[1 - b + \theta mv]. \qquad (14.13)$$

Equations (14.12a) and (14.13) describe the short-run deviations. But in the long run when $Y = Y^f$, the shocks may still cause inflation to deviate from target. Substitute $r^f = [a - (1 - \mathrm{b})Y^f]/\theta$ into Eq. (14.11b) to get r and then substitute r into Eq. (14.11a). This yields the following result for long-run inflation deviations.

$$(\pi - \pi^T) = \varepsilon/\theta m. \qquad (14.14)$$

The difference between the short-run determination and the long-run determination of the inflation deviation is based entirely on the fact that in the long run, the shock has no impact on output. Shocks affect AD (i.e., Z) but AS is fixed at $Y = Y^f$.

14.4 Summary

- The Central Bank can either set the money supply or the nominal interest rate but not both.
- Setting the nominal interest rate is equivalent to setting the real interest rate, given the expected rate of inflation.

- Except for the presence of an effective lower bound on the real interest rate, monetary policy can achieve full employment.
- The Central Bank is sometimes assumed to follow a feedback rule for the real interest rate which is based on deviations of inflation from target and output from its full employment value.
- Inflation and output dynamics can be analysed using AD/AS analysis. The role of inflation expectations in shifting short-run AS curves is crucial.

Chapter 15

Open Economy Macroeconomics

Up to now, the fact that most countries trade with each other has been ignored. In this chapter, we consider how international factors influence the macroeconomy and may constrain macroeconomic policy options. We consider the case of a **small open economy**, like the UK. The small open economy cannot influence the world economy but is influenced by events and policies in the world economy. For ease of exposition, we consider the macroeconomics of a domestic small open economy (the UK prototype) trading with the large "**rest of the world economy**" which we call ROW. The currency of the domestic economy is pounds (£) and that of ROW is dollars ($). They are linked by the concept of the **exchange rate**.

15.1 Exchange Rates

The exchange rate is a relative price that connects the two currencies. It is often defined as the number of units of foreign currency (dollars) per one unit of the domestic currency (pounds). Thus, if e is the exchange rate, then \$$e$ = £1. Of course, as the exchange rate is a relative price, we could equally define it as S where £S = \$1 whereby S is the number of units of domestic currency per unit of foreign currency. There is no agreed convention but as $S = 1/e$, it really does not matter. However, for clarity, we stay with \$$e$ = £1 definition throughout. Hence, a rise in e is an **appreciation** of the £ (more dollars per £) while a fall in e is a **depreciation** of the £. This exchange rate is sometimes called the nominal exchange rate because it links the price of two monies.

Parallel to this concept is the concept of the **real exchange rate**. If the domestic economy exports luxury cars (Rolls-Royce) to ROW which exports motorbikes to the UK, then the real exchange rate is the relative price of a luxury car (domestic good) in terms of a motorbike (foreign good). We denote this by ξ which means that each Rolls-Royce (the domestic good) is worth ξ motorbikes (the foreign good).

Example 15.1: If £p is the pound price of the domestic good (Rolls-Royce) and \$$p^W$ is the dollar price of the foreign good (motor bike), what is the relationship between e, ξ, p and p^W?

To buy 1 unit of the domestic good, you spend £p or \$$pe$ since \$$e$ = £1. But \$$pe$ buys (pe/p^W) motorbikes. Hence by definition, $\xi = pe/p^W$.

Example 15.2: If the price of a UK Rolls-Royce in terms of ROW motorbikes has remained constant over a period of time but in that same period Rolls-Royce price in £ has risen by 5% but price of motorbikes in dollars has risen by 25%, what has happened to the (nominal) exchange rate?

Since $\xi = pe/p^W$, we can take logs to get $\ln \xi = \ln p + \ln e - \ln p^W$. Then, differentiate to get rates of change so that

% change in p + % change in e – % change in p^W = % change in ξ = 0 (as ξ is constant) or % change in e = % change in p^W – % change in p.

Hence, plugging in the numbers, we get

$$\% \text{ change in } e = 25\% - 5\% = 20\%.$$

Hence, the £ has appreciated by 20%. The pound is worth 20% more dollars than before the prices of both goods changed.

This example shows the impact of differential inflation rates on nominal exchange rate if real exchange rate is constant which, under perfect arbitrage, should happen. This version of the law of one price is called **Purchasing Power Parity** (PPP). What in effect the hypothesis of PPP says is that it should not matter where in the world you buy a tradeable good since its price (barring transport costs) should be the same when evaluated at the going exchange rate. Thus, if a Big Mac costs \$3 in USA, and the exchange rate is £1 = \$1.5, then if PPP holds, a Big Mac in London should cost £2. Although our example was in terms of a specific good, the principle applies to a basket of traded goods too.

15.2 Exports, Imports and Capital Flows

Exports and **imports** affect the national income identity and the equilibrium condition. Again, for simplicity, assume that the single-good domestic economy produces Rolls-Royce only so that $Y = C + I + G$ is measured in Rolls-Royce. The first step in analysing how the open economy impinges on this is to convert imports (motorbikes) into equivalent Rolls-Royce using the real exchange rate. Thus, if level of Imports is IM motorbikes, then it is equivalent to (IM/ξ) Rolls-Royce. And if X denotes exports of Rolls-Royce, then the equilibrium condition for the domestic economy is given by domestic output (Y) equals expenditure on domestic goods (Z) or

$$Y = Z = C + I + G + X - \mathrm{IM}/\xi. \tag{15.1}$$

The reason for adding exports and subtracting imports is that exports are part of domestic production but imports are part of ROW production. Note that looking at expenditure on domestic goods, we include expenditure by foreigners on domestic goods, which is exports X. But since C includes all consumption by domestic residents (including consumption of foreign goods), we must subtract real volume of imports (IM/ξ) to arrive at the correct number for real expenditure on domestic goods. A rise in real exchange rate ξ means domestic goods are getting expensive so demand for exports (X) falls and demand for imports (IM) increases. Hence, we can write the export and import functions as

$$X = X(\xi, Y^W), \tag{15.2a}$$

$$\mathrm{IM} = \mathrm{IM}(\xi, Y), \tag{15.2b}$$

where Y^W is world income and is exogenous by the small open economy assumption. Furthermore, it is assumed that the partial derivatives of X and IM are given by

$$\delta X/\delta\xi < 0, \quad \delta X/\delta Y^W > 0, \quad \delta \mathrm{IM}/\delta\xi > 0 \quad \text{and} \quad \delta \mathrm{IM}/\delta Y > 0,$$

which merely says that X and IM are normal goods with "normal" demand functions. In many applications, we simplify further by assuming that the income variable in Eq. (15.2) is not significant and hence we can write, **net exports** which is the difference between X and imports (measured in Rolls-Royce!) as

$$NX = X - \mathrm{IM}/\xi = NX(\xi). \tag{15.3}$$

Example 15.3: Under what circumstances is NX a decreasing function of ξ?

Clearly, as ξ goes up, X falls from the assumptions following Eq. (15.2). But the term (IM/ξ) is more problematic. Does it rise or fall with an increase in ξ? As ξ rises, by assumption, IM increases but $1/\xi$ falls and hence the change in the product (IM)($1/\xi$) is ambiguous. If the "price effect" $1/\xi$ is large and the quantity effect (IM) is small, then (IM)($1/\xi$) could fall and fall by enough to drown the negative impact of the increase ξ on X. So, in principle, NX could go either way as real exchange ξ increases. We need to analyse further.

We start by differentiating $NX(\xi) = X(\xi) - \mathrm{IM}(\xi)/\xi$ with respect to ξ to get

$$dNX/d\xi = X'(\xi) - \mathrm{IM}'(\xi)/\xi + \mathrm{IM}(\xi)/\xi^2. \tag{15.4}$$

And then, we multiply the whole equation by ξ/X to get that

$$[dNX/d\xi](\xi/X) = [\xi X'(\xi)]/X - [\mathrm{IM}'(\xi)/X] + [\mathrm{IM}(\xi)/\xi X]. \tag{15.4a}$$

If we start close to an equilibrium with $NX = 0$ or $X = \mathrm{IM}/\xi$, then Eq. (15.4a) simplifies down to

$$[dNX/d\xi](\xi/X) = -\eta_X - \eta_{IM} + 1, \tag{15.4b}$$

where $\eta_X = -\xi X'(\xi)/X$ is the elasticity of exports with respect to the real exchange rate (and is positive) and $\eta_{IM} = \xi[\mathrm{IM}'(\xi)/\mathrm{IM}]$ is the elasticity of imports with respect to the real exchange rate (and is positive).

As X and ξ are both positive, it follows from Eq. (15.4b) that $dNX/d\xi < 0$ requires $-\eta_X - \eta_{IM} + 1 < 0$ or $\eta_X + \eta_{IM} > 1$. In words, it states that if the sum of the absolute values of imports and export elasticities with respect to the real exchange rate exceeds one, then a depreciation of the real exchange rate will increase net exports. This is tantamount to saying that quantity effects (which is what the elasticities measure) can't be too small if real depreciation is going to increase *NX*. This is the famous **Marshall–Lerner condition**.

But goods and services (cars, motorbikes, washing machines, etc.) are not the only traded goods. A very important category of goods is financial assets. ROW citizens may choose to buy UK securities like government bonds and vice versa. These flows in both directions are large. Their determinants are quite different from the determinants of exports and imports of physical goods (and services). UK purchases of ROW bonds are a capital outflow from the UK. Like UK imports, they use up **foreign exchange**. ROW purchases of British bonds denominated in pounds are a capital inflow (to the UK). They earn foreign exchange for the UK. The **balance of payments** (BP) is the total net receipts of foreign exchange (credit items less debit items). Since commodity exports and capital inflows add to foreign exchange while commodity imports and capital outflows use up foreign exchange, BP is defined as: gross value of exports less gross value of imports plus gross value of capital inflow less gross value of capital outflow. In net terms, therefore,

$$\mathrm{BP} = NX + \mathrm{NCI}, \tag{15.5}$$

where NCI is the net capital inflow = gross capital inflow less gross capital outflow.

A simple theory of net capital inflow is that it depends on the interest rate differential between the UK and ROW which allows BP to be written as

$$\mathrm{BP} = NX(\xi) + \mathrm{NCI}(r - r^{\mathrm{ROW}}), \tag{15.6}$$

where r^W is the world interest rate prevailing in ROW. In equilibrium, BP = 0.

Example 15.4: If NCI is given by NCI = $k(r - r^W)$, find the equilibrium relationship between r and NX. If NX is given by $NX = \varphi - \delta\xi$, find the relationship between r and ξ. Discuss the special case in which $k \to \infty$.

If BP = 0, then NCI = $-NX$ or $k(r - r^W) = -NX$ or $r = r^W - (1/k)NX$. Also, by Marshall–Lerner, NX is decreasing on the real exchange rate so that in linear form, $NX = \varphi - \delta\xi$. Then, $r = r^W - (\varphi/k) + (\delta/k)\xi$. This is an upward-sloping relationship. As ξ rises, NX will fall so NCI must rise which requires r to rise. If $k \to \infty$, then $(1/k) = 0$ and NX has no influence on r which is given by $r = r^W$. Since k can be interpreted as the ease of **capital mobility** so that $1/k$ represents barriers to capital mobility or friction in international capital movements, then the special case of $k \to \infty$ represents **perfect capital mobility**. Under this assumption, domestic interest rate r will equal world interest rate r^W. Even the slightest temporary excess of r over r^W would ensure a flood of capital inflow sufficient to match NX.

15.3 The Open Macroeconomy: Floating Exchange Rates

The functioning of the small open economy depends crucially on what type of exchange rate regime prevails. The most common type of exchange rate regime is called a floating exchange rate regime where the exchange rate is determined entirely in the foreign exchange market without interference from government or Central Bank. However, historically, there have been long periods when virtually all countries operated a fixed exchange rate regime. In such a regime, a country's government or Central Bank will intervene in the foreign exchange market by buying or selling foreign exchange to keep the value of the currency at a predetermined pre-announced constant level. For the most part, we assume a floating exchange rate.

Example 15.5: If prices are fully flexible, the exchange rate is floating and capital is perfectly mobile, what is the consequence of an increase in government spending? Illustrate diagrammatically. Compare the outcome with the closed economy.

Since capital is perfectly mobile, then $r = r^W$. Consequently, investment is fully determined by this and we denote the level of investment at the world interest rate as I^W. As prices are fully flexible, we are in a classical model framework, and output is pre-determined at full employment level Y^f. Since consumption depends on income and income is fixed at Y^f, then consumption is also fixed and we denote full employment consumption level as C^f. In equilibrium, $Y = C + I + G - NX$ which given assumptions made earlier reduces to $Y^f = C^f + I^W + G - NX(\xi)$ or $Y^f - C^f - I^W - G = NX(\xi)$. A rise in G lowers $Y^f - C^f - I^W - G$ and hence NX must fall by the same amount as G. But NX is decreasing in ξ and hence ξ must rise. Figure 15.1 illustrates fiscal policy with flexible prices.

In Figure 15.1, we plot real exchange rate ξ on the vertical axis and NX and output on the horizontal axis. The bold vertical line is the initial position for $Y^f - C^f - I^W - G$ which is a fixed quantity. As NX is downward

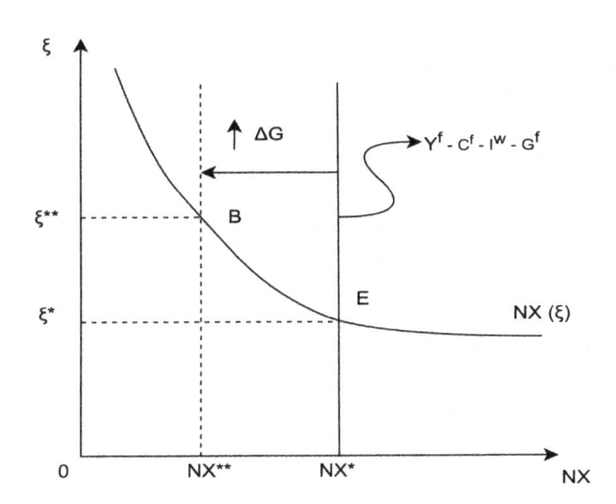

Fig. 15.1 Fiscal Policy with Flexible Prices

sloping in ξ, the equilibrium real exchange rate ξ^* is given by the intersection of NX with the vertical line at E. If G rises by ΔG, then the vertical line shifts inwards by ΔG to the dashed line. The new equilibrium is at B with real exchange rate ξ^{**} and the new value of NX is NX^{**} with $\Delta NX = \Delta G$. There is full crowding out! Output has remained at its pre-determined level, Y^f. Compared to closed economy, it is net exports that are crowded out, not investment.

Example 15.6: Suppose the consumption function is $C = C_0 + b(Y - T)$, where T is the lump sum, i.e., $T = T_0$, and b the marginal propensity to consume lies in (0, 1). Suppose further that the investment function is $I(r) = I_0 - \theta r$ and the money demand function is $L = \alpha Y - \beta i$. And the net export function is $NX = \phi - \delta\xi$. If prices are *fixed*, the exchange rate is floating and capital is fully mobile, what is the short run consequence of an increase in government spending and money supply?

We have three endogenous variables: Y, r and ξ. But perfect capital mobility implies a simple solution for r in terms of exogenous variables which is $r^* = r^W$. Consequently, $I^* = I_0 - \theta r^W$. We can write the equilibrium goods market condition as

$$Y = C_0 + b(Y - T) + I^* + G + \phi - \delta\xi, \tag{15.7}$$

which can be rewritten as

$$\xi = [C_0 - bT + I^* + G + \phi]/\delta - (1 - b)Y/\delta. \tag{15.7a}$$

This is the open economy IS curve which shows the downward-sloping relationship between ξ and Y. The intuition is that a rise in ξ lowers NX and hence Y for any I^*. We denote this curve as IS^{OPEN} to distinguish it from the standard IS curve in (r, Y) space.

The open economy LM curve is even simpler. Assume as before that inflation expectations are fixed at π^e. Since r is pre-determined at r^*, we have $i^* = r^* + \pi^e$, independently of Y. Hence, from the demand for money, we have $\alpha Y - \beta i^* = (M/P)$ which uniquely determines Y^* as $Y^* = [M/P + \beta i^*]/\alpha$. Note that the expression for Y^* is independent of the real exchange rate, ξ. The LM^{OPEN} curve is vertical at Y^*. A rise in G shifts IS^{OPEN} to the right raising ξ^* to $\xi^{*}+$ but leaving output at Y^* as before since the new IS^{OPEN} also intersects LM^{OPEN} at Y^*. A rise in M however causes LM^{OPEN} to shift to the right reflecting a higher Y at Y^{**} and simultaneously a lower ξ at ξ^{**}. Figure 15.2 illustrates policy with floating exchange rates.

In Figure 15.2, we measure ξ on the vertical axis and Y on the horizontal axis. The original IS^{OPEN} curve is the bold downward-sloping curve. The original vertical LM^{OPEN} curve is the bold line at Y^*. They intersect at E and determine the real exchange rate as ξ^*. A rise in G shifts IS^{OPEN} rightwards and upwards to the dashed line IS^{+OPEN}. The new equilibrium real exchange rate is $\xi^{*}+$. But output is still Y^*. An increase in M however shifts LM^{OPEN} to LM^{+OPEN}. Output is now Y^{**} which is higher than original output at Y^* and the real exchange rate is now ξ^{**} which is lower than the initial one at ξ^*. Why does ξ fall as M increases? The answer is that since Y rises but I is fixed and C rises less than Y, NX must rise as well. But in order for that to happen, ξ must fall. This model, which shows the very different impacts of fiscal and monetary policy in the floating

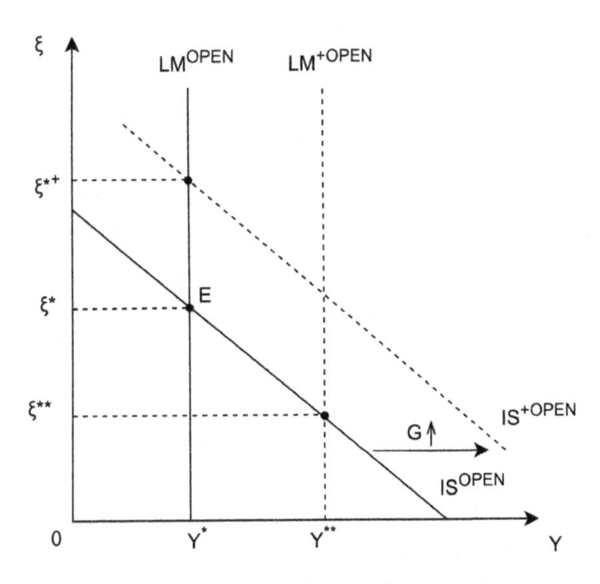

Fig. 15.2 Policy with Floating Exchange Rates

exchange rate economy, is known as the **Mundell–Fleming** model. Monetary policy influences output but fiscal policy only influences the exchange rate. The following example presents a modified and possibly more accurate version of Mundell–Fleming.

Example 15.7: If prices £p and \$$p^W$ are fixed and the exchange rate is floating, show how the consumer price level in the UK depends on the nominal exchange rate e. How is the LM^{OPEN} curve affected? What is the effect of fiscal expansion as compared to the standard Mundell–Fleming model described in Example 15.6?

Suppose UK consumers divide their consumption between UK goods and foreign goods with λ being the share of UK goods consumed. Then, writing P^C as consumption price facing UK consumers, we have

$$P^C = \lambda p + (1 - \lambda)(p^W/e). \tag{15.8}$$

In Eq. (15.8), the term (p^W/e) is the price of a foreign good costing \$$P^W$ measured in £ since the nominal exchange rate is \$$e$ = £1. Since the demand for money comes from consumers, it is reasonable to deflate money supply by consumer price P^C rather than GDP price deflator, p. Hence, the money market equilibrium is given by

$$\alpha Y - \beta i = M^S/[\lambda p + (1 - \lambda)(p^W/e)]. \tag{15.9}$$

Since $\xi = pe/p^W$ and both the domestic and foreign prices of goods are fixed, real and nominal exchange rates move together. Since i is fixed at i^* by perfect capital mobility and fixed expected inflation, then Eq. (15.9) can be rewritten as a relationship between ξ and Y which is the open economy LM curve. A rise in e lowers (p^W/e) and hence raises the real money supply which in equilibrium implies higher real money demand. But since interest rate is fixed by world conditions, the only way real money demand can rise is if income rises. Hence, LM^{OPEN} is upward sloping in (ξ, Y) space. Thus, a fiscal expansion will have the conventional impact of raising output Y. The rise in output raises demand for money, so real supply of money must rise. This can only happen through (p^W/e) falling or exchange rate rising as shown in Figure 15.3

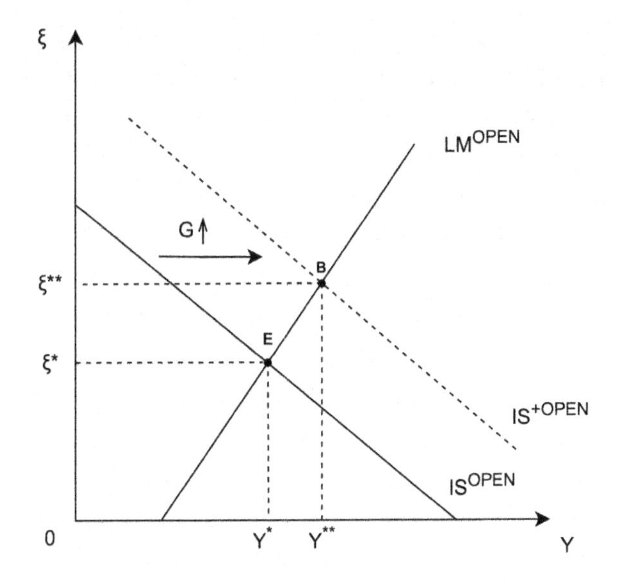

Fig. 15.3 Fiscal Policy in Modified Mundell–Fleming

In Figure 15.3, the LM^{OPEN} curve is upward sloping reflecting the fact that every rise in the exchange rate means a fall in the consumer price index and consequently a rise in the real money supply which expands equilibrium output. The initial equilibrium is at E with $\xi = \xi^*$ and $Y = Y^*$. Increased G shifts IS^{OPEN} outwards to IS^{+OPEN}. The new equilibrium is at B. Output has increased to Y^{**} and real exchange rate has appreciated to ξ^{**}. The modified Mundell–Fleming model has different predictions from the standard version.

15.4 The Open Macroeconomy: Fixed Exchange Rates

Up to now, we have considered floating exchange rates only. But many countries do use **fixed exchange rate** regimes. In this type of regime, the CB announces a target nominal interest rate e^T which it is committed to maintaining. This means the CB will intervene in the foreign exchange market, if necessary, in order to stabilise the value of the pound at $\$e^T$.

In practice, the CB sets the target as an acceptable band of variation and only intervenes if the market value of the pound moves outside the band. For expositional ease, we stick with the idea of a single valued target e^T.

The market for foreign exchange operates much like any other competitive market. The demand for pounds comes from ROW citizens wishing to buy UK goods (UK exports) and UK bonds (capital inflow) while supply of pounds comes from UK citizens wishing to import ROW goods and ROW bonds (capital outflow). It is against this background that intervention by the CB takes place. If e^T is lower than current market price e^M, then CB perceives the pound as overvalued. It intervenes by selling pounds (acquiring dollars) thus adding to the supply of pounds. Given constant demand for pounds, this additional supply of pounds drives the price of £ down to e^T. Conversely, if e^T is higher than current market price e^M, then CB perceives the pound as undervalued and buys pounds (selling dollars) adding to demand for pounds to drive the price of £ up to e^T. Note that to drive up the price of £, the CB needs a stock of dollars but in order to drive down the price of £, it can print pounds as needed. There is a fundamental asymmetry in the CB ability to operate in the foreign exchange market.

The following examples illustrate how the economy operates under a fixed exchange rate regime and what the policy options are.

Example 15.8: If capital is perfectly mobile and the domestic CB follows a fixed exchange rate policy, explain the major determinants of short-run output when prices are fixed. What happens as world interest rate changes? What is the role of fiscal and monetary policies?

Because of perfect capital mobility, investment is fixed at I^W — the investment that is generated at world interest rate. Fixed prices mean that real and nominal exchange rates are interchangeable. Nothing is lost by assuming $e^T = \xi^T$ so that $NX = \phi - \delta\xi^T - mY$ where the negative impact of Y arises because increased Y increases imports. Hence, we can write equilibrium output as

$$Y = H + bY + I^W - \delta\xi^T - mY + G, \tag{15.10}$$

where H is a constant incorporating taxation and the constant terms in the C and NX functions. This can be solved to give

$$Y^* = [1/(1 - b + m)][H + I^W - \delta\xi^T + G], \tag{15.11}$$

where $1/(1 - b + m)$ is the open economy multiplier. Clearly, the major determinants of equilibrium output are the world interest rate (r^W) which determines I^W, the target exchange rate e^T (or ξ^T) and government spending G. A rise in r^W lowers I^W and hence Y^* through the multiplier. A rise in the exchange rate target e^T lowers NX and hence Y^*. Finally, a rise in G is expansionary with a unit rise in G leading to a rise of $[1/(1 - b + m)]$ in Y^*.

As Y^* and i^* are already determined, then so is the demand for money and CB must adjust the supply of money to accommodate the desired exchange rate target. Money supply is endogenous.

There are strong limits to the use of fiscal policy to stimulate Y. We have seen that a rise in G leads to a rise in Y. From the NX equation, this also has the effect of lowering NX by sucking in more imports. Eventually, increasing G will raise imports to the point where demand for dollars (supply of pounds) rises so much that the dollar must appreciate or pound must depreciate. The CB has then to sell dollars and buy pounds in order to stabilise the pound at e^T. Its ability to do this is limited by its dollar reserves. When they run out, the government will have to either reverse its fiscal policy or devalue the pound by lowering the target. This is not an uncommon scenario under fixed exchange rates of government increasing output by increasing G but then having to cut back on its spending because foreign exchange reserves start to run out. It is sometimes referred to as the **stop-go cycle**.

Example 15.9: Consider an economy where output is at its full employment level $Y = 140$, $C = 100$, $I = 40 - 5r$, $G = 0$ and $NX = 20(1 - \xi)$. Capital is imperfectly mobile so that the domestic interest $r = r^W + \phi - 0.05NX$ where ϕ measures the risk of default of domestic bonds relative to ROW bonds. Find the real exchange rate. What happens to the real exchange under a floating exchange rate regime as risk goes up? What happens if the country has a fixed exchange rate (assuming ROW price is fixed) as risk goes up?

Substitute for r and NX into $Y = C + I + NX$ to get $\xi^* = 1 - [r^W + \phi]$. As ϕ rises, ξ^* falls by the same amount. Increased risk means some capital outflow (demand for dollars increases) and pound depreciates and NX increases.

With fixed nominal exchange rate, the adjustment falls on domestic price level p. Since $\xi^* = ep/p^W$, it follows that ep falls as ϕ rises so that since e is fixed, p must fall by the same percentage as ξ^* falls.

The following final example provides a means of combining the floating and fixed exchange rate models.

Example 15.10: A small open economy has a fixed price level = 1 so that all nominal and real magnitudes are the same. Expected inflation is zero so that real and nominal interest rates are the same. Capital mobility is perfect. The real money demand is $L = \alpha Y - \beta i$. The real money supply, m^s, is controlled by CB according to the policy rule $m^s = \Upsilon + \lambda(e - e^T)$.

(a) Explain the importance of the parameter λ in determining the equilibrium relationship between e and Y (the open economy LM curve).

(b) With standard consumption and investment and net export functions and $G = 0$, find the impact of a reduction in the world interest rate.

(a) By perfect capital mobility and zero expected inflation, we have $i^* = r^* = r^W$. Solving for the open economy LM, we have $\alpha Y - \beta i^* = m^s = \Upsilon + \lambda(e - e^T)$ which can be rewritten equivalently as either

$$Y = (1/\alpha)\,[\Upsilon + \beta r^W - \lambda e^T] + (\lambda/\alpha)e. \tag{15.12a}$$

or

$$e = e^T + (1/\lambda)\,[\alpha Y - \beta r^W - \Upsilon]. \tag{15.12b}$$

Clearly, for $\lambda > 0$, these represent an upward-sloping curve LM^{OPEN} curve in (e, Y) space. The slope is controlled by λ. From Eq. (15.12b), the slope is flatter the bigger is λ. As Y increases, money demand rises and so supply must rise too which can only happen if e rises. If $\lambda \to \infty$, the slope is zero and we have a horizontal line at $e = e^T$. This is the fixed exchange rate case. If $\lambda = 0$, we get vertical LM^{OPEN} curve in (e, Y) space with $Y = (1/\alpha)[\Upsilon + \beta r^W]$. This is the floating exchange rate/fixed money supply case.

(b) With standard functions, we can write the equilibrium condition as in Eq. (15.7) reproduced as follows:

$$Y = C_0 + b(Y - T) + I + G + \phi - \delta\xi. \tag{15.7}$$

Making the following substitutions in Eq. (15.7), viz. $e = \xi$ (as domestic price level = 1) and $e = e^T + (1/\lambda)[\alpha Y - \beta r^W - \Upsilon]$ (15.12b) from Eq. (15.12b) and $I = I - \theta r^W$ into Eq. (15.7), collecting constants into H, and simplifying gives us

$$Y^*[(1 - b + (\alpha\delta/\lambda)] = H - \delta\xi^T + [(\beta\delta/\lambda) - \theta]r^W. \tag{15.13}$$

Thus, we see that the impact of the world interest rate calculated as dY^*/dr^W is given by

$$dY^*/dr^W = [(\beta\delta/\lambda) - \theta], \tag{15.14}$$

which is positive only when λ is small enough for $[(\beta\delta/\lambda) - \theta]$ to be positive. In the extreme cases of fixed money supply, $\lambda = 0$ and $dY^*/dr^W > 0$ — the standard Mundell–Fleming result with floating exchange rates/fixed money supply. On the other extreme when $\lambda \to \infty$, $dY^*/dr^W < 0$ — the standard Mundell–Fleming result with fixed exchange rates/endogenous money supply. The importance of the monetary policy regime is paramount.

15.5 Summary

- The exchange rate is a relative price that connects the two currencies. The real exchange rate adjusts the nominal exchange rate by relative prices to provide the real price of tradeable goods.
- The small open economy cannot influence the world economy but is influenced by events and policies in the world economy.

- Tradables include goods and services as well as paper assets like bonds.
- Net exports and net capital inflows are opposite sides of the same coin and must sum to zero.
- The exchange rate influences net exports while interest rate differentials influence net capital flows.
- The special case of perfect capital mobility has acquired special importance in recent times.
- The impact of policy — both monetary and fiscal — depends crucially on the exchange rate regime in place.
- Fiscal policy has greater impact in fixed exchange rate regimes while monetary policy is more powerful in floating exchange rate regimes.

Chapter 16

Capital Accumulation and Economic Growth

In our analysis of macroeconomics so far, we have distinguished between the short run and the long run. The short run is conceived as a period of time in which prices are fixed and cannot change. By contrast, the long run has been conceived of as a period of time in which prices can fully adjust. However, both in the short-run as well as in the long-run analyses, we have maintained the implicit assumption that the productive capacity of the economy is unchanged. The capital stock is assumed to be constant. Investment adds to aggregate demand but its impact on capital accumulation and hence capacity has been ignored. In this chapter, we analyse the role of capital accumulation in moving the economy forward. Investment is the source of additions to the capital stock or capital accumulation. This in turn leads to greater output which in turn leads to greater savings. If these savings are partly or wholly converted into investment, the process continues driving output upwards. This may be thought of as the economics of the very long run.

16.1 Basic Growth Concepts

Continuous rises in output are what we mean by economic growth. If $Y(t)$ stands for output at time t, and if dY is the change in output over a small interval of time dt, then the rate of economic growth is defined as

$$G_y(t) = (dY/dt)/Y(t), \tag{16.1}$$

where (dY/dt) is the derivative of output with respect to time and measures the change in output per unit of time while Gy measures the proportional change in output (often expressed as a percentage). In principle, the growth rate could be changing over time and this is indicated by writing it as $G_y(t)$.

Example 16.1: If $Y(t) = a + bt^2$, find the growth rate of output.

Since $(dY/dt) = 2bt$, hence $G_y(t) = 2bt/[a + bt^2]$. Note that in this example, G_y initially increases as t gets larger starting from a low value, it then reaches a maximum when $t = \sqrt{(a/b)}$ before declining as t gets even larger beyond this level.

In this example, the rate of economic growth will become zero as t gets large. This leads naturally to the question of whether it is inevitable that growth comes to an end or can it continue indefinitely but not be explosive. In other words, is it possible that economic growth is a constant forever? This question is at the heart of growth theory.

Example 16.2: If G_y is a constant independent of time, say g, then what is the path that describes the evolution of output?

The answer is given by

$$Y(t) = Y_0 \exp(gt), \tag{16.2}$$

where Y_0 is the initial value of output and "exp" stands for exponential.

To verify, note that $dY(t)/dt = gY_0 \exp(gt) = gY(t)$ and hence dividing both sides by $Y(t)$, we get $[dY(t)/dt]/Y(t) = g$.

Example 16.3: Sketch the graph of $Y(t) = Y_0 \exp(gt)$ with t on the horizontal axis and Y on the vertical axis. Redraw with ln Y on the vertical axis.

Taking logs on both sides of $Y(t) = Y_0 \exp(gt)$, we have $\ln Y = \ln Y_0 + gt$. Thus, the exponential curve becomes linear after taking logs on both sides. Figure 16.1 illustrates constant growth rate.

In Figure 16.1, the left panel shows the path of $Y(t)$ for constant growth rate g. In the right panel, the same relationship is described but using $\ln Y(t)$ on the vertical axis. It is linear with (constant) slope g. Both are alternative representations of the same relationship.

Example 16.4: Show that if $Y(t) = Y_0 \exp(gt)$, then $G_y = g$ by log differentiation.

Taking logs on both sides, we get $\ln Y = \ln Y_0 + gt$ and then differentiating this equation with respect to t, we get $d \ln Y/dt = g$. But by using the chain rule for differentiation, $d(\ln Y)/dt = [1/Y(t)][dY/dt]$ which is the definition of the growth rate.

What is true of output is equally true of any other variable: if the growth rate of any variable is constant, then its path in levels must be exponential. Since the ultimate drivers of output are labour and capital, we will define an economy to be in **steady state** if its output, employment and capital stock are growing exponentially and its capital/output ratio is constant as well. This last condition of course requires that the constant growth rates of capital and output are the same.

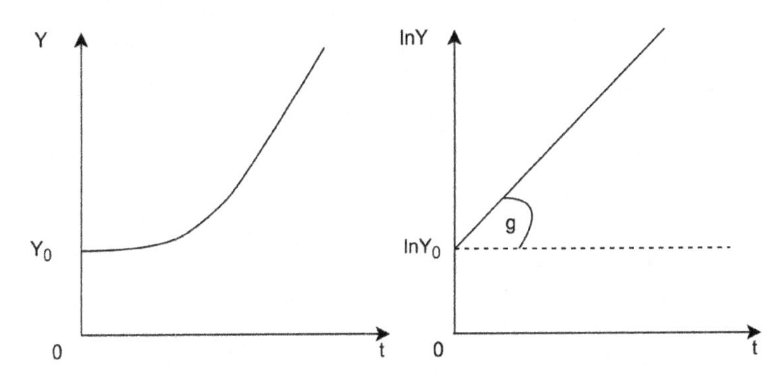

Fig. 16.1 Constant Growth Rate

16.2 Production and Technology

In common with other areas of economics, the production process is described by a production function which its most general form can be written as

$$Y = F(K, L), \tag{16.3}$$

which asserts simply that output Y is produced by the inputs labour L and capital K. In the simple one-good economy, we are required to imagine that K stands for the number of units of output used as machines. The process of converting output into machines is assumed costless so that K units of output will if needed produce exactly K machines.

A key assumption about the technological process described by the production function is that is characterised by **constant returns to scale** which means that if we "scale up" all the inputs by any factor z, we will increase output by the same factor. Formally, we write this assumption as

$$zY = F(zK, zL). \tag{16.4}$$

Returns to scale are about the impact on output of increasing all factors simultaneously by the same proportion. This is in contrast to the impact of increasing only one factor (holding all others constant) which is measured by the marginal product of that factor. Diminishing marginal product of each factor is entirely consistent with constant returns to scale. If in Eq. (16.4) we set the scale factor $z = 1/L$, we conveniently arrive at a production function which is expressed entirely in per worker terms as

$$y = f(k), \tag{16.4a}$$

where $y = Y/L$ and $k = K/L$ are output per worker and capital per worker respectively and $f(k) = F(K/L, 1)$. This device of writing the output–capital relationship in per capita terms is only valid when the original two-input production function is of the constant returns to scale type.

Example 16.5: For the production function $Y = F(K, L) = BK^{\alpha}L^{\beta}$,

(a) show that F exhibits constant returns to scale (CRS) if $\alpha + \beta = 1$;
(b) show that marginal products of K and L are both diminishing; what happens to marginal product of capital as $K \to \infty$ (with fixed L)?
(c) show that $y = Bk^{\alpha}$ if CRS holds.

(a) Starting from an arbitrary choice of K and L, say, $K = K_0$ and $L = L_0$, then since $Y = BK^{\alpha}L^{\beta}$, we have $Y_0 = BK_0^{\alpha} L_0^{\beta}$. Multiply each input by the factor $z > 0$, then we have $Y(z) = F(zK_0, zL_0) = B(zK_0)^{\alpha} (zL_0)^{\beta} = z^{\alpha+\beta} BK_0^{\alpha} L_0^{\beta} = (z^{\alpha+\beta})Y_0 = \lambda Y_0$, where $\lambda = z^{\alpha+\beta}$. Clearly, if $\alpha + \beta = 1$, then $\lambda = z$ so that $F(zK_0, zL_0) = zY_0$ which is CRS. If $\alpha + \beta > 1$, we have increasing returns to scale. The production function $Y = F(K, L) = BK^{\alpha}L^{\beta}$ is known as the **Cobb–Douglas production function**.
(b) The marginal product of K is as usual given by the partial derivative $\partial Y/\partial K = \alpha BL^{\beta}K^{\alpha-1} = (\alpha BL^{\beta})/(K^{1-\alpha})$, which clearly diminishes as K increases since $0 < 1 - \alpha < 1$. This can be further verified by differentiating $(\partial Y/\partial K)$ with respect to K again to obtain the second partial derivative. As $K \to \infty$, $K^{1-\alpha}$ also $\to \infty$ so that marginal product of capital goes to zero.
(c) $Y/L = BK^{\alpha}L^{\beta}/L = BK^{\alpha}L^{1-\alpha}/L$ if $\alpha + \beta = 1$ (CRS). Hence, $y = Y/L = BK^{\alpha}/L^{\alpha} = B(K/L)^{\alpha} = Bk^{\alpha}$. And marginal product of k given by $(dy/dk) = Bk^{\alpha-1} = B/k^{1-\alpha}$ is also diminishing in k and tending to zero as k gets large.

Example 16.6: Does the augmented Cobb–Douglas production function given by $Y = AK + BK^{\alpha}L^{1-\alpha}$ exhibit CRS? Is marginal product of labour diminishing?

Multiply all inputs by z and we get $Y(z) = AzK + B(zK)^{\alpha}(zL)^{1-\alpha} = zAK + zBK^{\alpha}L^{1-\alpha} = z[AK + BK^{\alpha}L^{1-\alpha}] = zY$ and hence CRS. Marginal product of capital is $A + (\alpha BL^{1-\alpha})/(K^{1-\alpha})$ which diminishes with increasing K BUT tends to a finite limit $A > 0$ as $K \to \infty$. Thus, both Cobb–Douglas and augmented Cobb–Douglas production functions have diminishing marginal product of capital, but in the augmented case, there is a lower bound for the marginal product which exceeds zero.

16.3 Capital Accumulation

An implication of constant returns to scale is that we can think of the macroeconomy in a rather simple way. One might think of each factory as employing only one worker who works with k units of capital to produce y units of output according to the production function $y = f(k)$. The whole economy then consists of L such (identical) factories. To understand growth under constant returns to scale, all that is needed is to analyse (i) growth of output in each one-worker factory and (ii) what drives growth in number of such single-worker factories — and these two processes can be analysed separately.

Growth in output clearly depends on the growth in the capital stock which is "produced" by investment. But not all investment adds to the capital stock. Some of it is used to merely replace "worn out" or "collapsed" capital — known as **depreciation**. Suppose the depreciation *rate* is δ so that the number of machines "dying" per period is δK, then the net addition to the capital stock, dK/dt, is given by

$$dK/dt = I - \delta K. \tag{16.5}$$

If the savings ratio is s so that total savings $= sY$ and if we make the heroic assumption that all savings are automatically invested, then $I = sY$. Substituting $I = sY$ in Eq. (16.5) and dividing both sides by K, we get the growth of total capital as

$$g_K = (dK/dt)/K = s(Y/K) - \delta. \tag{16.6}$$

Note that since $Y/K = y/k$, we can replace $s(Y/K)$ on the RHS of Eq. (16.6). And since $k = K/L$, or $K = kL$, it follows (by taking logs and then differentiating $\ln K = \ln k + \ln L$) that $(dK/dt)/K = (dk/dt)/k + (dL/dt)/L$. Hence, $g_k = g_K - g_L$ which states that rate of growth of per capita capital equals rate of growth of capital less rate of growth of labour force. If we assume that rate of growth of labour force is exogenous and equals n, then we can write the equation which drives per capita accumulation as

$$g_k = (dk/dt)/k = s(y/k) - \delta - n. \tag{16.6a}$$

This is the fundamental equation of per head capital accumulation. Since s, δ and n are all constants, the shape of g_k is driven by (y/k) which can be thought of as output per unit of capital or **capital productivity**.

Example 16.7: For each of the production functions (a) $Y = BK^{\alpha}L^{1-\alpha}$ and (b) $Y = AK + BK^{\alpha}L^{1-\alpha}$, derive capital productivity (y/k) and illustrate diagrammatically.

(a) If $Y = BK^{\alpha}L^{1-\alpha}$, then from Example 16.4, $y = Bk^{\alpha}$ and hence capital productivity, $(y/k) = Bk^{\alpha-1} = B/k^{1-\alpha}$. Since α is a fraction, this function is decreasing as k gets bigger. Furthermore, as $k \to \infty$, capital productivity tends to zero.
(b) If $Y = AK + BK^{\alpha}L^{1-\alpha}$, then $y/k = A + B/k^{1-\alpha}$, which is also a declining function of k. But in this case, as $k \to \infty$, capital productivity tends to its lower bound A. Figure 16.2 illustrates both cases.

In the Cobb–Douglas case, the productivity of capital is declining but tends to zero as k gets larger and larger but in the augmented Cobb–Douglas

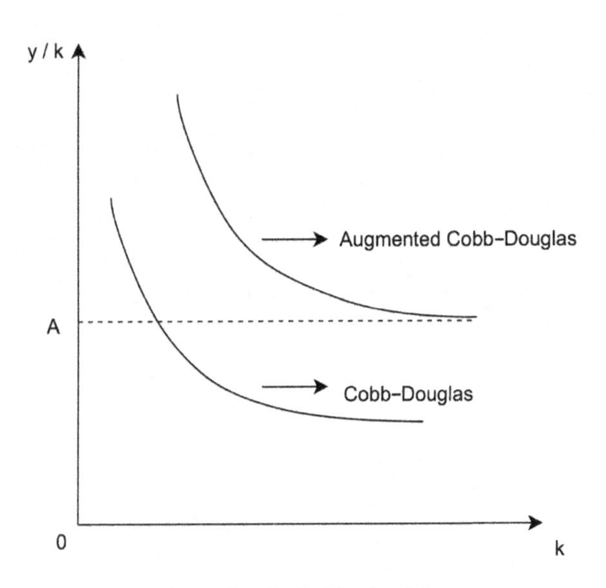

Fig. 16.2 Capital Productivity

case, capital productivity is also declining but has a lower bound $A > 0$. In both cases, capital productivity asymptotes towards a lower bound, but in the Cobb–Douglas case this lower bound is zero whereas in the Augmented Cobb Douglas case, it is A which exceeds zero. Diminishing marginal product of capital is enough to ensure that in Eq. (16.6a), capital productivity is decreasing, but its lower bound is not zero in all cases.

16.4 Steady State and Dynamics

Will the economy converge to a steady state in which output, employment and capital stock are growing exponentially *and* capital/output ratio is constant? Constant capital–output ratio requires constant k or $g_k = 0$. From Eq. (16.6a), this requires $g_k = s(y/k) - \delta - n$ to equal zero or $y/k = [\delta + n]/s$. Does this equation have a solution? The following examples illustrate.

Example 16.8: For each of the production functions (a) $Y = BK^{\alpha}L^{1-\alpha}$ (Cobb–Douglas) and (b) $Y = AK + BK^{\alpha}L^{1-\alpha}$ (augmented Cobb–Douglas), discuss whether a steady state exists. Illustrate diagrammatically.

(a) For Cobb–Douglas, we require $y/k = B/k^{1-\alpha} = [\delta + n]/s$ which solves for k as $k^* = [Bs/(\delta + n)]^{[1/(1-\alpha)]}$. Per capita capital stock is indeed constant in the very long run. The higher the $(s/\delta + n)$, the larger the k^*.
(b) For Augmented Cobb–Douglas (ACD), we require $y/k = A + B/k^{1-\alpha} = [\delta + n]/s$ which can only solve for a positive k^* if $[\delta + n]/s > A$ or $sA < \delta + n$. For a sufficiently high savings ratio s, there is no steady state! Since $g_k = s(y/k) - (\delta + n)$, in the ACD case, $g_k = [s(A + B/k^{1-\alpha}) - (\delta + n)]$ which equals $sA - (\delta + n)$ as $k \to \infty$. Even in the very long run, growth of capital per capita is positive and equals $sA - (\delta + n)$. Figure 16.3 illustrates existence of steady state.

In Figure 16.3, we measure k on the horizontal axis and y/k on the vertical axis. The downward-sloping curve CD is the Cobb–Douglas capital productivity curve. It asymptotes to the horizontal axis for large k.

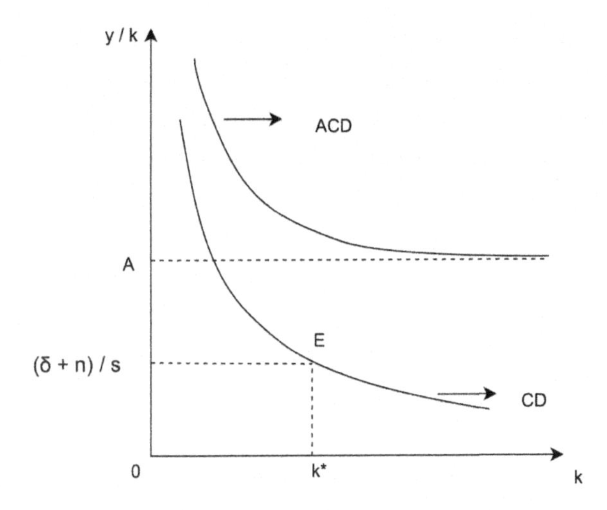

Fig. 16.3 Existence of Steady State

It cuts the horizontal line $[(\delta + n)/s]$ at E giving steady-state capital per worker as k^*. The curve ACD is the capital productivity curve for augmented Cobb–Douglas. It is everywhere higher than the CD curve due to the presence of the augmenting factor A. This curve asymptotes to the horizontal line $y/k = A$. As drawn, A is bigger than $[(\delta + n)/s]$ and hence there is no steady state. If A was smaller than $[(\delta + n)/s]$, then the horizontal line at A would intersect the ACD curve at some finite value of k and a steady state would exist.

The following example illustrates the properties of the steady state and the dynamics of growth.

Example 16.9: For the Cobb–Douglas production functions $Y = BK^{\alpha}L^{1-\alpha}$, find the steady-state values of output, capital stock and per capita capital stock. Will the economy converge to this steady state? Illustrate diagrammatically.

It has already been shown (in the previous example) that the steady-state value of k is given by $k^* = [Bs/(\delta + n)]^{[1/(1-\alpha)]}$. From this, steady-state value of per capita output y is given by $y^* = k^* [(\delta + n)/s] = \{B^{[1/(1-\alpha)]} [s/(\delta + n)]^{[\alpha/(1-\alpha)]}\}$ which shows that steady-state output per capita increases with $[s/(\delta + n)]$ which is intuitive. The benefit of higher savings ratio comes in higher output per capita but NOT in higher output growth per capita. Total output in steady state is $Y^* = Ly^*$, where L is the labour force or employment. Hence, we cannot solve for Y^* without knowing L. What $Y^* = Ly^*$ implies is that $g_{Y*} = g_L + g_{y*}$ or $g_{Y*} = n + 0$ which asserts that in steady state, total output grows exponentially at the same rate as the labour force. But note there is no growth in per capita output. The only way we can have growth in per capita income is through technical progress. Since in steady state $y^* = B(k^*)^{\alpha}$, then $g_{y*} = g_B + \alpha g_{k*}$ so that per capita output grows at the rate g_B since $g_{k*} = 0$ in steady state. So, unless there is some exogenous force driving technical progress, there can be no improvement in per capita income (living standards) once steady state is reached in the very long run.

Will convergence to this steady state occur? We have shown in Eq. (16.6a) that the rate of growth of output per capita is given by $g_k = s(y/k) - \delta^{-} n$. For $k < k^*$, (y/k) must exceed (y^*/k^*) since y/k is decreasing in k. But when $y/k = (y^*/k^*)$, $g_k = 0$. Hence, when (y/k) exceeds (y^*/k^*), g_k must exceed 0. Whenever k is $< k^*$, capital accumulation occurs which drives the economy to k^*. A similar argument works if we start with $k > k^*$ in which case, capital decumulation occurs which drives the economy to $k = k^*$. Figure 16.4 illustrates convergence and catching up.

In Figure 16.4, we measure k on the horizontal axis and pure numbers (percentages) on the vertical axis. The declining curve is $s(y/k)$. Steady state is at k^*, where $s(y/k) = (\delta + n)$ and $g_k = 0$. Consider any value of k such that $k < k^*$ such as k_1. At k_1, (sy_1/k_1), the vertical height of the declining curve exceeds $(\delta + n)$, thus gk at $k = k_1$ is positive and this drives capital accumulation and growth. To the left of k^*, the further away the initial position is from k^*, the greater the gap representing a positive g_k and hence the faster the growth. This is the basis of the so-called "**catching up**" argument. Consider two countries which are identical in all respects except that one country has a lower k and hence a lower y than the other.

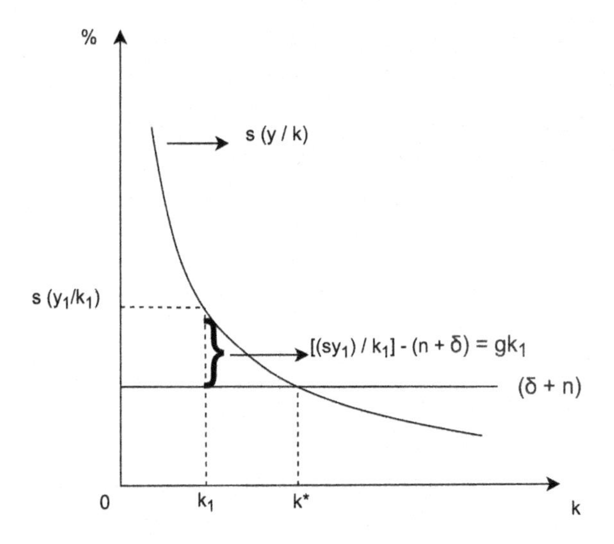

Fig. 16.4 Convergence and Catching up

The country with the lower initial y is the "poor" country. The other country (higher k and y) is the rich country. The poor country must grow faster than the rich country and eventually both will converge to the same steady state in the very long run. This argument is an interesting theoretical point but not of much practical relevance to policy design.

16.5 The Golden Rule

Given the values of s and δ and the production function, the value of k^* is determined by the requirements of steady growth from Eq. (16.6a). Obviously, as s changes, so does the value of k^* Thus, an increase in savings ratio s will increase k^* and steady-state output per worker y^*. Can we compare the infinite number of different steady states (each corresponding to a different value of s) to choose the one which is "best" by appropriately choosing the savings ratio? This is the problem of finding the **golden rule of accumulation**.

Note that as s changes, so does the value of consumption per head c since in this simple economy, $c + s = y$. Or $c = y - s = y - i$ (since all savings are invested). We restrict attention to steady states only so that $c^* = y^* - i^*$. But in steady state, k^* is a constant which implies investment per worker simply replaces capital (per worker) "lost" due to depreciation and population growth, and hence there is no change in capital per worker. Thus, $i^* = (\delta + n)k^*$. Consequently, we may write steady-state consumption per head as

$$c^*(k^*) = y^* - (\delta + n)k^*. \tag{16.7}$$

Equation (16.7) tells us that as the (endogenously determined) value of k^* changes across steady states as savings ratio s varies, so does consumption per worker. A natural target for policy might be to select that steady state at which consumption per worker is maximised. Does such an "optimal" steady state exist? From Eq. (16.7), we can see that as k^* increases, so does y^* and hence consumption increases initially. But since y^* is characterised by diminishing returns, each higher value of k^* leads to a smaller increment in c^*. By contrast, the term which reduces c^*, viz. $(\delta + n)k^*$, increases at a constant rate. Eventually, this negative component will get bigger than the ever-diminishing positive increment from y^* and so c^* will eventually start to fall. Thus, c^* has a maximum for some k^*. To find this maximum, differentiate c^* with respect to k^* and set it equal to zero which implies that the maximum occurs at that value of k when $dy/dk = f'(k^*) = \delta + n$. It is easily checked that the second-order conditions for a maximum are satisfied. The golden rule for maximising steady-state consumption per worker thus states that the marginal product of capital per worker must equal the sum of population growth rate and depreciation rate. If the value of k which solves for the golden rule is k^{**}, then the optimal policy is to find s^{**} — the value of s that just supports a steady state in which $k = k^{**}$.

Example 16.10: For the production function $Y = K^{\alpha}L^{1-\alpha}$ (Cobb–Douglas), find the savings ratio which satisfies the golden rule and interpret.

The per worker production $y = Y/L = k^{\alpha}$ and MPK $= \alpha k^{\alpha-1}$. For the golden rule, we require MPK $= (\delta + n)$ and hence we have $\alpha k^{\alpha-1} = (\delta + n)$.

But in every steady state, we also have $s[f(k)/k] = (\delta + n)$ or $s(k^{\alpha}/k) = \delta + n$. From the two results just derived, we have MPK $= \alpha k^{\alpha-1} = \delta + n = s(k^{\alpha}/k)$. Hence, $\alpha k^{\alpha-1} = s(k^{\alpha}/k)$ or $s^{**} = \alpha$ as the optimum savings ratio. If the planners want to maximise consumption per head in the steady state, they must manipulate (by taxes or other incentives) the savings ratio to exactly equal α, the exponent of capital in the production function.

16.6 Summary

- The engine of capital accumulation is savings.
- So long as savings exceed depreciation of capital, capital per worker and output per worker will grow.
- Under constant returns to scale, the marginal product of capital falls continuously as k increases, and hence the existence of a steady state can be shown provided marginal product of capital has a lower bound of zero (the Cobb–Douglas case).
- If the marginal product of capital falls but is bounded below, steady state only exists for large enough s.
- If a steady state exists, the economy will converge to it at a speed which depends on how far away from steady state the starting position is.
- Convergence also implies poor countries eventually catching up with richer countries, all at the same steady state if all countries are identical save for their starting position.
- In steady state, there is no growth of per capita output unless there is exogenous technical progress.

Index

O

P

Printed in the United States
by Baker & Taylor Publisher Services